Political Rhetoric, Social Media, and American Presidential Campaigns

Lexington Studies in Political Communication

Series Editor: Robert E. Denton, Jr., Virginia Tech University

This series encourages focused work examining the role and function of communication in the realm of politics including campaigns and elections, media, and political institutions.

Recent Titles in This Series

Political Rhetoric, Social Media, and American Presidential Campaigns

Candidates' Use of New Media

Janet Johnson

LEXINGTON BOOKS

Lanham • Boulder • New York • London

Published by Lexington Books
An imprint of The Rowman & Littlefield Publishing Group, Inc.
4501 Forbes Boulevard, Suite 200, Lanham, Maryland 20706
www.rowman.com

6 Tinworth Street, London SE11 5AL, United Kingdom

British Library Cataloguing in Publication Information Available

Library of Congress Control Number: 2020949433

ISBN: 978-1-4985-4083-4 (cloth)
ISBN: 978-1-4985-4085-8 (pbk)
ISBN: 978-1-4985-4084-1 (electronic)

I dedicate this book to my Mom, Patricia Jean Johnson. She gifted me my voice and gave me the courage to use it. I will always be grateful.

Contents

Acknowledgments

When you commit to writing a book, you find out the experience is lonely. Fortunately, I had an excellent support team that made the experience a bit less isolating. I want to thank Dr. Melissa Hernandez-Katz, who convinced me my voice was important enough to write a book. Dr. Helen McCourt whose "Go, Janet!" texts made me smile and motivated me to keep moving forward.

Writing a book is also enjoyable. Thank-you to MaryAnn McClung, who reminded me to keep hygge in my writing by creating a cozy writing space. Our hygge brunch talks and strategy sessions, which usually ended up with notes written on napkins, inspired me. You reminded me that rest was the most critical aspect of reaching my goal.

I would also like to express my gratitude to Dr. Carie King, who helped me navigate through revisions and coached me through the rough spots. She is a talented writer and editor.

And, to Dr. Anthony Spencer. I can't thank him enough for his advice and encouragement when I needed it the most.

I am grateful to all my friends, colleagues, and students who are too numerous to name. If you followed my journey on social media, know your supportive messages helped me finish this book.

Finally, I want to thank my dad, Ted Johnson. I am thankful for his love and support, no matter if I had written this book or not. Oh, and I can't forget Lucy. She's the best writing partner—but after every word demands a treat.

Introduction

I remember entering my elementary school library to visit my mom working the polls in the 1980 presidential election. Ronald Reagan ran against incumbent President Jimmy Carter. My mom and my neighbor discussed how they were not allowed to eat peanuts because that could be perceived as an endorsement for President Carter, a former peanut farmer. I still remember a classmate stating Reagan would send our country to war. I am sure those were their parents' opinions. I remember my mom showed me the voting booth—a big metal machine with levers and a curtain to add a bit of privacy. Through a third-grader's eyes, voting looked complicated. One could not eat peanuts while voting, and one had to decide which presidential candidate would not send us to war.

Voters have to make hard decisions every four years. As media technology progresses it makes communication faster and information more abundant. The Founding Fathers gifted us with the freedom of free speech and a free press to ensure democracy prevails. We are not only U.S. citizens, but we are now digital citizens. We interact online with our presidential candidates and the press. We are creators and disseminators of our own media messages. As digital citizens, we have a responsibility to understand that language is powerful, and not all information is created equal.

In 2008, I noticed how technology changed the way U.S. presidential candidates talked to the electorate and how the electorate responded. This book explores the role of media in presidential campaign rhetoric. Not only did each media technological innovation deliver information quickly, but it also created a political rhetoric shift with each milestone creating a dialogic interaction between presidential candidate and voter.

I experienced firsthand social media's impact on the presidency. In both 2014 and 2015, the White House selected a few social media leaders to live-tweet the State of the Union at the White House. I was honored to be invited to the White House to tweet and honored that the experience allowed me to be part of social media history. President Barack Obama's administration found it essential to use social media to its advantage—and America noticed the change in the flow of information from the White House to their house.

Later, I was lucky enough to be invited on a private, exclusive tour of the West Wing. President Obama was the first president to allow tours of the West Wing. After the president retired to the residence to spend time with his family, White House staffers could book tours for family and friends. My host told me President Obama had wanted people to experience the White House and felt the West Wing tour was notable for White House staffers to share the vital work they did for Americans daily.

I stood in the doorway of the Oval Office in awe. I could see President Obama's personal touches to the office. That day, the Oval Office looked very comfortable; fresh flowers, elegant wallpaper, regal curtains, and superb artwork. Behind the Resolute Desk, I noticed personal pictures—one was a black-and-white photo of the president and first lady. I looked over to the center of the room and saw the hue of the red apples sitting on the coffee table between the couches. The Oval Office is the best-lit room in America. It is not as big as you would expect and is cozy. At that moment, I felt the significance of that room: no matter what your political beliefs may be, the Oval Office is an influential room, keeper of our nation's most important decisions and our nation's worries. I stood there, imagining presidents of the past standing in that office, making the most crucial decisions that have affected each of us at some point in history. I know others have had many more experiences in that office more significant than mine: I stared in the doorway, my toes touching the inside of the office so I could say I stepped in.

Nevertheless, I, who just loved to tweet about social media, rhetoric, journalism, and politics, was able to stand in the doorway of history. Because of Twitter, I was a White House guest. When people ask me what they can gain by using social media, I say, "Maybe one day, you will be invited to the White House."

Presidential campaign rhetoric evolves with every media advancement. People are sometimes fearful and hesitant about any new media. Politicians hesitated to broadcast over the radio because they had to prepare not just one standard speech but suddenly needed several addresses, so they did not sound redundant. Television became a nuisance for politicians; they had to sound good and look good. Charisma became part of the presidential campaign rhetorical strategy. This book takes a rhetorical criticism perspective to show how persuasive language, through media, influences and motivates the electorate. History shows that with every new media advancement comes communication upsets and chaos until that change becomes ingrained in our culture. Time usually reveals the media's impact on political rhetoric.

A rhetoric and media critic "reveals meanings that are shared but not universally and also meanings that are known but not articulated."[1] By revealing the layers of political rhetoric through new media, the purpose of rhetorical criticism "is to teach or enlighten those who hear or read the critique."[2] I will explore the ways presidential campaigns persuade voters through new media.

RHETORIC

Rhetoric is the art of communication. Not only through words but also how visuals influence an audience during a specific moment. Each moment we exist, we experience a rhetorical situation: reading the newspaper, listening to a presidential address, tweeting, texting, choosing a new wall color for your favorite room, designing a website, or watching a movie. Rhetoric is everywhere. Every day we are influenced by words and visuals. Words and visuals make us understand, think, inform, persuade, and emote.

Social media can sometimes feel like a whirlwind filled with information that can overwhelm even the most passive user. For example, when we read a book, we take part in a rhetorical act. We are interacting with the author and the story they created. The polyphony of voices on social media, on the other hand, makes it harder to figure out how to respond. Language is powerful, and it encourages audiences to move to action. A political candidate most often wants readers to give money, volunteer, and vote.

This book examines the influence of political rhetoric through the media's advancements, but "the goal of rhetoric is never to be 'scientific,' or to be able to categorize persuasion for all times and all places. The power of rhetorical analysis is its immediacy, its ability to talk about the particular and the possible, not the universal and the probable."[3] Instead of a diverse and anonymous audience (such as the audiences drawn to television and radio), social media allows presidential candidates to have a more transactional audience and a more targeted audience.[4] The digital citizen is not only a reader but a writer.[5] Each online reader becomes a potential rhetor, "and the audience communicates with itself, potentially eclipsing in frequency and volume any original message."[6] The Internet's delivery ability to the virtual audience "is radically transformed, as the speed of the medium accelerates the dynamics of social movements, coupled with the internet's ability for 'narrowcasting.'"[7] Politicians use social media channels to target digital citizens where they consume media and where users are more likely to share, comment, and like their messages. The speed of delivery on social media creates a more active and engaged audience where "media politics encourages public officials to engage in cosmetic rather than genuine problem-solving behavior."[8] Political candidates now realize the digital citizen's rhetorical power, who persuades their own audiences by commenting and sharing posts. Media users do not consume information on one media source, and politicians have to respond to those rhetorical demands.

In 2008, "blogs took the 2008 election by storm."[9] By the 2016 presidential election, candidate websites only served as a "hub for information and organization."[10] Changes in technology and evolving media used by campaigns may change the dynamics of a candidate's rhetorical choices. Candidates' websites and social media use become text artifacts to study and show the influence of words on a screen. Sonja K. Foss, in *Rhetorical Criticism: Exploration & Practice*, explains,

> Knowledge of the operation of rhetoric also can help make us more sophisticated audience members for messages. When we understand the various options available to rhetors in the construction of messages and how they function together to create the effects they produce, we are able to question the choices others make in the construction of acts and artifacts. We are less inclined to accept existing rhetorical practices and to respond uncritically to the messages we encounter. As a result, we become more engaged and active participants in shaping the nature of the worlds in which we live.[11]

In the end, Foss states, "Rhetorical criticism is a contribution to the improvement of our abilities as communicators."[12] By examining the evolution of campaign rhetoric through media advancements, candidates can learn to construct targeted messages, and the electorate becomes wiser in consuming and responding to political messages. Learning about the relationships between text, producer, and intended audience helps explain the texts' persuasive aspects.[13] Presidential candidates have changed their rhetorical styles to fit the needs of new media.

CHAPTER SUMMARIES

The first two chapters review the historical foundation of presidential candidates' rhetoric from traditional media to new media choices. Chapter 1 traces media history as a dialogical tool in presidential campaigns, and chapter 2 explains the rise of the political press. These two foundational chapters examine the ways history has shaped our future political landscape. As the media technology progressed, so did the rhetorical impact on presidential campaigns and changed how the press covered the "horserace."

Chapter 3 discusses the rhetorical influence of President Obama's 2008 campaign website blog posts. In 2008, Obama's digital campaign style was far superior to his opponents', Republican senator John McCain and Democrat senator Hillary Clinton. Barack Obama's campaign team understood the power of viral media to build a strong grassroots campaign and strong ethos for their candidate.

Chapter 4 analyzes the 2012 election and how Mitt Romney took advantage of the rhetorical situation through his Twitter feed, which showed he evolved from candidate to Republican nominee. Romney's message was consistent, but his campaign against an incumbent proved challenging. President Obama had the advantage of the White House as a backdrop and social media campaign experience.

Chapter 5 explains the 2016 presidential campaign and how the ritualistic, conventional presidential campaign narrative was challenged. Americans learned a new style of campaigning—one that took the conventional story frame and broke it to pieces, redefining and rewriting the story to fit a candidate's rhetorical style.

Chapter 6 discusses how Democratic nominee Hillary Clinton's *ethos* became her major obstacle. Clinton distanced herself from the media. Clinton became a cyborg, a fictional character within digital media, in which foreign influencers may have helped manipulate. In the end, Clinton did not gain control of her campaign story—a story she defined years ago.

Chapter 7 examines the bombastic, controversial rhetrickery of Donald Trump and how he broke the traditional political campaign narrative. Trump used repetition, propaganda, and media to control his campaign narrative. His aggressive colloquial style moved people to action in protest or support.

Finally, chapter 8, the conclusion, is a reflection. This chapter examines the implications of how much information is too much information. This chapter also shows how vital journalism and truth are to upholding democracy in the age of social media.

Democracy flourishes because of our freedom of speech and press. New media changes our political rhetoric, both online and offline. The words presidential candidates say online often influence the words candidates use offline. Social media has revealed that not all information is created equal, and it can alter a U.S. presidential campaign's outcome.

NOTES

1. Barry Brummett, *Techniques of Close Reading* (Los Angeles, CA: Sage, 2019), 15.
2. Ibid., 17.

3. Joan Leach, "Rhetorical Analysis," in *Qualitative Researching with Text, Image and Sound,* ed. Martin W. Bauer and George Gaskell (London: Sage Publications, 2000), 211.

4. Robert L. Heath and Jennings Bryant, *Human Communication Theory and Research* (Mahwah, NJ: Lawrence Erlbaum Associates, Publishers, 2000), 377.

5. Joseph B. Walther, "Virtual Audiences," in *Encyclopedia of Rhetoric,* ed. Thomas Sloan (Oxford: Oxford University Press, 2001), 72.

6. Ibid., 73.

7. Ibid., 74.

8. Shanto Iyengar, *Media Politics: A Citizen's Guide* (New York: W.W. Norton, 2016), 16.

9. "Election 2016: Campaigns as a Direct Source of News," *Pew Research Center,* July 18, 2016, http://www.journalism.org/2016/07/18/digital-news-devel opments-in-u-s-presidential-campaigns-2000-2016/.

10. Ibid.

11. Sonja K. Foss, *Rhetorical Criticism: Exploration & Practice* (Long Grove, IL: Waveland Press, 2004), 8–9.

12. Ibid.

13. Bonnie S. Brennen, *Qualitative Research methods for Media Studies* (New York: Routledge, 2013), 205.

Chapter 1

Media Use in American Presidential Campaigns

In March 2008, three presidential candidates dominated the American political primaries. Of the three, Barack Obama connected to voters using new media more successfully than Hillary Clinton or John McCain. Online fundraising is one way to measure if a political candidate's message is compelling. Using new media[1] resources, Obama raised nearly $750 million in campaign contributions, which exceeded John McCain's by more than 30 percent.[2] To stimulate interest in contributing to his campaign, Obama took advantage of emerging new media: to create a powerful, possibly even unique, dialogic connection with his supporters. New media's current capabilities are a digital form of media that enables users to communicate frequently and instantaneously. Obama was unique in the 2008 presidential campaign to tap into the most compelling new media. Scholar Lee Thornton believes that "Obama's grasp of the power of new media—and those most likely to use it—helped fuel his victory."[3] Many presidential candidates and elected presidents have connected dialogically with their supporters using the new media of their time. One-way mass communication evolved into a polyphony of voices.

Obama used what past presidents used to spread his message—all available media. He used the media as a tool to help create dynamic dialogical messages while using strategic rhetorical techniques. In this way, Obama revolutionized campaigning by delivering his messages through every available means to all possible audiences. Obama's administration helped set the standard for developing a social media plan for the White House. Remember, it takes a while for new media to develop fully into the fabric of mass communication. Barack Obama used social media to communicate directly to citizens; the 2016 election created a new rhetorical standard. As we look through over 230 years of presidential administrations and campaigns, there is one constant: The persuasive use of media is always evolving.

The evolution of Twitter from Obama's 2008 campaign to Donald Trump's 2016 campaign changed significantly. Unlike Barack Obama, Donald Trump used his own personal Twitter account to create a connection to voters. Trump used his personal Twitter account to respond directly to the citizens and maintains that connection as president of the United States. He used Twitter to garner media buzz and to interact directly with citizens. His rhetorical use of social media in delivery and style is much different from Barack Obama's. As new media evolves, the rhetorical styles evolve. The connection gaps between rhetor and audience start to shrink. Once new media settles into a routine, the communication standards change. Presidential administrations have to create new rhetorical standards that carry into the campaign season. Presidents also have to communicate while in office while trying to use new media to persuade voters to take action.

POWER IN WORDS

Media such as social media channels allow a dialogue between the candidate and the electorate. However, not all dialogue is dialogic. Dialogical interaction is often a well-thought-out message in which the messenger considers the audiences' expected response while creating the message. Print, radio, and television allow for one-way communication, which delays the interaction between politicians and citizens; however, social media and smartphone technology allow for nearly instantaneous interaction.

Mikhail Bakhtin says the one constant throughout political communication is the importance of a social collective to interpret, discuss, evaluate, refute, support, and develop ideas.[4] Media allows the electorate to interpret, discuss, evaluate, refute, support, and develop ideas. Candidates can dialogically engage with the electorate to create a more intimate experience, especially with social media channels such as Facebook and Twitter. Also, presidential campaigns use big data collected through social media to create more powerful strategic messages. As Seth Stephens-Davidowitz explains in *Everybody Lies: Big Data. New Data. And What the Internet Can Tell Us about Who We Really Are*, "Certain online sources get people to admit things they would not admit anywhere else. They serve as a digital truth serum."[5] Presidential campaigns can use this knowledge to send people targeted messages. For example, social media channels can help remind readers to vote, volunteer, and attend events or even reinforce a search keyword.

Moreover, social media channels allow American citizens to have a voice. Social media allows politicians to attract that voice through different styles, delivery, and rhetorical techniques. Multiple political voices, such as politicians and citizens, become empowered at the same time. Bakhtin asserts:

> The word (or in general any sign) is interindividual. Everything that is said, expressed, is located outside the "soul" of the speaker and does not belong only to him. The word cannot be assigned to a single speaker. . . . The word is a drama in which three characters participate (it is not a duet, but a trio). It is performed outside the author, and it cannot be introjected into the author.[6]

Once the word flows through the media channels, the author's or orator's words are now part of a broader conversation that creates a life of its own.

Moreover, for each type of media, we now have different genres. For each "particular function . . . and the particular conditions of speech communication specific for each sphere give rise to particular genres, that is, certain relatively, stable, thematic, compositional, and stylistic types of utterances."[7] There is always a time, place, and circumstance for a politician to use a specific media channel. New media creates new opportunities for current presidents and future presidential candidates.

In "Power in Dialogic Interaction," Edda Weigand writes, "As social individuals, we pursue self-interests but need to take account of social concerns. We depend on other individuals and try to influence each other."[8] The rhetorical political game is about pursuing self-interests, taking into account social concerns and, finally, persuasion. New media allowed new opportunities to create different dialogical interactions throughout presidencies and especially how candidates ran for office.

For example, in 1788, when George Washington "stood" for election, he did not interact with the electorate but only anticipated the final vote. When Abraham Lincoln used the telegraph in the 1860s to send messages to the Republican Convention, he might not have anticipated a response back. The evolution of media evolved from little to no interaction between politicians and citizens to where we are today, instantly communicating back and forth. Paul Levinson, in *New New Media*, explains, "Wherever we may be, whether online or offline, whether tweeting about our actions in the real world or about something we just encountered online, we inhabit a new new media world in which both the digital and physical are close at hand."[9] The online world and the offline world merge. We connect with people involved in our offline world, and we connect with people we only know in the online world. These interactions are still new and filled with complex rhetorical situations that people sometimes handle poorly. Leszek Koczanowicz explains, "The dialogical character of language is a reflection of a complex, social situation of communication in which misunderstandings and conflicts are as common as understanding and reconciliation."[10] As media channels evolve, so do the rhetorical effects and messages. Digital citizens are now navigating new ways to approach misunderstandings and conflicts through digital media. The once monologic media has evolved into a polyphony of voices that create nothing other than noise. Both politicians and citizens need to navigate the complexities of the online social situation of communicating.

MEDIA AND THE PRESIDENTIAL CAMPAIGN MESSAGE

Past American presidents used media as a persuasive strategy to reach the masses during America's hardships. Presidents have long recognized that communicating with citizens was essential and used the media available to them. This realization transcended into presidential campaigns. Presidential candidates and presidents in office during the rise of a new medium became accidental rhetorical influencers for that medium. During the first presidential election, print media was one of the few sources for information that American citizens used and could access. The first presidential election was not only historical but also uneventful. In 1788, General Washington became the first and only presidential candidate who ran with no opposition. He refused to campaign because he did not want citizens to believe that he wanted to be king after the United States won its freedom from England.[11]

> Presidential candidates were supposed to "stand" for election, not "run." They did not make speeches. They did not shake hands. They did nothing to betray the slightest ambition for office. Candidates were supposed to stay on their farms in dignified silence, awaiting the people's call as George Washington had done.[12]

Washington was the only president who truly stood for the presidency with little to no media influence. George Washington was considered a war hero and did not campaign. The newly formed Electoral College chose Washington as president and John Adams as vice president. Washington served two terms before deciding in 1796 to retire to his home in Mount Vernon. After that, every candidate had to run "to advance his own cause somehow."[13] The campaigns and presidential rhetorical influence grew as the press did.

The second presidential race was not as honorable. The 1796 presidential campaign between Thomas Jefferson and John Adams "is considered one of the most virulent and personally abusive campaigns in the history of American politics."[14] Print media fueled this first negative campaign. The Federalist Party branded Jefferson an atheist, and Democratic-Republicans branded Adams a monarchist and a friend of England. Both political parties disseminated information through print media such as newspaper editorials, leaflets, and political rallies.[15] These newspapers and the pamphlets "would shape public opinion."[16] The emotional appeals made by the two candidates did shape public opinion. William H. Riker writes:

> A campaign is not directed at the people who have decided to vote. A campaign is directed at the people who haven't decided . . . . The first thing a rhetor has to do with such people is get their attention. One good way to do that is to frighten them by prophesying disaster if the other side wins.[17]

Those negative emotional appeals created drama and a motive for voters to take action out of fear—a rhetorical style that has since become a mainstay in American politics.

American citizens read in their newspapers and other print media about these negative presidential campaigns and, as a result, worried that politics were corrupt. To ease tensions, Thomas Jefferson tried to communicate with and assure both Federalists and Democratic-Republicans through newspapers. Jefferson's eloquence and persuasive commentaries, according to scholar Ryan Tetan, were "viewed as so important to the American people that the press consistently published them so that they could be disseminated to the larger public."[18] Jefferson, the Democratic-Republican candidate, demonstrated a grassroots campaign as well as choosing state campaign committees to disseminate news to the citizens throughout the new states.[19] Before Jefferson took the Presidential Oath of Office, he provided a written draft of his speech to newspaper editor Samuel Harrison Smith so the newspaper could publish Jefferson's speech, and citizens could read the speech in the newspaper by the end of that day.[20] This proactive measure demonstrates Jefferson's connection to the electorate. Jefferson said:

> During this course of administration, and in order to disturb it, the artillery of the press has been leveled against us, charged with whatsoever its licentiousness could devise or dare. These abuses of an institution so important to freedom and science, are deeply to be regretted, inasmuch as they tend to lessen its usefulness, and to sap its safety; they might, indeed, have been corrected by the wholesome punishments reserved and provided by the laws of the several States against falsehood and defamation; but public duties more urgent press on the time of public servants, and the offenders have therefore been left to find their punishment in the public indignation.[21]

Jefferson knew the importance of connecting with the American people. He reassured them the negative campaign that the Nation had just endured was a sign that Americans were free to write and speak their opinions.[22] Both politicians and citizens were learning new rhetorical techniques during the beginnings of the American political process. Politicians knew they needed to appeal to a citizen's emotional side to create a dramatic effect to motivate them to vote. The printers of newspapers and pamphlets learned how to target an audience and deliver strategic messages to support their chosen candidate.

Print media was the only outlet that presidential candidates could use to communicate with the electorate until face-to-face campaign techniques evolved. New campaign techniques, which did not involve any media, were being used; these techniques included town meetings, parades, and, in Andrew Jackson's campaign in 1829, a hickory pole raising.[23] Jackson's campaign created a zestful community atmosphere. During Jackson's second campaign in 1832, political parties held the first conventions. Moreover, for the first time, campaigns targeted specific communities to garner votes. During this campaign, the newspapers also "encouraged local groups to meet and pass resolutions. The resolutions were then often published in newspapers and sent to nearby communities and states."[24] Jackson's campaign used newspapers. However, this time a campaign created a movement within the community. During the 1800s, newspapers were extremely biased, and newspaper owners and editors had political agendas, which made the newspapers more powerful during these campaigns.

Lincoln and the Telegraph

In the 1860s, technology boomed, and the Industrial Revolution flourished. During this time, communities built schools and libraries, which increased Americans' literacy.[25] Literacy rates soared and created more newspaper readers, creating a more informed and educated electorate.

Lincoln used the telegraph during the Civil War to broadcast his message and, as a result, unified a divided country. The telegraph enabled the nation to discover Lincoln's excellent communication skills. Author Tom Wheeler, who wrote *Mr. Lincoln's T-mails*, explains,

> The telegraph, which had given Lincoln unprecedented capability for a chief magistrate, also brought to the American people an unprecedented awareness of and vicarious participation in both battlefield events and political intrigue.[26]

Lincoln, Wheeler writes, knew he needed to "mold public sentiment" to triumph over the war,[27] so he communicated his message through the telegraph. The telegraph allowed Lincoln to be the first president to send and receive electronic messages.[28] The telegraph led to more precise messages, especially for sending information to newspapers. Journalists started formatting and writing news articles in a new way. The format for a print news article stayed the same all these years later. Marshall McLuhan proclaimed in *Understanding Media: The Extensions of Man*:

> [...] characteristic of all media, means that the "content" of any medium is always another medium. The content of writing is speech, just as the written word is the content of print, and print is the content of the telegraph.[29]

More importantly, information started to move faster across the country.

Lincoln took advantage of new media. He was a quiet man, but he knew how to reach American citizens. Ronald C. White Jr., the author of *A. Lincoln*, writes,

> Before the modern press conference, he became skilled in shaping public opinion by courting powerful newspaper editors. During the Civil War, he learned how to reach a large audience through the writing of "public letters.'" He understood the potential of the chattering new magnetic telegraph, which allowed him to instantly communicate with generals in the field and become a hands-on commander in chief.[30]

Overall, White explains, Lincoln embraced all media. Lincoln may have also used new media to stay home in Springfield, Illinois, during the 1860 campaign. He believed, as did Washington, in keeping a low profile during a campaign. White explains that Lincoln's speeches were bundled together in campaign pamphlets.[31] In addition to pamphlets and newspapers, surrogates would campaign for the candidates. However, Lincoln, who did not attend the 1860 Republican Convention in Chicago, stayed in touch by the telegraph.[32] Lincoln would "report in with updates via wire, and occasionally the candidate would respond with directives such as, 'I authorize no bargains and will be bound by none.'"[33] Lincoln's rhetorical style was perfect for sending messages through the telegraph because his rhetoric had a "plainness of language."[34] During this time, "an imposing vocabulary was the acknowledged mark of learning and refinement."[35]

Nevertheless, Lincoln as a candidate and as president kept his language simple, clear, and brief because "Lincoln's theory was that you must talk their language."[36] His rhetorical style was perfect for short, brief messages sent through the telegraph to communicate in his political career. The media matched the rhetorical techniques already applied by Lincoln. The already instilled rhetorical techniques within political leaders shine through when introducing the use of new mass communication. The delivery, style, and moment in time make a presidential candidate or a president a great communicator. Both media and rhetorical techniques merge to create the gold standard that politicians use in future circumstances.

McKinley's Front Porch Media Campaign

Thirty-six years later, during the 1896 campaign, President William McKinley borrowed President James Garfield's strategy to campaign from his front porch. McKinley staged media events at his home. He would step out on his porch and make speeches to invited advocacy groups because new media allowed him to do this. The press set up a telegraph office near his home to disseminate McKinley's speeches to the masses. As his opponent made his way across the country by railroad, McKinley conducted a "Front Porch Campaign." The Front Porch Campaign "shaped what McKinley said and how he said it, as he created the impression of *identification* between the voters and himself."[37] McKinley used the Aristotelian strategy. Aristotle stressed a rhetor must always think about his audience and identify with their audience through language. George Lakoff writes,

> Language does not merely express identity; it can change identity. Narratives and melodramas are not mere words and images; they can enter our brains and provide models that we not merely live by, but that define who we are.[38]

With every pseudo-event, McKinley and his campaign created, the speech identified with the intended audience. The mastermind behind President McKinley's campaign strategy was campaign manager Marcus Hanna.[39] Hanna created staged events, such as parades and what seemed to be extemporaneous front porch speeches, which in turn created "a feeling that he cared about each visitor, that he welcomed each one warmly to his home."[40]

The first president on film was McKinley. Jonathan Auerbach, who wrote "McKinley at Home: How Early American Cinema Made News," explains,

> unlike the telegraph, the news of the cinema, a potential new national medium, was made up of moving images. When we turn from transmission to reception, we begin to see how the reading of images, rather than print, could transform perceptions of public and private.[41]

Moving pictures created a connection between the U.S. president and the public, mostly when McKinley ran for a second term. Auerbach believes Hanna created a campaign where the press came to McKinley, which Hanna believed maximized fundraising efforts.[42] The strategy was to reach as many people as possible by creating an entertaining atmosphere with speeches, parades, and visitors.[43]

McKinley spoke about the issues related to the members of the organizations who traveled to his home. McKinley created an atmosphere in which people believed he was speaking extemporaneously. His speeches were methodically produced speeches to send specific messages out to the masses. McKinley's campaign mass-distributed his prewritten speeches to the press. For example, when McKinley was nominated, he started his campaign with a conversation with the crowd. On many occasions, a representative from the organization visiting McKinley introduced the candidate before McKinley's speaking engagement. In return, McKinley spoke to the individuals in the crowd in response to their well-wishes:

> There is nothing, it seems to me, more gratifying or more honorable, to any man, than to have the regard of his fellow townsmen, and in this I feel that I am and have always been peculiarly blessed. Never were neighbors more devoted or unfaltering in their support to anyone than you have been to me. You have made my cause your cause, and my home among you has been in consequence one of constant and ever-increasing pleasure.[44]

Most of McKinley's speeches created a dialogue between the people and McKinley because his speech was in response to the represented group. He allowed the audience to participate. The film newsreel created a buzz and a want to be part of the crowd gathered around his front porch. McKinley's campaign knew how to attract a crowd as well as make them feel welcomed. He also knew the telegraph allowed for speeches to travel across the country faster. He wanted to spread shared common sentiments throughout the country. McKinley's delivery of preplanned speeches made each seem extemporaneous. In reality, the speeches targeted specific audiences during a time and place that was appropriate. McKinley's campaign's rhetorical strategy created an interaction that considered the audience's intended response.

RADIO'S INFLUENCE ON PRESIDENTIAL CAMPAIGN RHETORIC

McKinley used the Front Porch Campaign because the campaign-style was consistent with the tradition that candidates did not "campaign." It also matched McKinley's rhetorical style of creating what seemed to be extemporaneous speeches. He wanted to connect to the audience without having it look like he was campaigning.

Most of the time, a candidate would send out surrogates to represent his party's platform. Not until the late 1920s and 1930s was radio used as a campaign tool; Herbert Hoover was the first to use it in his 1928 campaign. Louis W. Liebovich says that neither Hoover nor his running mate, Al Smith, "electrified" radio audiences.[45] Liebovich explains, "Hoover was a shy person whose voice sounded timid and distracted over the radio. He read his addresses word-for-word from sheets of paper, and his monotone voice was flat and emotionless."[46] In 1930, *The New York Times* reported that if Marc Hanna had this type of technology in the 1896 campaign, he would "spend that money in buying a nation-wide hook-up for the McKinley of today."[47]

In 1928, the press wrote about radio as the press wrote about Obama's 2008 use of Facebook and Twitter. Radio opened the world to people. Radio informed farmers of urban issues and informed city dwellers of rural issues.[48] When Hoover accepted the Republican candidate nomination, he was capable of reaching out to the Nation instantly because radio stations aired his acceptance speech.

While radio provided candidates a mass audience, it also provided a new type of oratory. Hoover's and Smith's styles differed from those styles necessary for radio speeches. According to *The New York Times* in 1928, Hoover read prepared speeches, whereas opponents Al Smith used only notes.[49] Major J. Andrew White, president of Columbia Broadcasting System during the 1928 campaign, critiqued Hoover's and Smith's radio styles:

> we pass on to a comparison of deliveries. Here we find that Smith, in spite of certain handicaps, has a slight advantage. Hoover is cold in his radio delivery. He speaks as he would to an audience in a hall, rather than using the warm, friendly type of speech, which is appropriate to the home. Practically, all of the radio sets in the country are in the homes where people talk with warmth and cordiality. Smith's delivery is warm—too dynamic perhaps for the placidity of the home circle—but studded here and there with a sparkling gem of humor or human-interest anecdote. His delivery is as interesting and gripping at the fireside or on the front porch as it is in a hall with thousands present. Radio transmits his magnetic personality, whereas it even further chills Hoover's delivery of cold facts.[50]

After White explains that Smith's overall delivery is quite inviting, he writes about how Hoover never forgets he is speaking into a microphone. In contrast, Smith once moved the microphone out of his way and caused the audience to lose his intended message. Smith also did not like to read from a script. According to R. L. Duffus, Smith had little national exposure, but White expected radio to increase political exposure to the public.

By contrast, Hoover was a national and international figure. Also, Hoover's Republican Party aired more radio speeches than did Smith's Democratic Party. In his 1928 *The New York Times* article, Duffus also reports that the Republican Party had 6,000 "minute-men" whom each gave one five-minute speech that 151 stations ran daily.[51] Although Smith may have created a more dialogical interaction between himself and the audience, Hoover's numerous campaign messages, and his no-nonsense approach contributed to his winning the presidency, despite his lack of radio broadcasting skills.

Hoover thought he had mastered radio as a campaign tool until the 1932 presidential election, when he ran against Franklin D. Roosevelt, one of the greatest orators of our time. Roosevelt campaigned for Al Smith in 1928 and, at the time, was governor of New York and used radio to talk to New York citizens.

Roosevelt was fifteen years old when Guglielmo Marconi invented the wireless telegraph.[52] Then inventors developed the radio, which transformed campaign rhetoric. Russell D. Buhite and David W. Levy explain, "Radio and Roosevelt came to maturity together."[53] Roosevelt was governor of New York from 1929 to 1933, and he occasionally used radio to speak to the people of New York and pressure the Albany legislature.[54] Irving J. Rein writes, "Roosevelt found that radio allowed [politicians] to use a conversational style that was personal and informal with an emotional quality not experienced before in American politics."[55] Gil Troy, who wrote *See How They Ran: The Changing Role of the Presidential Candidate*, points out Roosevelt mastered radio only after one mishap:

> After speaking over [the radio] in 1924, he had embarrassed himself by asking "How did it sound?" while he was still on air. But after over seventy-five talks during four years as governor, Roosevelt delivered textbook examples of how to combine a genial tone and familiar language for maximum effect.[56]

Later, during his time as president, Roosevelt liked to invoke mystery on whether he was running for president for a second term.[57] When he did begin to run for president, Roosevelt created a candidate-centered campaign. Roosevelt was not a passive candidate who sat at home while surrogates campaigned on his behalf. He was an active candidate who campaigned with rigor. Radio allowed candidates to converse with the electorate on a different, more personal, level. Roosevelt had a robust dialogical interaction in each of his "Fireside Chats": listeners invited him into their homes, who appreciated becoming a part of the political process. Roosevelt used the media to enhance his rhetorical style to connect to citizens. Citizens could only respond one way—by voting. Roosevelt's voice made him a success on the radio.[58] Roosevelt's voice exuded confidence, yet friendliness. Each Fireside Chat was polished and wellrehearsed before he went on air.[59] Betty Houchin Winfield, in *FDR and the News Media*, writes, "Roosevelt used simple, fluid language and reached the American people with the most direct, technologically efficient means then available for both words and images—radio, photography, and newsreels."[60]

On September 6, 1936, Roosevelt addressed the nation in a Fireside Chat as a preelection appeal to farmers and laborers. Roosevelt began his campaign speech with stories of his visit to the drought-laden lands:

My Friends, I have been on a journey of husbandry. I went primarily to see at first-hand conditions in the drought states, to see how effectively federal and local authorities are taking care of pressing problems of relief and how they are to work together to defend the people of this country against the effects of future droughts. I saw drought devastation in nine states.

I talked with families who had lost their wheat crop, lost their corn crop, lost their livestock, lost the water in their well, lost their garden and come through to the end of the summer without one dollar of cash resources, facing the winter without feed or food—facing a planting season without seed to put in the ground.[61]

Notice how Roosevelt begins his radio chat with "My Friends." In radio, Roosevelt believed his rhetoric should reflect visiting the audience at home. Connecting to the audience also allowed the audience to connect to the problems people faced around the country. Radio allowed Roosevelt "to bring political culture back to the common citizen. In radio, he found the ideal means to speak to Americans in their most intimate surrounding, without journalistic interference."[62] Roosevelt continued to discuss the help the government would try to provide. At the end of this speech, Roosevelt discussed the importance of Labor Day, a discussion that he hoped would unite laborers and farmers. Overall, Roosevelt's rhetoric created a bond with the agriculture community through this preelection Fireside Chat on the radio. The farmers may have felt that, because Roosevelt discussed his experiences in drought-devastated areas, he understood the importance of the farmers' situation. As a result, he carried every agricultural state in America.[63]

After Roosevelt's death, Vice President Harry S. Truman became president of the United States. He did not have to campaign in 1944, but in 1948, Truman ran for reelection and was the first sitting president to campaign "energetically."[64] Truman's energetic campaign involved traveling across the country by train. Because Truman traveled by train, his campaign was labeled "The Whistle-Stop Campaign," and traveled cross-country while stopping at various towns to give campaign speeches. He also tested the extemporaneous style of speech and succeeded.[65] Truman's aides wanted to test how his new speaking style would sound on the radio. Truman seemed "comfortable, direct and even affable,"[66] as evident in this excerpt from Truman's last national radio address on November 1, 1948, before Election Day:

During the past two months, the Senator and I have been going up and down the country, telling the people what the Democratic Party stands for in government. I have talked in great cities, in State capitals, in county seats, in crossroad villages and country towns.

Everywhere the people showed great interest. They came out by the millions. They wanted to know what the issues were in this campaign, and I told them what was in my mind and in my heart.

I explained the meaning of the Democratic Party platform. I told them that I intend to carry it out if they will give me a Democratic Congress to help.

From the bottom of my heart, I thank the people of the United States for their cordiality to me and for their interest in the affairs of this great Nation and of the world. I trust the people because when they know the facts, they do the right thing. I have tried to tell them the facts and explain the issues.

Now it is up to you, the people of this great Nation, to decide what kind of government you want—whether you want government for all the people or government for just the privileged few.

Tonight I am at my home here in Independence—Independence, Missouri— with Mrs. Truman and Margaret. We are here to vote tomorrow as citizens of this Republic. I hope that all of you who are entitled to vote will exercise that great privilege. When you vote, you are in control of your government.[67]

In the first part of this speech, Truman discussed his Whistle-Stop Campaign tour, in which Truman was warm and inviting. He asked for Americans' votes as if he was waiting for their response to his hard work on the campaign trail. Truman's extemporaneous speeches created a more accessible Truman, and the 1948 speech excerpt shows that he was anticipating the reaction of a vote that he hoped the American people would bestow. Truman used the train and radio as tools to spread his message; however, as Steven R. Goldzwig, who wrote *Truman's Whistle-Stop Campaign*, argues,

> Truman's rhetorical legacy is one that may not translate well in an electronic environment where television and the Internet now dominate the modern election. But Truman may yet have a few lessons for the sophisticated postmodern politician. At the very least, a focus on his campaign teaches us that there is no substitute for old-fashioned human contact.[68]

President Truman scholar Gary A. Donaldson agrees that Truman made more effort to deliver his presidential campaign and his petition for votes to the American people than did any other president in history.[69] Moreover, Truman's campaign was the last campaign that did not take full advantage of the newest technology: television.

TELEVISION'S INFLUENCE ON PRESIDENTIAL CAMPAIGN RHETORIC

By 1952, televisions started to appear in American homes. The 1952 presidential campaign used television, but Dwight D. Eisenhower's vice presidential nominee Richard Nixon's "Checkers" speech proved how powerful a tool television would become for candidates. Nixon's speech was in response to the accusation that Nixon received secret monies totaling $18,000 between his 1950 Senate election and the 1952 presidential election.[70] Nixon appeared on television with his wife and his dog as he spoke to the American people. He used the speech to address the questions about his integrity and to relate to his audience:

> One other thing I probably should tell you, because if I don't they'll probably be saying this about me, too. We did get something, a gift, after the election. A man down in Texas heard Pat on the radio mention the fact that our two youngsters would like to have a dog. And believe it or not, the day before we left on this campaign trip we got a message from Union Station in Baltimore, saying they had a package for us. We went down to get it. You know what it was? It was a little cocker spaniel dog, in a crate that he had sent all the way from Texas, black and white, spotted, and our little girl Tricia, the six-year-old, named it Checkers. And you know, the kids, like all kids, love the dog, and I just want to say this, right now, that regardless of what they say about it, we're gonna keep it . . .
>
> And now, finally, I know that you wonder whether or not I am going to stay on the Republican ticket or resign. Let me say this: I don't believe that I ought to quit, because I'm not a quitter. And, incidentally, Pat's not a quitter. After all, her name was Patricia Ryan, and she was born on St. Patrick's day, and you know the Irish never quit. But the decision, my friends, is not mine. I would do nothing that would harm the possibilities of Dwight Eisenhower to become President of the United States. And for that reason, I am submitting to the Republican National Committee tonight through this television broadcast the decision, which it is theirs to make. Let them decide whether my position on the ticket will help or hurt. And I am going to ask you to help them decide. Wire and write the Republican National Committee whether you think I should stay on or whether I should get off. And whatever their decision is, I will abide by it.[71]

In this speech, Nixon creates a deeper interaction with the audience. He starts by confiding in the audience that he received a dog as a gift for his family. Nixon asks questions and then answers them. He discusses personal finances and personal decisions. Nixon seems to care about the audience's perception of him. Nixon made sure to read an excerpt from a letter from an auditor who concluded that Nixon did not violate any federal laws in his personal or campaign finances. Presidential scholar Kathleen Hall Jamieson, in *Packaging the Presidency*, argues,

> The genius of the speech is that it successfully defined the test that would determine whether Nixon would stay on the ticket and then fashioned an appeal that would ensure that the test was met. Neither could be accomplished in a

pre-broadcast age, for both required a national audience able to respond to an appeal such as the one Nixon made.[72]

In response to the "Checkers" speech, a 1952 *New York Times* headline said, "Nixon's Speech 'Shot in Arm' to the G.O.P., Survey Finds."[73] The article said the reactions to Nixon's speech varied. However, one reaction was more potent than the others: "The address appeared to have had an emotional effect on women listeners, many of whom wept while watching Senator Nixon and his wife on television."[74] The televised speech was only a part of Eisenhower's campaign, which introduced the first television campaign advertisement. Short, frequent images of Eisenhower entered people's homes daily and, in the end, won Eisenhower the presidency. The Republican Party had large amounts of money to advertise, and the organization blasted radio and television with advertisements.[75]

In his 1956 campaign, Eisenhower used television to prove that he was healthy enough to serve a second term. The campaign decided to celebrate Eisenhower's sixty-fifth birthday on television. The televised birthday celebration was similar to "This Is Your Life."[76] To create an intimate experience for viewers, "the audience was explicitly invited to see itself as part of Ike's extended family, particularly when the president's granddaughter introduces a cherubic little boy who carries a large piece of cake to the president."[77] This television program created a familial feeling and emphasized Eisenhower's commitment to his family. In contrast, Eisenhower's opponent, Adali E. Stevenson, was divorced and, therefore, would seem to be less of a "family man." Eisenhower connected with the American people through what seemed to be a private family event. Eisenhower liked to share keyhole moments where audiences felt as if they were acting as voyeurs.

Additionally, on October 12, 1956, a television show entitled "The People Ask the President" aired. The television show was similar to a modern press conference: The audience members raised their hands and asked Eisenhower questions. During the broadcast, Eisenhower said:

> It is really a great privilege to welcome you here tonight. I have looked forward for a long time to a chance to talk to a sort of a cross-section of America and talk about the things that are on their minds, except those that are on mine, thinking that I know what you are thinking.
>
> Now, I know that among you there are Republicans and Democrats and Independents, and first voters, everything. And I am not going to ask you to vote for anyone, except this I will ask you, the only request: please vote, that is all, please vote.[78]

The dialogical interaction between Eisenhower, the studio audience, and the home audience created a strong bond between the president of the United

States and citizens of the United States. People at home could identify with the citizens who were present at the broadcast. Overall, during the 1956 presidential campaign, the Republican Party spent $2.8 million on television ads, while the Democratic Party spent only $1.7 million.[79]

Televised Debates

As the 1956 campaign foreshadowed the current campaign, the 1960 campaign solidified the style and efforts of future campaigns. John F. Kennedy and Richard Nixon took part in the first televised presidential debates. Even before the debates, Kennedy took full advantage of television. Gary A. Donaldson, the author of *The Modern Campaign*, explains:

> Television exposure in the primaries was particularly important to Kennedy because he was generally unknown outside of New England. For Kennedy to show his face to the voting nation while running in the Wisconsin and West Virginia primaries—and then winning three primaries—was a major advantage over a candidate like Lyndon Johnson who chose to remain in Washington in hopes that his success in running the Senate would be enough to appeal to voters.[80]

Kennedy used television to create recognition with the audience. The more American citizens saw Kennedy campaigning on television, the more of a connection Kennedy had with the home audience.

Nixon did not take full advantage of television, as did Kennedy. Because Nixon was received well on television in 1952 for his "Checkers" speech, he did not need to worry about the televised presidential debates. Additionally, Nixon did not receive an official endorsement from former President Eisenhower. Kennedy's campaign created television advertisements highlighting Eisenhower's hesitance to endorse Nixon as the Republican candidate. Kennedy's campaign advertisement said:

Announcer: Every Republican politician wants you to believe that Richard Nixon is quote "experienced." They even want you to believe that he has actually been making decisions in the White House. But listen to the man who should know best, the president of the United States. A reporter recently asked President Eisenhower this question about Mr. Nixon's experience.

Reporter: I just wondered if you could give us an example of a major idea of his that you had adopted in that role as the decider and final . . . ah . . .

Eisenhower: If you give me a week, I might think of one. I don't remember.

Announcer: At the same press conference, Eisenhower said . . .

Eisenhower: No one can make a decision except me.

Announcer: And as for any major ideas from Mr. Nixon?

Eisenhower: If you give me a week I might think of one. I don't remember.

Announcer: President Eisenhower could not remember, but the voters will remember. For real leadership in the sixties, help elect Senator John F. Kennedy president.[81]

This advertisement damaged Nixon's campaign because the advertisement showed Eisenhower speaking the words, "No one can make a decision except me." Before television, a candidate would have struggled to capture such a quote, but television allowed Kennedy's campaign to capture the quote and share it with American voters. Because the audience witnessed Eisenhower expressing his inability to answer, on television, Eisenhower's words were far more damaging than if a newspaper article had quoted him. These new campaign techniques—using direct quotes in advertisements—started to reach more people and affect public opinion.

On September 26, 1960, seventy million Americans watched the first Kennedy-and-Nixon debate.[82] Additionally, millions more listened to the debate on the radio. Television audiences believed Kennedy won the debate, whereas radio audiences reported that Kennedy and Nixon performed equally well. The television audiences saw a tired, ill-looking Nixon debating a young, charismatic Kennedy.[83] The debates boosted Kennedy's public image and helped audiences relate and thus connect with Kennedy.

As a result of the televised debates and advertisements and recorded quotes, the modern American presidential campaign was born. Gary Donaldson points out, "What Truman achieved in months of whistle-stop campaigning, Kennedy, and Nixon in 1960 could achieve with one televised speech or on a Sunday morning interview on national television."[84]

Television played an important role in presidential elections from the 1960s on. Ronald Reagan, the first actor to become president of the United States, showed how powerful such exposure could influence a presidential campaign. Reagan knew how to perform for an audience and use television to his advantage.[85] In a speech on October 24, 1980, he connected to the audience when he quoted a fifth-grader who saved money for roller skates only to find the price increased:

Throughout this campaign, I've been saying that the economy concerns more than mere statistics—it concerns people, families, human hopes, and human suffering.

Each American family has its own story about what the Carter economy has done. But the other day I came across a story that sums up what the American people have been through. The story is all the more poignant because it concerns a child's disappointment.

It appeared in the Fort Wayne, Indiana, *News-Sentinel* and concerns a Fort Wayne fifth-grader named Andrea Baden, who wanted to buy a pair of roller skates. So, in the great American tradition, she saved her allowance until she had the money to buy them.

Andrea put it this way: "When I went back to the store, the price had gone up. I saved more money, but when I got back again, the price had gone up again. It's just not fair."

That's right, Andrea: What Mr. Carter has done to this country's economy just isn't fair. It just isn't right.[86]

Reagan knew how to engage an audience through his speech. His campaign strategy was to identify with the American public, and he did this through his televised speeches and advertisements. Reagan also knew he had to schedule a televised debate carefully because the timing was critical.[87]
An excerpt from Reagan's book explains:

When Carter finally agreed to a debate, the date was set for October 28, one week before the election, and we were delighted. The debate went well for me and may have turned on only four little words.

They popped out of my mouth after Carter claimed that I had once opposed Medicare benefits for Social Security recipients.

It wasn't true, and I said so:

"There you go again. . ."

I think there was some pent up anger in me over Carter's claims that I was a racist and warmonger. Just as he'd distorted my view on states' rights and arms control, he had distorted it regarding Medicare, and my response just burst out of me spontaneously.

The audience loved it, and I think Carter added to the impact of the words by looking a little sheepish on the television screen.

To me, the finish of the debate was probably more significant: In my closing statement, I asked people if they thought they were better off now than they had been four years earlier. If they were, I said they should vote for my opponent; if not, I said I thought they'd agree with me that it was time for a change. (221)[88]

Reagan had an advantage over incumbent President Jimmy Carter when they debated because Reagan knew *how* to perform in front of the camera. President Carter did not have that experience. Carter's televised reaction to Reagan's extemporaneous remark during this debate told audiences plenty.

INTERNET'S INFLUENCE ON PRESIDENTIAL CAMPAIGN RHETORIC

Throughout the 1980s and into the 1990s, television dominated the publicity of activities in the American political sphere. However, a new media—the Internet—became available. The Internet allowed audiences with instant access to information. Just as radio and television slowly developed into a campaign tool, the Internet slowly found its way as a campaign tool. In the 1992 presidential campaign, candidates Bill Clinton and George Bush first used the Internet: both candidates used email. In the 2000 presidential campaign, candidates started to use the Internet for fundraising. John McCain was the first presidential candidate to raise over $1 million in his effort to win the Republican Party's nomination. Then, in the 2004 election, Howard Dean, who sought the Democratic Party's nomination, raised over $40 million online.[89]

Presidential candidates only dabbled with the Internet as a campaign tool until the 2008 campaign. A new campaign tradition was born when Hillary Clinton announced her bid for the presidency by posting the news online. At the beginning of the 2008 presidential campaign, new media became a source for voters to gather news and information about the candidates. Supporters could interact on the candidates' blogs and donate money directly to any candidate. During the 2008 presidential campaign, campaign writers created true dialogical interactions between presidential candidates and the American electorate and established the Internet (with print, radio, and television) as an influential campaign tool. The Internet allows for two-way communication. This two-way communication allows candidates to create a dialogical interactive atmosphere to motivate readers to vote, donate, or volunteer. The Internet allows citizens to share candidate's messages, to react, and to create dynamic content. Print, radio, and television allowed only one-way interaction, whereas public opinion was more challenging to measure. The reaction from Internet users following campaign messages are now instantaneous as well as can go viral.

Web 2.0

Web 2.0 is when the Internet went from static web publishing to interactive participation.[90] However, as shown through history, Obama's campaign became an extension of what presidents before him did when they faced using new media. Past presidents embraced the newest media and used the available mass communication tools to interact and identify with the electorate—just as Obama did. Unlike past presidents, Obama's campaign could use Web 2.0's most influential power—dialogical interaction. Again, technology changed the rhetorical resources future presidential candidates could apply to persuade the electorate.

The 2008 presidential election is the first genuinely digital dialogic inter- active campaign. Both Barack Obama and Hillary Clinton took advantage of social networking sites during the Democratic primaries, as did Republican candidate John McCain. Past campaigns did not have access to such new media, which allows for near-instantaneous responses from both candidate and electorate. The Internet allows real-time interaction, during which the candidate can post messages and receive almost instant feedback about their policies and issues. Of all three campaigns in 2008, "Obama's campaign has thus far shown that the Web can enable greater participation in the political process and, hopefully, the process of the government."[91]

Even though McCain was one of the first political candidates to fundraise online, his web campaign was poorly executed, which lacked the personal connection that establishes a successful online campaign. McCain failed to connect to his audience. Obama, on the other hand, created an interactive campaign through his campaign blog, which became a social hub for Obama supporters. Because of Obama's tone, subjects, and language, his readers felt as if Obama cared about them and their opinions. Because Obama seemed to care, grassroots organizations rewarded Obama's dialogic interaction with planned events and phone-bank participation.

Because Obama won the election, it would seem Obama used the Internet to better connect with the American electorate. In contrast, neither McCain nor Clinton used the Internet to create an online dialogic network. Obama used the Internet to establish new methods to fundraise; his campaign was among the first to embrace shareable widgets that allowed users to host the equivalent of "donate here" buttons on the users' sites. Visitors to My.BarackObama.com could copy codes to post photos, campaign logos, and icons on their websites. Obama did not only use his website for fundraising, but he also gave people the tools to post code to their Web hangouts.[92] This strategy helped Obama use new media and rhetorical figures of speech to motivate readers to act independently.

McCain tried to follow suit and added widgets to his campaign website for his supporters to use; however, he made his efforts too late in the campaign. Although fundraising and volunteer opportunities were easy to access for the American citizens who chose to participate, neither McCain nor Clinton cre- ated a meaningful dialogue with their supporters as did Obama. That dialogue helped enlist volunteers from accessible online tools to build a grassroots community.

When Obama announced Senator Joe Biden as his vice-presidential choice via Twitter, the electorate received Obama's message at the same time that the press received the message. Obama's campaign bypassed the media and interacted with the citizens directly. As a result of Obama's methods, candidates learned that they could respond to their opponents and discuss their issues directly with the electorate without the "middleman," specifically the press. Because of the candidates' online presence, the Internet flourished in the 2008 presidential campaign, just as radio flourished when Roosevelt connected with Americans through engaging speeches. Obama connected with Americans because he created a media network that incorporated print, broadcast, and the Internet to motivate supporters to take action, which is no different than when Roosevelt used radio to pressure the legislature to take action.

Future presidential candidates will emulate Obama's Internet campaign; however, Obama is just one of many past presidents who had uncovered the dialogical and rhetorical secrets to successful campaigns via interactive media to influence public opinion. McCain used the media throughout the 2008 campaign, but because of McCain's rhetorical techniques, he failed to use interactive media to connect with and motivate American citizens. McCain made the same mistake made by Herbert Hoover's opponent, Al Smith, in 1928: he turned his head away from the microphone.

CONCLUSION

The Obama campaign showed how a candidate could interact in new ways with citizens. The Pew Research Center reports that six in ten American adults use a mobile device to consume news.[93] As Americans rely more on their mobile devices, the more politicians will try to find new ways to use this new media frontier to create meaningful, rhetorical messages.

Big data is one way. During the 2012 campaign between President Obama and Republican nominee Mitt Romney, the Obama campaign created a television rating system, "a kind of Nielsen in which the only viewers who mattered were those not yet fully committed to a presidential candidate."[94] Obama's campaign's goal was to target various demographics across different types of media.[95] Obama's 2012 campaign created a more effective and dialogic campaign by:

> reducing every American to a series of numbers. Yet those numbers somehow captured the individuality of each voter, and they were not demographic classifications. The scores measured the ability of people to change politics—and to be changed by it.[96]

Furthermore, emerging new media allows both candidates and citizens to influence the political landscape. As media evolves, so do the means that allow politicians to bypass the mass media, such as by creating a television rating system or an interactive campaign website, to create and send messages directly to the voter.

On the other hand, candidates must remember that as much as campaigns are using digital media to track the electorate, their same audience uses smartphones and are always nearby to capture the moment of any snafus that occur on the campaign trail. Moreover, American citizens are used to instant gratification. American citizens are becoming more impatient. Politicians and the news media have to deliver information Americans need as soon as the information is available. Ignoring social media as a campaign tool is not an option, as John McCain's campaign did in 2008. Social media engages the voter as a participant. American citizens are now digital citizens who expect politicians and journalists to use interactive media to create a dialogical experience. The 2008 election was the beginning of the power of social media's influence in presidential campaign rhetoric. As social media evolves and becomes an influential information source, the presidential candidates' rhetorical styles also change.

NOTES

1. "New media," according to the *Oxford Dictionary*, is any new mass communications.

2. According to the Center of Responsive Politics (opensecrets.org), Clinton's total fundraising efforts the end of May were $229.4 million.

3. Lee Thornton, "New Media and the Man," *American Journalism Review,* December/January 2009, http://ajrarchive.org/Article.asp?id=4654.

4. Bakhtin discusses in *The Dialogic Imagination*, "Our speech is filled to overflowing with other people's words, which are transmitted with highly varied degrees of accuracy and impartiality. The more intensive, differentiated and highly developed the social life of a speaking collective, the greater is the importance attaching, among other possible subjects of talk, to another's word, another's utterance, since another's word will be the subject of passionate communication, an object of interpretation, discussion, evaluation, rebuttal, support, further development and so on" (337).

5. Seth Stephens-Davidowitz, *Everybody Lies: Big Data, New Data, And What The Internet Can Tell Us About Who We Really Are* (New York: HarperCollins, 2017).

6. M. M. Bakhtin, *Speech Genres & Other Late Essays*, trans. Vern W. McGee, ed. Caryl Emerson and Michael Holquist (Austin: The University of Texas Press, 1986), 121–122.

7. Ibid., 64.

8. Edda Weigand, "Power in dialogic interaction," *Language and Dialogue* 1, no. 2 (2011): 234.

9. Paul Levinson, *New New Media* (Boston, MA: Pearson, 2013), 2.

10. Leszek Koczanowicz, "Beyond Dialogue and Antagonism: A Bakhtinan Perspective on the Controversy in Political Theory," *Theory and Society* 40, no. 5 (2011): 558.

11. Joseph J. Ellis, *His Excellency: George Washington* (New York: Alfred A. Knopf, 2004), 182–83.

12. Ibid., 7.

13. Gil Troy, *See How They Ran: The Changing Role of the Presidential Candidate* (New York: Free Press: Toronto, 1991), 11.

14. John P. Todsen, "Presidential Election 1796," in *Encyclopedia of American Political Parties and Elections*, ed. Larry J. Sabato and Ernst Howard (New York: Checkmark Books, 2007), 298–299.

15. Ibid.

16. Sean Wilentz, *The Rise of American Democracy: Jefferson to Lincoln* (New York: Norton, 2005), 50.

17. William H. Riker, "Campaign Rhetoric," *Bulletin of the American Academy of Arts and Sciences* 46, no. 5 (1993): 41.

18. Ryan Teten, "Presidential Election 1804," in *Encyclopedia of American Political Parties and Elections*, ed. Larry J. Sabato and Ernst Howard (New York: Checkmark Books, 2007), 301.

19. Ibid.

20. Wilentz, *The Rise of American Democracy*, 95.

21. Thomas Jefferson, "Second Inaugural Address—March 4, 1805," in *The Life and Selected Writings of Thomas Jefferson*, ed. Adrienne Koch and William Peden (New York: Random House, 1993), 316.

22. Wilentz, *The Rise of American Democracy*, 95.

23. President Andrew Jackson was known as "Old Hickory." Allison Clark Odachowski explains, "Besides the hickory pole raisings, they also used hickory brooms as a symbol for Jackson sweeping out filth and corruption." Allison Clark Odachowski, "Presidential Election 1828," in *Encyclopedia of American Political Parties and Elections*, ed. Larry J. Sabato and Ernst Howard (New York: Checkmark Books, 2007), 309.

24. Ibid., 310.

25. Troy, *See How They Ran*, 63.

26. Tom Wheeler, *Mr. Lincoln's T-Mails: The Untold Story of How Abraham Lincoln Used the Telegraph to Win the Civil War* (New York: Collins, 2006), 95.

27. Ibid.

28. Ibid., xviii.

29. Marshall McLuhan, *Understanding Media: The Extensions of Man* (Cambridge, MA: MIT Press, 2001), 8.

30. Ronald C. White, *A. Lincoln: A Biography* (New York: Random House, 2009), 6.

31. Ibid., 332.

32. Wheeler, *Mr. Lincoln's T-Mails*, 34.

33. Ibid.

34. Douglas L. Wilson, "Lincoln's Rhetoric," *Journal of the Abraham Lincoln Association* 34, no. 1 (2013): 5.

35. Ibid., 5–6.

36. Ibid., 6.

37. William D. Harpine, *From the Front Porch to the Front Page: McKinley and Bryan in the 1896 Presidential Campaign* (College Station: Texas A&M University Press, 2005), 38.

38. George Lakoff, *The Political Mind: A Cognitive Scientist's Guide to Your Brain and Its Politics* (New York: Penguin Books, 2008), 231.

39. Robert Butts, "Presidential Election 1896," in *Encyclopedia of American Political Parties and Elections*, ed. Larry J. Sabato and Ernst Howard (New York: Checkmark Books, 2007), 332.

40. Harpine, *From the Front Porch to the Front Page*, 38.

41. Jonathan Auerbach, "McKinley at Home: How Early American Cinema Made News," *American Quarterly* 51, no. 4 (1999): 800.

42. Ibid., 802.

43. Harpine, *From the Front Porch to the Front Page*, 38.

44. William McKinley and Joseph P. Smith, *McKinley, the People's Choice* (Canton, OH: The Repository Press, 1896), 4.

45. Louis Liebovich, *Bylines in Despair: Herbert Hoover, the Great Depression, and the U.S. News Media* (Westport, CT: Praeger, 1994), 73.

46. Ibid.

47. Charles Willis Thompson, "Radio Takes the Bunk Out of Campaigns," *New York Times,* October 26, 1930, SM6.

48. "Radio is Changing Campaign Tactics-Broadcasting Has Taken Politics into the Family Circle, Contends Major White—Five More Talks by Smith: Two by Hoover Radio Is Switching Votes. Final Speeches on Nov. 5," *New York Times,* October 28, 1928, 154.

49. Ibid.

50. J. Andrew White, "Hoover vs. Smith as Radio Orators," *New York Times,* September 16, 1928, 164.

51. R. L. Duffus, "Our Radio Battle for the Presidency," *New York Times,* October 28, 1928, 139.

52. Russell D. Buhite and David W. Levy, "Introduction," in *FDR's Fireside Chats*, ed. Russell D. Buhite and David W. Levy (Norman, OK: University of Oklahoma Press, 1992), xiii.

53. Ibid.

54. Ibid., xiv.

55. Irving Rein, "Campaigns," in *Encyclopedia of American Political Parties and Elections*, ed. Larry J. Sabato and Ernst Howard (New York: Checkmark Books, 2007), 77.

56. Troy, *See How They Ran*, 163.

57. Ibid., 187.

58. Betty Houchin Winfield, *FDR and the News Media* (New York: Columbia University Press, 1994), 105

59. Ibid.

60. Winfield, *FDR and the News,* 103.

61. Franklin D. Roosevelt, "123-Fireside Chat," on *The American Presidency Project,* online by Gerhard Peters and John T. Woolley, September 6, 1936, http://www.presidency.ucsb.edu/ws/index.php?pid=15122.

62. Huub Wijfjes, "Spellbinding and Crooning: Sound Amplification, Radio, and Political Rhetoric in International Comparative Perspective, 1900–1945," *Technology and Culture* 55, no. 1 (January 2014): 165.

63. Russel D. Buhite and David W. Levy, "A Pre-Election Appeal to Farmers and Laborers," in *FDR's Fireside Chats,* ed. Russell D. Buhite and David W. Levy (Norman, OK: University of Oklahoma Press, 1992), 74.

64. Daniel Ballard, "Presidential Election 1948," in *Encyclopedia of American Political Parties and Elections,* ed. Larry J. Sabato and Ernst Howard (New York: Checkmark Books, 2007), 353.

65. Steven R. Goldzwig, *Truman's Whistle-Stop Campaign* (College Station: Texas A&M University Press, 2008), 18.

66. Ibid.

67. Harry S. Truman, "Harry S. Truman: Radio Remarks in Independence on Election Eve, Santa Barbara CA, November 1, 1948," *The American Presidency Project,* online by Gerhard Peters and John T. Woolley, September 16, 2009, http://www.presidency.ucsb.edu/ws/?pid=13082.

68. Goldzwig, *Truman's Whistle-Stop Campaign,* 123.

69. Gary Donaldson, *The First Modern Campaign: Kennedy, Nixon, and the Election of 1960* (Lanham, MD: Rowman & Littlefield, 2007), vii.

70. Philip R. VanderMeer, "The Election of 1952," in *Encyclopedia of American Political Parties and Elections,* ed. Larry J. Sabato and Ernst Howard (New York: Checkmark Books, 2007), 824

71. Richard Nixon, "Address of Senator Nixon to the American People: The "Checkers Speech" Santa Barbara, CA, September 23, 1952," in *The American Presidency Project,* online by John T. Woolley and Gerhard Peters, September 16, 2009, http://www.presidency.ucsb.edu/ws/index.php?pid=24485.

72. Kathleen Hall Jamieson, *Packaging the Presidency* (Oxford: Oxford Press, 1996), 77.

73. James A. Haggerty, "Nixon's Speech 'Shot in Arm' to the G.O.P., Survey Finds," *New York Times,* September 29, 1952, 1.

74. Ibid.

75. Jamieson, *Packaging the Presidency,* 86.

76. Ibid., 107.

77. Ibid.

78. Dwight D. Eisenhower, "241-Television Broadcast: 'The People as the President' 1956," in *The American Presidency Project,* ed. John T. Woolley and Gerhard Peters, October 5, 2009, http://www.presidency.ucsb.edu/ws/index.php?pid=10640&st=Eise nhower&st1=television.

79. Danny Hayes, "Has Television Personalized Voting Behavior," *Political Behavior* 31 no. 2, (2008): 355.

80. Donaldson, *The First Modern Campaign*, 46.

81. "1960 Kennedy vs. Nixon," *The Living Room Candidate: Presidential Campaign Commercials 1952–2016,* Accessed August 24, 2018. http://www.livi ngroomcandidate.org/commercials/1960/nixons-experience.

82. Craig R. Coenen, "The Election of 1960," in *American Presidential Campaigns and Elections,* ed. William G. Shade, Campbell C. Ballard, and Craig R. Coenen (Armonk, NY: Sharpe Reference, 2003), 856.

83. Ibid.

84. Donaldson, *The First Modern Campaign*, 157.

85. Coenen, "The Election of 1960," 946.

86. Ronald Reagan, "Televised Campaign Address A Visual Economy: Jobs, Growth, and Progress for Americans," in *The American Presidency Project*, ed. John T. Woolley and Gerhard Peters, November 18, 2009, http://www.presidency.ucsb.edu /ws/?pid=85201.

87. Ronald Reagan, *An American Life* (New York: Simon and Schuster, 1990), 221.

88. Ibid.

89. Danny Hayes, "Media and Elections, Internet," in *Encyclopedia of American Political Parties and Elections*, ed. Larry J. Sabato and Howard R. Ernst (New York: Checkmark Books, 2007), 224.

90. For an in-depth discussion about Web 2.0 see Tim O'Reilly, "What Is Web 2.0," *O'Reilly*, September 30, 2005, https://www.oreilly.com/pub/a/web2/archive/wh at-is-web-20.html?page=1.

91. Ibid., 13.

92. David Talbot, "How Obama Really Did It," *Technology Review*, August 19, 2008, https://www.technologyreview.com/s/410644/how-obama-really-did-it/.

93. Sophia Fedeli and Katerina Eva Matsa, "Use of Mobile Devices for News Continues to Grow, Outpacing Desktops and Laptops," *Pew Research Center*, July 17, 2018, http://www.pewresearch.org/fact-tank/2018/07/17/use-of-mobile-devices-for-news-continues-to-grow-outpacing-desktops-and-laptops/.

94. Sasha Issenberg, "How Obama's Team Used Big Data to Rally Voters," *MIT Technology Review*, December 19, 2012, https://www.technologyreview.com/s/ 509026/how-obamas-team-used-big-data-to-rally-voters/.

95. Ibid.

96. Ibid.

Chapter 2

Brief History of Political Media

Aristotle, in his work *Politics*, explains, "Man is more of a political animal . . . Endowed with the gift of speech."[1] With this gift of speech, today's political animals have the gift of the Internet. Traditional news media, once seen as truth-seekers, are changing their rhetorical habits to compete with hashtags, likes, and follows.

The Internet allows individuals to have a voice—sometimes a LOUD voice. When Aristotle said people were "endowed with the gift of speech," he meant people had the gift of communication. John Dewey said, "To learn to be human is to develop through the give-and-take of communication an effective sense of being an individually distinctive member of a community."[2] The Internet allows people to participate in a larger conversation—nationally and worldwide. Because more people are participating in the media community, the messages are sometimes muddled and confusing. People talk over each other, and the traditional media regularly includes tweets as newsworthy components to a story.

Journalism has always had strong ideologies—and, "like all ideologies, it serves as a guide to thought and political and social action."[3] Journalism has a set of stringent practices, but now the Internet is filled with citizen journalists who lack the formal training of disseminating information to the public. William James's philosophy could explain citizen journalism because people using social media "is more or less dumb sense of what life honestly and deeply means. It is only partly got from books; it is our individual way of just seeing and feeling the total push and pressure of the cosmos."[4] When one looks at their Facebook newsfeed or Twitter feed, they will see their online community trying to figure out what life honestly means. Moreover, with the gift of speech—and the right technology—people will continue to seek meaning and contribute their opinions.

The journalistic tradition is to help find balance—to share all sides to a story. Especially during the presidential campaign season, the role journalism plays is sometimes not as unbiased as we would hope. The media has succumbed to social media, which creates murky waters for digital citizens to navigate. Social media is noisy, and traditional journalistic values are declining. Social media creates an atmosphere where the term "clickbait" determines a story's success.

The digital citizen is excited to participate in these stories. The digital citizen wants to contribute their opinion—but is social media ruining political news with digital citizens' contributions? Today's candidates do not need the press. Candidates use Facebook Live, Twitter, and Instagram to inform constituents. The role of journalism has changed. As of 2018, 77 percent of Americans owned a smartphone.[5] Smartphones capture pictures, video and allow the user to post to social media channels quickly. The average American citizen that documents breaking news becomes a citizen journalist. Professional journalists will rarely break news stories before social media users. Journalists are our truth-seekers. The journalist's role in new media is to fact-check and tell the story in more than 280 characters.

Both presidential candidates and the press compete with social media messages that either divert or inflate their intended message. Either way, the rhetorical impact of new media creates a more dynamic interactive atmosphere among the candidate, the press, and digital citizenry.

TRADITIONAL NEWS MEDIA

The Internet is new, but the spread of news is not. A cave dweller used petroglyphs, Ancient Greeks shouted the news in the middle of the town square, and in colonial times printers tried to report the news without being put in jail.

In the seventeenth century, England's coffeehouses were specialized depending on the location of the community. "Londoners would often visit more than one coffeehouse each day to sit, drink, and exchange news."[6] Through these coffeehouses grew underground newspapers. Coffeehouses acted as the first Internet, connecting people from all over the city who gathered information, whether it be gossip, shipping news, or financial news.

The fight for the freedom of the press spurred a rash of political pamphlets and publications written by anonymous authors. One of the most well-known and daring political pamphlets is *Common Sense*, which appeared in 1776 and was authored by Thomas Paine. Paine and other political activists used the printing press to spread their message because "to them, the newspapers and pamphlets were simple tools for their activism, not their means of sustenance."[7] In today's terminology, Paine's pamphlet went viral because of his simplistic writing style. He was a writer, unlike most pamphleteers, who had other trades. People resonated with his words more so than any other pamphleteers writing about the same issues. Overall, these types of pamphlets created an atmosphere to protect the freedom of the press because "a free press can arm the people to protect their liberties against the grasping, aggressive nature of centralized power."[8] During this time, Thomas Jefferson became a strong advocate for journalism:

> The basis of our governments being the opinion of the people, the very first object should be to keep that right; and were it left to me to decide whether we should have a government without newspapers or newspapers without a government, I should not hesitate a moment to prefer the latter.[9]

The Founding Fathers encouraged the press to grow and flourish.

Information flowed more rapidly with better communication abilities such as updated and efficient printing presses, which lowered printing costs. Furthermore, the railroad and the telegraph all helped information flow more rapidly. The invention of the telegraph in the mid-nineteenth century changed the delivery of news and the writing style of news. The telegraph stripped away the newspaper's "tall story, the hoax, much humor, irony, and satire."[10] Words fed through the telegraph cost money, which led to shorter messages. Tom Standage argues that the sound bite was born because of the telegraph: "This new telegraph writing style also influenced public speaking: short sound bites became popular because they were easier for the stenographers to transcribe, and cheaper and quicker for reporters to transmit."[11] The story became a blurb in the newspaper and "led journalism without the luxury of detail and analysis."[12] The telegraph kept people connected to the world—not just their community. To further connect communities, the Associated Press was founded in 1848 to decrease the high cost to send messages by telegraph. To this day, this service connects news organizations to share information globally. American journalism as an honorable profession can be traced as far back as 1869.[13] For the first time, "instead of being *participants* in politics, however the papers now saw themselves as *reporters* of politics."[14]

The ways the press influenced public opinion bear many similarities to the criticisms we hear today. William Randolph Hearst and Joseph Pulitzer both had successful papers linked by the telegraph. The two men competed for the top position in the news. Because their newspapers competed against each other, the two publishers were known for their sensationalistic news accounts, which many now know as *yellow journalism*. The two men, especially Hearst, would fake news and doctor photos. Hearst is also blamed for starting the Spanish-American War.[15] Hearst was "demagogic and inflammatory, and everything about him was oversized: his rhetoric and his headlines

... The big money he spent on his newspapers, and not least of all, his lavish homes and private life."[16] All the while, Pulitzer was determined "to use his newspaper as an instrument of reform."[17]

Radio

Once the flow of information fell across the country with much more ease, the invention of the radio made information more personal. Paul Starr notes that radio was first met with skepticism because "radio invaded the sanctity of the home."[18] Many predicted that radio would end the rallies and town hall meetings. People would gather around the radio for entertainment and news. On June 29, 1924, *The New York Times* reported:

> Who will get the radio vote, and how can the votes be won by an invisible speaker? It will be the first time in political history that a candidate for president comes into contact with the voice with a large percentage of the voters.[19]

President Calvin Coolidge reportedly had a "good radio voice," and because radio listeners heard Coolidge several times on the radio, they may have felt as if they knew him.[20] The radio also helped audiences who had felt excluded from participating in politics before feel connected to the issues. *The New York Times* reported that women who typically did not attend speeches could "sit comfortably at home and hear the speeches by radio."[21] Women who campaigned could talk into a microphone, and audiences across the country could hear their messages.[22] Otherwise, their voices in loud town hall platforms were not understood as well as a man's voice.[23]

Politicians realized radio was a much different venue than stumping the traditional way, with long-winded speeches. Radio allowed people options. The audience could turn the radio to a more entertaining station rather than listen to a politician's speech. Politicians had to learn new ways to talk to constituents. For instance, politicians would often repeat the same speech as they made their way across the country. Radio broadcasted to a mass audience. Presidential candidates had to create compelling and distinct messages each time they spoke.[24]

Politicians also had difficulty not appearing fake or, in the expression, many newspapers used at the time, using the "bunk and hokum" technique. Politicians had to stick to facts and remember the audience could not see their facial expressions or hand gestures. Their voice was the only tool to persuade, which meant many candidates tried to have a polished radio voice. Consequently, politicians (and broadcasters) learned that content mattered when monotone presidential candidate Herbert Hoover won without the most polished radio voice.

Television

The success of the radio predicted the success of television. *The Washington Post* in 1928 predicted that television "promises so much in the way of drawing the American people more closely together."[25] Politicians had to think about their speaking ability and their overall physical appearance. Citizens could read about candidates in the newspapers, but television allowed citizens to watch and listen to the candidate. Listening to the radio required more "active participation,"[26] whereas television required "less effort by viewers," and, in turn, dominated more of their time.[27] Television influenced how people view politics today: "Candidates have learned how to stage media events that will land them on the tube."[28] Many people thought television would not be as sophisticated as radio. Media critics assumed that television's images would captivate the audience more than the facts of the story. Television images "can be draining because it can be energizing."[29] The early critics of television predicted that "when public ceremonies can be televised, fewer people will journey to witness them. The majority of people will prefer to admire at a minimum by all home comforts."[30] Not only would television stimulate the audience, but it would also create homebodies.

In 1949, ten years after the first significant television broadcast, *The New York Times* surveyed to see how television affected family unity, radio listening, reading, conversation, the influence on children, movie attendance, theater attendance, sports attendance, and the "night out."[31] The newspaper found television brought families together every evening, while radio listening, movie attendance, and reading declined. Television changed viewers' habits. At the time, "if the ultimate effects of such a social phenomenon are cloaked in uncertainty, there is a good reason. It never has happened before."[32] With any new media, it takes time to adjust and to understand the consequences. *The New York Times* points out, "The fact that one medium can pre-empt the complete attention of millions of persons simultaneously is what gives television both its unprecedented opportunity and responsibility."[33] Television made information more accessible and allowed national and world events to unfold in the privacy of one's home.

Overall, television and the presidency expected to "establish a greater rapport between the nation and its potential leaders."[34] And it did. In the 1950s, viewers knew what they wanted to watch, and politics was not always their top choice. When President Eisenhower broke into a popular television show, people complained: "A flood of telegrams proved that Americans 'liked' Ike, but they 'loved' Lucy."[35] The way citizens viewed the presidency was forever changed.

Longtime CBS News anchor Walter Cronkite, in his 1996 autobiography, said, "Television began to influence politics from the beginning."[36] The 1952 campaign, Cronkite said, was the last convention on television that looked chaotic, but by 1956, both party's conventions were more polished and organized. Because of television's influence, "delegates were even told what to wear and how to behave so as to present a more dignified appearance."[37] Cronkite would report from the convention, narrating the events for viewers. Viewers experienced what was once a mysterious process.

Broadcast news soon evolved into 24/7 cable news networks; cable stations targeted specific audiences with targeted themes. Narrowcasting changed television-viewing habits. On June 1, 1980, Ted Turner launched CNN, the first 24/7 news channel. CNN told news stories quickly—spending no more than two minutes on one story. The "CNN Effect" started affecting how people received and processed the news. The CNN Effect is "the tendency for a certain kind of intensive, highly emotional coverage to drive public policy."[38] CNN had a way of setting their news agenda to reach the president to create policy change.[39] Furthermore, the talk show format became less journalistic and more opinionated and editorial. Aaron Barlow explains that the television pundits "have no interest in resolution or reconciliation, but do everything they can to fuel discord knowing that will best bring viewers."[40]

Most recently, shows such as *The Daily Show*, which are satire, comedy news programs based on real news, began to appear. Satire news programs allow "the method to engage in serious political criticism; the label of 'fake news' enables Comedy Central's *The Daily Show* to say that which the traditional journalist cannot."[41] *The Daily Show* is framed just like a cable news program. Shows like *The Daily Show* are "also an informative examination of politics and media practices, as well as a forum for the discussion of substantive public affairs."[42] *The Daily Show* allows viewers to see that no matter how bad the world may seem, there is another side to the daily news that is laughable.

INTERNET

In 1969 the Department of Defense created the Advanced Research Projects Agency Network (ARPANET). ARPANET allowed researchers, government officials, and others to communicate and connect in different locations. Today, many would call this method of communication "email." ARPANET connected people in different geographical areas to share information. Finally, in 1991, Tim Berners-Lee developed the World Wide Web, which then grew into the intricate communication system that would allow people to read and write on the Internet.[43] When the Internet became more user-friendly, communication flowed more easily across the Web that Berners-Lee envisioned.

Not only did significant broadcast news outlets become sources of information, but so did Internet users. For the first time, the audience could start conversations with the media. The Internet's polyphony of user voices made the Internet a conversation that created a new way to consume news. This new way to consume news changed the political process, making politicians more accessible to the citizen and changed the way journalists told a story.

The Internet became a game-changer for campaigns: the more technological advances, the more distracted the voter. Not only did voters change how they gathered information, but campaigns had to start to rethink campaign strategies every four years. Campaigns now have to consider that younger voters do not rely on broadcast news or the newspaper as they did in the 1970s and the 1980s. Campaign phone banks saw a decline in engagement because citizens started using Caller-ID to filter calls from telemarketers. Television channels originally consisted only of CBS, ABC, NBC, and FOX, but now online streaming networks, including Hulu, Netflix, and Amazon Prime, provide commercial-free entertainment. Subscribing to cable is optional. The Internet rapidly grew from emails to websites to mobile phone applications. When the Internet first became more popular in the 1990s, people were skeptical that the Web was a reliable news source.

The 1992 campaign was the first campaign to use the Internet as a resource. Bill Clinton's campaign sent emails and posted them to Listservs to reach potential voters. The Internet slowly became an essential aspect of campaigning, but many people believed the Internet did not create the same effect of television, print, and direct mailings. People held on to the past. Slowly, people realized the Internet's influence; many media critics predicted the Internet would bring like-minded people together and that candidates would need to consider the Internet as a viable source to reach voters.

During the 1996 campaign, the first campaign websites appeared. As much as the Internet provided information, the 1990s "relied on paid media and waves of direct mail and paid phoning, which made voter contact more of a vote-harvesting operation."[44] The Internet allows the same vote-harvesting atmosphere, but "sometimes the use of old media helps increase the effectiveness of the new media campaign."[45] The Internet allowed people in the 1990s to compare and contrast the candidates more thoroughly than just listening to the soundbites the press provided. *The Wall Street Journal* predicted in 1996 that the Internet would become a haven for information:

Television broadcasting may one day be replaced by Internet "narrowcasting:" leaving people to get their news from and share views with only those who believe essentially what they believe.[46]

Twenty years later, this sentiment is why research studies show that social media conversations have become so polarized.[47]

In a 1999 study, Carole Anne McKeown and Kenneth D. Plowman studied Robert Dole's campaign and President Bill Clinton's campaign websites. Because the first campaign websites appeared in 1996, McKeown and Plowman found that by "incorporating interactivity in their websites, an option not available through television, candidates had an opportunity to increase voter activity."[48] The websites provided a way to expand the sound bites heard through broadcast news and print media. The website allowed voters to peruse the candidates' full agenda while not relying on television news to mediate the information.[49] Traditional news became a resource and not a necessity to learn about the 1996 presidential campaign. Voters could turn to the candidate's websites and bypass the media for any information. The candidates' websites provided a deeper understanding of each candidate's position on major campaign issues—not the horserace aspect the media usually showcases.[50]

The most exciting part of the Internet—and what Tim Berners-Lee envisioned—is an authentic participatory culture. The participatory culture of the Internet allows anyone to contribute. Howard Rheingold says, "Your voice is what distinguishes your views from others who hold the same opinions."[51] The participatory culture of the Internet is what makes the medium unique from other traditional media. Unfortunately, people participate in online discussions—only to find like-minded people. People tend to filter the news they are interested in while not viewing other sides of the conversation. No matter what, "People have always made the choice about what to pay attention to."[52]

Online News

In the late 1990s, established news brands CNN.com, MSNBC.com, ABCNews.com, and others created websites. The Internet's pivotal moment came when Kenneth Starr released a report about Bill Clinton and his affair with White House intern Monica Lewinsky.[53] The report was released on September 11, 1998, and created high Internet traffic, which proved people were reading the report. The Starr report was the first time the press was notified of breaking news simultaneously as the public. The Starr report's lesson to online news organizations was that they too should be in the trenches with both print and broadcast news reporters. People bypassed the media and went straight to the source. Before the Internet went mainstream, no one "could have envisioned a presidential scandal that played out over computer screens."[54] Each new news story became an Internet event—no one could predict which story would become the Internet's gleaming moment in journalism. Three years after the Starr report—on the same day, September 11—the Internet's real power was tested.

People were still skeptical of the influence the Internet had on journalism until September 11, 2001, when terrorists brought down the World Trade Towers in New York City and crashed an airliner into the U.S. Pentagon in Washington, DC. America stood still—in shock—looking for answers. In fact, "In the aftermath of September 11, then, it is not surprising that several online news commentators have been quick to declare the attacks to be the biggest story to break in the Internet Age."[55] September 11 shut down news websites such as CNN.com and MSNBC.com, because of high traffic. For the first time, news organizations saw the impact a big news story had on the Internet. People did not turn to television, but the Internet for more information. Many people learned about the news while at work. Since people's access to traditional media was limited, the Internet was accessible from their desks. During the aftermath, people also started learning about September 11 from major news outlets and actual observers and victims in New York City. September 11 "produced the most dramatic decline in the availability of the major news sites yet witnessed."[56] As news sites' availability was nonexistent, people started to share their stories on diary-type websites known as weblogs. On September 11, 2001, the Internet became a credible news medium.

Soon after the September 11 attacks, the Iraq War began. The Pew Research Center reported that "77% of online Americans have used the Internet in connection with the war."[57] The war showed that many people still relied on television, but "reliance on the Internet is many times greater than after the 9/11 attacks."[58] The Iraq War helped solidify the Internet as a resource to get up-to-the-minute news. Many alternative news sources emerged, which led to "the Internet's role in shaping the American public's perception of the War."[59] *The Guardian* reported on an alternative news source, a blog created by Salam Pax, a twenty-nine-year-old Iraqi man:

> While the world's leading newspapers and television networks poured millions of pounds into their coverage of the war in Iraq, it was the Internet musing of a witty young Iraqi living in a two-story house in a Baghdad suburb that scooped them all to deliver the most compelling description of life during the war.[60]

Salam Pax said the blogging world fascinated him: "Bits of news started having texture and, most amazingly, these blogs talked with each other."[61] Journalists can report the facts, but their experience to share the real narrative is sometimes limited; most importantly, traditional media is known to be one-way communication.

On the other hand, the Internet created a dialogical discourse that allowed many voices to talk, react, and question the traditional news media. Even American soldiers blogged about their experience, although the Pentagon discouraged blogging.[62] As Walter Lippmann said, "All the reporters in the world working all the hours of the day could not witness all the happenings in the world."[63] Traditional media still had problems with alternative online news; "mainstream media viewed alternative news websites like horoscopes: fine for entertainment, but not a good basis for actual decision-making."[64] This same viewpoint carried over into the 2004 election. The Internet's milestones were becoming more frequent and less important, and the Internet became an everyday medium people relied on no matter how big or small the stories. The 2004 election made the Internet a viable campaign outlet that could not be ignored or discounted.

During the 2004 election cycle, the Internet's reputation began to blossom because more people accessed the Internet as an informational and communication portal. More people relied on the Internet and felt comfortable sifting through different resources other than the usual mainstream media brands. Since the Internet allows for different viewpoints, people started to gravitate to like-minded online voices.

The 2004 Campaign

The Internet allowed for outside, unknown political candidates to gain notoriety more easily. A candidate's website "can supply voters with information for a fraction of the cost of televised ads."[65] The Internet also bypasses mainstream media outlets that typically cover only high-profile candidates. It allows people to surf to candidates they may not know and learn about their stance on issues. One research study found, "Respondents who reported visiting a candidate's website saw that candidate more favorably than those who did not visit."[66] In the 2004 election, the Internet proved to be a valuable fundraising tool and "facilitating communication with the electorate."[67] Both President George W. Bush and Senator John Kerry had campaign websites that proved useful in informing the electorate of their stance on the issues; their campaign blogs engaged with the electorate.

Both Bush and Kerry used the Internet the same way to push their issue agendas and "to use the Web as a platform to discuss many of the same issues facing the country."[68] Both President George W. Bush and Senator John Kerry's websites had blogs that highlighted more personal stories about the candidates. The study also found that the candidate's blogs did not correlate with the Web pages. One form did not reinforce the other, making it seem as if the Web pages were issue-oriented, and the blog was created to establish a personal bond.[69] Beyond the two candidates' websites, the online 2004 presidential campaign proved to be engaging in other ways, with two significant online events that defined the online influence in both campaigning and journalism.

Howard Dean

Howard Dean, governor of Vermont, is known for the scream everyone heard around the world. Well, maybe just Iowa, until the media decided to make Dean's scream a "thing" on January 19, 2004. First, before discussing Howard Dean's downfall, an essential aspect of the importance of Howard Dean is that he helped set the standard on how to communicate to voters over the Internet. Howard Dean's campaign created an Internet grassroots following that many candidates today emulate. Dean set the standard for the modern digital campaign that President Obama later executed to win in 2008.

The example of Howard Dean explains that if a candidate has a strong message, a politician can create a robust online following:

> Individuals who clearly wanted something very different in the country were meeting up of their own accord to support a candidacy that had a very strong message about change, a campaign that was confronting wrong policy and wrongdoing.[70]

Howard Dean's campaign showed the power the Internet had "as an organizing tool, with the Web spawning an extensive network of volunteers who seem as willing to pound the pavement as well as the keyboard for him."[71] Dean's campaign used the Internet as a tool to grasp a grassroots following. Joe Trippi, Dean's campaign manager, used the website "for a telethon of sorts, with frequently changing messages urging people to pull out their credit cards."[72] The campaign posted to Meetup.com, a website to connect like-minded people for different events. Meetup's founder Scott Heiferman said, "He never expected politics to be one of the service's markets."[73] The 2004 election cycle would change the way candidates campaigned in 2008, thanks to Joe Trippi, Howard Dean's campaign manager. Trippi knew the Internet was becoming as important as the television became in the 1960 election. Within three months, Dean's campaign raised $14.8 million from small donations. However, Dean's campaign succeeded by having a candidate who moved people to action and knew the Internet was mature enough. Therefore, Dean succeeded by realizing how to handle the grassroots aspect.[74] A study of Dean's blog showed "the candidate blog was primarily used as a place for supporter grassroots organizing."[75] The study also found that Dean encouraged participants "not only to share their opinions but also to engage in the act of Web content creation."[76] Even as fast as the information can spread—and as useful it is to organize groups—unless a campaign has a relatable candidate and a powerful message that moves people to action, the Internet can only do so much for a candidate with no charisma.

The news media started covering Howard Dean more closely, which meant his rhetorical mistakes were up for scrutiny. His message carried him further than expected—until he screamed. His scream in January 2004 was not unusual at rallies—but for some reason, this night was different. After the rally, the media kept replaying Howard Dean's scream. Howard Dean became the first political Internet meme, which, at the time, portrayed a less than ideal presidential image that damaged Dean's credibility. The caucus's actual video footage, which is available on YouTube, the viewer will see an excited candidate. Dean was not angry; he was rallying the crowd to create excitement. Unfortunately, the media took the scream and isolated the image of him throwing a fist up, screaming. The rhetorical influence this image showed was Howard Dean was not a stoic person whom citizens might see as presidential. Unfortunately, a scream should not have brought down a candidate so quickly. Dean's overall message was for change, but his overall message and reputation were not strong enough to survive his opponents, President George W. Bush, and seasoned politician Senator John Kerry. When a candidate's campaign combusts because of an innocent extemporaneous act, "The right thing done at the right time must also be done by the 'right person.' This means that one must judge whether one is the right person to seize an opportunity."[77]

Dan Rather

During this time, political blogs became standard and more abundant. Liberal bloggers tried to blog their candidate, Sen. John Kerry, to victory. The blogosphere during this time helped take down Dan Rather after he reported on President George Bush's questionable service in the Texas National Guard during the Vietnam War. The 2004 election is the first time the Internet played a significant role in changing the course of an election—and a veteran anchor's career.

The influence of the blogosphere was abundant in the 2004 campaign. After September 11, people started to see blogs as viable resources for information. Official presidential campaign websites housed blogs that discussed issues and other campaign news. Political blogs also created public opinion venues. For the first time in 2004, national conventions handed out press passes to political bloggers. Public opinion was now being influenced by media that was owned by large conglomerates, but also by citizen journalists.

On September 8, 2004, Dan Rather presented a story about President George W. Bush and his lack of service in the Texas National Guard. Dan Rather presented memos allegedly from President Bush's commander, Lt. Col. Jerry Killian. After the story aired, "a swarm of right-wing blogs assailed Rather's documents, claiming their typeface and spacing was inconsistent with any known typewriter of the early seventies."[78] The bloggers put questionable doubt in the public's minds, and their accusations helped destroy the credibility of longtime CBS News anchor Dan Rather. This incident could have cost President Bush the election. "Memogate" was the first instance where the users of the Internet discredited journalism. The bloggers concentrated on proving the evidence was false. However, in the end, Dan Rather still believes that the crux of the story is factual because of other evidence, and other news sources reported the story before CBS did, minus the Killian documents. Dan Rather, in his book *Rather Outspoken: My Life in the News*, explained the significance of the Internet at the time of the report:

> Although it is commonplace today, it bears mentioning that in September 2004, using the Internet as a political tool was in its infancy. We didn't realize it at the time, but what we were seeing was the beginning of a well-orchestrated Internet campaign, what has since become known as a blogswarm. And we were in the crosshairs. At the time, CBS News had no Internet presence of its own and was not accustomed to the new rules of engagement in cyberspace.[79]

The blogswarm of conservative bloggers showed a divided country and that President Bush "was the most divisive candidate during this era."[80] President Bush did win the 2004 election—but not by a landslide. Bloggers claimed victory in casting doubt in the public's minds about the authenticity of the documents. Peggy Noonan, a columnist for *The Wall Street Journal* and a political analyst, said:

> It was to me a great historical development in the history of politics in America. . . . Someday, when America is hit again, and lines go down, and media are hard to get, these bloggers and site runners and independent Internetters of all sorts will find a way to file, and get their word out, and it will be part of the saving of our country.[81]

In the end, CBS was criticized for how they handled the situation because "CBS News immediately should have reassured skeptics—however politically motivated they might have been—that it would investigate allegations about the *60 Minutes Wednesday* segment."[82] The Internet changed the course of the story by raising questions about the authenticity of the memos. If CBS had followed standard protocol with a statement to the public on how they would avoid presenting false information on air, their journalistic integrity would still have been intact.[83] The Internet won that time. Journalism had to catch up.

SOCIAL MEDIA

Welcome to the world of Web 2.0—where Americans are bombarded by messages from all directions. Henry Jenkins, in his book *Convergence Culture: Where Old and New Media Collide*, writes, "When people take media into their own hands, the results can be wonderfully creative; they can also be bad news for all involved."[84] Jenkins's dichotomy shows the instability of the media landscape. Jenkins explains:

> No one seems capable of describing both sets of changes at the same time, let alone showing how they impact each other. Some fear that media is out of control, others that it is too controlled. Some see a world without gatekeepers, others a world where gatekeepers have unprecedented power. Again, the truth lies somewhere in between.[85]

Where is that middle ground in a world of Twitter, Facebook, Snapchat, YouTube, and now live-streaming capabilities? Information floods citizens' social media feeds, in which people gravitate to like-minded opinions. The media, which used to consist of only three broadcasting networks, is now filled with 24/7 news channels, online news, and smartphones. Anyone who has a smartphone has his or her own media hub. People can now stream events live from their phones and broadcast over Twitter or Facebook, or people can live tweet events such as a Donald Trump rally. Memogate set the example that the Internet is capable of manipulating a presidential campaign. As Peggy Noonan said, the Internetters will find a way to get their word out.

Blogging was the introduction of people with no formal media training creating content. However, the Internet showed how influential digital voices could become during Memogate. In today's social media world, where a hashtag can turn into a news event, the Internet's influence over journalism is prevalent. Digital citizens have to navigate through credible information and public opinion. Blogs started the online conversation; social media helps spread the conversation. Social media is now a presidential campaign standard and a White House tool to set message agendas.

Twitter and Facebook

Twitter is a microblogging Web application that limits the user to 280 characters. Twitter allows a user to Retweet (RT) another user's tweet, Quote a tweet from another user, and Direct Message (DM) to another user. The one communication phenomenon Twitter is known for is the hashtag (#), or, as some people may call the symbol, a pound sign or an octothorp. The hashtag "is created by online users to discuss specific events and relevant issues."[86] Hashtags create an easy way to categorize conversations. For example, Hillary Clinton supporters used #Imwithher, and Donald Trump supporters used #MakeAmericaGreatAgain during the 2016 campaign. The hashtags were then hyperlinked for users to click to view Twitter users using the same hashtags. The hashtag helps categorize conversations. A hashtag is visible to a user's followers and visible to anyone else following the hashtag.[87]

Twitter slowly emerged as an intricate part of presidential campaigns. In the 2008 campaign, blogs were still a dominant form of engagement. Since the 2008 election, Twitter has allowed politicians to find their voice. Presidential candidates can bypass the media and create a quick Twitter comment, which previously could have been a sound bite in the daily newspaper or nightly newscast. Twitter allows the candidate to control their sound bites.

Additionally, Twitter allows for candidates to communicate directly with the electorate. Journalists now find out information at the same time as a candidate's Twitter followers. Candidates can "also utilize new media tools as a means to defend themselves. With the help of electronic alerts, they have near-immediate access to almost everything that is written about their campaigns."[88] The press, the candidate, and Twitter followers all have access to the information at the same moment. The most crucial aspect of a political reporter's job is "very much about ferreting out information that is important to the functioning and future of our democracy."[89] That is one aspect in this social media world journalism cannot lose sight of—it is the journalist's job to dig deeper than a 280-character tweet. Political reporters should "get to the bottom of a story, to root out the truth . . . whether it is delivered in a 140-character tweet, a 240-word blog post, a 10- or 20- or 50-inch story or a two-minute video."[90] The good news for the press is that research has found that Twitter and traditional news sources complement each other.[91]

The Pew Research Center reports that 9 percent of American adults learned about the 2016 presidential election from one type of media source—but 45 percent of American adults learned from five or more types of media sources.[92] The rankings of media sources where people learned about the 2016 presidential election are television (78 percent), digital (65 percent), radio (44 percent), and print newspaper (36 percent).[93] Pew's data shows the media complementarity theory—where people will gather information on a particular topic from not just one information source, but many. As Mohan J. Dutta-Bergman explains:

> The idea of media complementarity suggests that media outlets, instead of being conceptualized as being in direct opposition to one another, may be seen as complementary in the information gathering process. The individual, according to this approach, is loyal to the content and used media only to the extent they satisfy the need for content.[94]

People who are interested in political news will fill in the gaps of information with multiple media outlets.[95] Social media has shifted the media from a one-way informational source to a two-way informational source. Mainstream media are conversing with their audience as well as gathering information about stories from their audience. Jason Gainous and Kevin M. Wagner explain:

> Social media has created a different news paradigm alongside, and in some ways replacing, the traditional model. It operates in both directions, allowing the parties to communicate with each other, rather than one side speaking and the other listening. Further, the conversation works in a remarkably open environment that allows information that is perceived as the most interesting or appealing to be distributed to the widest audience. The user chooses not only what to access but also what content is worth redistributing across the network.[96]

This new shift in media consumption to media production allows Americans to become involved in the conversation during election season. Instead of reading about a candidate, listening to a speech, or watching a debate, Americans can create a dialogue to discuss the candidate, a speech, and a debate. Americans do not just listen, read, and watch—digital citizens create, inform, and share.

As Americans proceed through an election season with this new paradigm in news consumption, citizens must become more media savvy and remember trusted news sources are fact checked and well researched. Unfortunately, with more communication sources, there is still media bias and the occasional hoax that misinforms. People rely on a tweet rather than double-check other sources. Yes, in today's digital world, people who use social media should not take a 280-character tweet as fact from unreliable sources. People are sometimes misguided when they think their friends who shared a story over Twitter or Facebook vetted the story. Digital citizens must beware of the share and learn how to "read" media in this participatory media culture.

Recently, Facebook faced scrutiny because *Gizmodo* reported former Facebook workers claimed they "routinely suppressed news stories of interest to conservative readers from the social network's influential 'trending' section."[97] Facebook had a news algorithm managed by gatekeepers, whom they called "news curators." *Gizmodo* reported:

> Several former curators said that as the trending news algorithm improved, there were fewer instances of stories being injected. They also said that the trending news process was consistently being changed, so there's no way to know exactly how the module is run now. But the revelations undermine any presumption of Facebook as a neutral pipeline for news, or the trending news module as an algorithmically-driven list of what people are actually talking about.[98]

Most often, the gatekeepers in news organizations pick the news to report. Facebook claimed that an algorithm curated the stories that appeared in the trending section—but algorithms "are all human choices. Sometimes they're made in the design of the algorithm, sometimes around it."[99] No matter how well the algorithm works, humans create the algorithms. Facebook is a social media site and does not claim to be a news organization. Facebook is in the sharing business, not the news business. Still, with millions of people who visit Facebook daily, Facebook is smart to create a one-stop media experience—socialize and inform at the same time. Facebook users should know to seek news elsewhere from online brand-name news organizations that have established, high-quality journalistic reputations.

CONCLUSION: MEDIA'S POWER

Aristotle said in *Metaphysics*, "All men by nature desire to know."[100] As mass communication technology evolves, the more people who are in the know, the more people feel engaged, and the more people participate in the political process. As Facebook and Twitter allow people to share and opine, one must realize that Facebook and Twitter control the flow of information as print, radio, and television have done for years. Aristotle wanted us to use knowledge for good, but "it has always been recognized that anyone who could control the flow of information was in a position to exercise power over receivers of *news*."[101]

Now more than ever, people distrust traditional news media. When NBC's *Nightly News* anchor Brian Williams admitted that he fabricated a story about the Iraq War, one had to wonder, where does one find credible information? Never before have people been able to challenge the press and mainstream media as they can today. Americans have a voice, and the media must gain trust in different ways. Bill Kovach and Tom Rosenstiel, in their book *Blur: How to Know What's True in the Age of Information Overload*, suggest:

The press must become more transparent about how it verifies the news so that the public can know why the press should be trusted and can develop their process of verification. The voice of the omniscient narrator in news, simply assuring the audience is now insufficient. Since the press is no longer the only source of news, its authority must come from how it gathers and authenticates its facts.[102]

A journalist's job is to tell a factual story as well as a balanced and fair story. As messages bombard digital citizens' news feeds, the press must help people find the truth in those messages.

Every technological advancement has had people on edge, questioning how technology will affect America's current political culture. News travels fast. The audience talks back. The press is trying to fit into this new technological boom. Technology—unlike before—is more personal and engaging. People are immune to the radio, and even television's "peek-a-boo world it has constructed around us no longer seems even strange."[103] These technological immunities take time. The Internet is a tool still being inducted into our media cultural realm. The first generation of digital natives does not remember a time when the Internet was not available. There will come a time when the Internet will be as passé as radio and television. With technology evolving faster than during the height of the beginning of the radio and television era, there is always an ever-changing learning curve on how to communicate messages effectively.

The 2008 presidential election used Twitter, which was only two years old, not to the capacity that the 2016 presidential candidates used Twitter. Media takes time to integrate into society. The 2016 presidential election had candidates using Twitter to gain momentum. Presidential candidates' tweets are now considered news.

@realDonaldTrump: Why does the media, with a strong push from Crooked Hillary, keep pushing the false narrative that I want to raise taxes. Exactly opposite! (May 10, 2015)

Candidates created their own media opportunities separate from mainstream media:

@HillaryClinton: Live on Facebook: Hillary leads a round table discussion with working families in Virginia. Watch—https://t.co/qM16OacO9H (May 9, 2016)

Presidential candidates who use social media are now using social media to its full capacity. Social media and mainstream media are powerful when used to move a message. That power can hinder or help a presidential candidate as long as the candidate has a clear and understandable message that connects to the right audience. The new-media climate is one where the electorate engages in conversation with the candidate, creates media for or against the candidate, and participates in the political process that takes them beyond the mainstream media sound bite. What digital citizens must remember is to tweet with intention, consume different viewpoints, and verify before they hit share. As Walter Lippmann said:

> The world that we have to deal with politically is out of reach, out of sight, out of mind. . . . He is learning to see with his mind vast portions of the world that he could never see, touch, smell, hear or remember. Gradually he makes for himself a trustworthy picture inside his head of the world beyond his reach.[104]

Oh, but Walter Lippmann, the world is within our reach.

NOTES

1. Aristotle, "Rhetoric," in *The Basic Works of Aristotle,* ed. Richard McKeon (New York: The Modern Library, 2001), 1129.

2. John Dewey, *The Public & It's Problems* (Athens: Swallow Press, 1927), 154.

3. J. Herbert Altschull, *From Milton to McLuhan: The Ideas Behind American Journalism* (New York: Longman, 1990), 17–18.

4. William James, *Pragmatism: A New Name for Some Old Ways of Thinking* (1907: Project Gutenberg, 2004), Lecture 1, http://www.gutenberg.org/files/5116/5116-h/5116-h.htm#link2H_4_0003.

5. Paul Hitlin, "Internet, Social Media Use and Device Ownership in U.S. Have Plateaued after Years of Growth," *Pew Research Center*, September 28, 2018, http://www.pewresearch.org/fact-tank/2018/09/28/Internet-social-media-use-and-device-ownership-in-u-s-have-plateaued-after-years-of-growth/.

6. Mitchell Stephens, *A History of News* (Fort Worth: Harcourt Brace, 1997), 35.

7. Aaron Barlow, *The Rise of the Blogosphere* (Westport, CT: Praeger, 2007), 21.

8. Christopher B. Daly, *Covering America : A Narrative History of a Nation's Journalism* (Amherst: University of Massachusetts Press, 2012), 43.

9. Thomas Jefferson, *Thomas Jefferson* (New York: Library of America, 1984), 880.

10. James W. Carey, *Communication as Culture: Essays on Media and Society* (New York: Routledge, 1989), 210.

11. Tom Standage, *Writing On The Wall,* (New York: Bloomsbury, 2013), 184.

12. Carey, *Communication as Culture*, 210.

13. Daly, *Covering America*, 151.

14. Barlow, *The Rise of the Blogosphere*, 76.

15. See Rodger Streitmatter, *Mightier than the Sword: How the News Media Have Shaped American History* (Oxford: Westview Press, 1997), 68–84, for an in-depth look at how William Randolph Hearst promoted the Spanish-American War. The chapter also discusses the differences between Hearst and Pulitzer and the rise of yellow journalism.

16. Paul Starr, *The Creation of the Media : Political Origins of Modern Communications* (New York: Basic Books, 2004), 259.

17. Daly, *Covering America*, 150.

18. Starr, *The Creation of the Media*, 364.

19. "Candidates to Use Radio in Presidential Campaign," *New York Times,* June 29, 1924, XX15.

20. Ibid.

21. Ibid.

22. Ibid.

23. Ibid.

24. Willis Thompson Charles, "Radio Takes The Bunk Out Of Campaigns," *New York Times*, October 26, 1930.

25. "Seeing Hoover By Radio," *The Washington Post*, September 8, 1928.

26. Ibid.

27. Ibid.

28. Carl P. Leubsdorf, "Reporting the Tube Campaign," *Columbia Journalism Review* 14, no. 6 (1976): 8.

29. Ibid., 8–9.

30. T. Coulson, "Is Television Ripe For Picking?" *Forum and Century* XC, no. 1 (1933): 35.

31. Jack Gould, "What is Television Doing to Us?" *The New York Times*, June 12, 1949.

32. Ibid.

33. Ibid.

34. Ibid.

35. Troy, *See How They Ran*, 200.

36. Walter Cronkite, *A Reporter's Life* (New York: Alfred A. Knopf, 1996), 178.

37. Ibid., 182.

38. Ibid., 408.

39. Ibid., 408.

40. Barlow, *The Rise of the Blogosphere*, 126–127.

41. Geoffrey Baym, "The Daily Show: Discursive Integration and the Reinvention of Political Journalism," *Political Communication* 22, no. 3 (2005): 273.

42. Ibid., 263.

43. See Dan Gillmor, *We the Media: Grassroots Journalism By the People, For the People* (Sebastopol, CA: O'Reilly, 2004), 23–43.

44. Will Robinson, "The Digital Revolution: Campaigns and New Media Communications," in *Margin of Victory: How Technologists Help Politicians Win Elections*, ed. Nathaniel G. Pearlman (Santa Barbara, CA: Praeger, 2012), 5.

45. Ibid., 13.

46. Jason Fry, "The Age of Internet Politics," *Wall Street Journal*, November 6, 1996.

47. See Mark Jurkowitz, Amy Mitchell, Elisa Shearer, and Mason Walker, "U.S. Media Polarization and the 2020 Election: A Nation Divided," January 24, 2020, https://www.journalism.org/2020/01/24/u-s-media-polarization-and-the-2020-electi on-a-nation-divided/.

48. Carol Anne McKeown and Kenneth D. Plowman, "Reaching Publics on the Web During the 1996 Presidential Campaign," *Journal of Public Relations Research* 11, no. 4 (October 1999): 342.

49. Ibid., 341.

50. Ibid., 340.

51. Howard Rheingold, *Net Smart* (Cambridge, MA: MIT Press, 2012), 122.

52. Ibid., 127.

53. See Jon Ronso, "Monica Lewinsky: 'The Shame Sticks to You Like Tar,'" *The Guardian,* April 22, 2016, https://www.theguardian.com/technology/2016/apr/16 /monica-lewinsky-shame-sticks-like-tar-jon-ronson. Monica Lewinsky discusses in a rare press interview her life after being a White House intern as well as being publicly shamed. Lewinsky's anti-bullying campaign has given her a voice to help others who may be cyberbullied or publicly shamed.

54. Kelly Heyboer, "Web Feat," *American Journalism Review* 20, no. 9 (November 1998): 26.

55. Stuart Allan, "Reweaving The Internet: Online News of September 11," in *Journalism After September 11*, ed. Barbie Zelizer and Stuart Allan (New York: Routledge, 2002), 119–140.

56. Ibid., 123.

57. Susannah Fox, Lee Rainie, and Deborah Fallows, "The Internet and the Iraq War," *Pew Research Center Internet, Science & Tech,* April 1, 2003, http://www .pewInternet.org/2003/04/01/the-Internet-and-the-iraq-war/#.

58. Ibid.

59. John W. Jordan, "Disciplining the Virtual Home Front: Mainstream News and the Web During the War in Iraq," *Communication & Critical/Cultural Studies* 4, no. 3 (September 2007): 277.

60. Rory McCarthy, "Salam's Story," *The Guardian*, May 30, 2003, http://www .theguardian.com/world/2003/may/30/iraq.digitalmedia.

61. Salam Pax, "I Blame the Profane Perfect Arab Blogger," *The Guardian,* September 9, 2003, http://www.theguardian.com/world/2003/sep/09/iraq.biography.

62. Ari Melber, "Web War," *The Nation,* September 15, 2008, 25.

63. Walter Lippmann, *Public Opinion* (New York: Free Press Paperbacks, 1922), 214.

64. John W. Jordan, "Disciplining the Virtual Home Front," 277.

65. Philip Paolino and Daron Shaw, "Can the Internet Help Outsider Candidates Win the Presidential Nomination?" *Political Science and Politics* 36, no. 2 (April 2003): 193.

66. Ibid, 195–196.

67. Andrew Paul Williams, Kaye D. Trammell, Monica Postelnicu, Kristen D. Landreville and Justin D. Martin, "Blogging and Hyperlinking: Use of the Web to Enhance Viability during the 2004 US Campaign," *Journalism Studies* 6, no. 2 (2005): 177.

68. Ibid., 183.

69. Ibid., 185.

70. Howard Dean, interview by Thomas Streeter and Zephyr Teachout, "How the Internet Taught Me that You have the Power: Interview with Howard Dean." In *Mousepads, Shoe Leather, and Hope,* ed. Zephyr Teachout and Thomas Streeter (Boulder, CO: Paradigm Publishers, 2008), 15.

71. Julie Kosterlitz, "The Internet Shows Its Muscles," *National Journal* 35, no. 40 (October 4, 2003): 3060.

72. Michael Janofsky, "Internet Helps Make Candidate a Contender," *New York Times*, July 5, 2003, A8.

73. Dan Gillmor, *We the Media: Grassroots Journalism by the People, for the People* (Sebastopol, CA: O'Reilly, 2004), 95.

74. Ibid., 95–96.

75. Sharon Meraz, "Analyzing Political Conversation on the Howard Dean Candidate Blog," in *Blogging, Citizenship, and the Future of Media*, ed. Mark Tremayne (New York: Routledge, 2007), 77.

76. Ibid., 77.

77. Amelie Frost Benedikt, "On Doing the Right Thing at The Right Time: Toward an Ethics of Kairos," in *Rhetoric and Kairos: Essays in History, Theory, and Praxis*, ed. Phillip Sipiora and James S. Baumlin (Albany, NY: State University of New York Press, 2002), 232.

78. Joe Hagan, "Truth or Consequences," *Texas Monthly*, May 2012, http://www.texasmonthly.com/story/truth-or-consequences.

79. Dan Rather, *Rather Outspoken: My Life in the News* (New York: Grand Central Publishing, 2012), Nook e-book, chap. 2.

80. Alan I. Abramowitz and Walter J. Stone, "The Bush Effect: Polarization, Turnout, and Activism in the 2004 Presidential Election," *Presidential Studies Quarterly* 36, no. 2 (June 2006): 153.

81. Peggy Noonan, "So Much to Savor," *Wall Street Journal*, November 4, 2004, http://www.wsj.com/articles/SB122460651917154585.

82. Michael Bugeja, "Making Whole: The Ethics of Correction," *Journal of Mass Media Ethics* 22, no. 1. (2007): 56.

83. Ibid., 62.

84. Henry Jenkins, *Convergence Culture: Where Old and New Media Collide* (New York: New York University Press, 2006), 6.

85. Ibid., 18.

86. Vanessa Doctor, "Hashtag History: When and What Started it?" *Hashtags.org,* May 30, 2013, https://www.hashtags.org/featured/hashtag-history-when-and-what-started-it/.

87. Axel Bruns and Jean Burgess, "Researching News Discussion on Twitter: New Methodologies," *Journalism Studies: The Future of Journalism 2011: Developments and Debates* 13, no. 5/6 (2012): 804.

88. Jodi Enda, "Campaign Coverage in the Time of Twitter," *American Journalism Review* 33, no. 2 (2011): 18.

89. Ibid., 21.

90. Ibid., 21.

91. Itai Himelboim, Derek Hansen, and Anne Bowser, "Playing in the Same Twitter Network," *Information, Communication & Society* 16, no. 9 (2013): 1393.

92. Jeffrey Gottfried, Michael Barthélemy, Elisa Shearer, and Amy Mitchell, "The 2016 Presidential Campaign—A News Event That's Hard to Miss," *Pew Research Center: Journalism & Media*, February 4, 2016, http://www.journalism.org /2016/02/04/the-2016-presidential-campaign-a-news-event-thats-hard-to-miss/.

93. Ibid.

94. Mohan J. Dutta-Bergman, "Complementarity in Consumption of News Types Across Traditional and New Media," *Journal of Broadcasting & Media* 48, no. 1 (March 2004): 49.

95. Ibid.

96. Jason Gainous and Kevin. M. Wagner, *Tweeting to the Power: The Social Media Revolution in American Politics* (Oxford, Oxford University Press, 2014), Kindle e-book, chap 1.

97. Michael Nunez, "Former Facebook Workers: We Routinely Suppressed Conservative News," *Gizmodo*, May 9, 2016, http://www.gizmodo.com.

98. Ibid.

99. Tarleton Gillespie, "Algorithms, Click Workers, and the Befuddled Fury around Facebook Trends," *Neiman Lab*, May 19, 2016, http://www.niemanlab.org/ 2016/05/algorithms-clickworkers-and-the-befuddled-fury-around-facebook-trends/.

100. Aristotle, "Metaphysics," in *The Basic Works of Aristotle,* ed. Richard McKeon (New York: The Modern Library, 2001), 689.

101. Altschull, *From Milton to McLuhan,* 329.

102. Bill Kovach and Tom Rosenstiel, *Blur: How to Know What's True in the Age of Information Overload* (New York: Bloomsbury, 2010), 185.

103. Neil Postman, *Amusing Ourselves to Death: Public Discourse in the Age of Show Business* (New York: Penguin Books, 1985), 79.

104. Walter Lippmann, *Public Opinion* (New York: Free Press Paperbacks, 1922), 18.

Chapter 3

Blogs and Barack Obama's Rhetoric

The beginning of Barack Obama's influence on running a multimedia presidential campaign started when the then-senator announced his run for the presidency in February 2007 at the Old State Capitol in Springfield, Illinois. The top of the campaign sign attached to his podium included the URL BarackObama.com. Obama's campaign manager, David Plouffe, said the announcement setting looked good on television, and "the message was a clear and distinctive frame for his candidacy."[1] The overarching message that day, both visually and rhetorically, was about "Change."

Barack Obama's message was about change for the country and a change in political rhetoric: Change in engagement and change in citizenship. In his speech that day, Obama exclaimed:

> That is why this campaign can't only be about me. It must be about us—it must be about what we can do together. This campaign must be the occasion, the vehicle, of your hopes, and your dreams. It will take your time, your energy, and your advice—to push us forward when we're doing right, and to let us know when we're not. This campaign has to be about reclaiming the meaning of citizenship, restoring our sense of common purpose, and realizing that few obstacles can withstand the power of millions of voices calling for change.[2]

Throughout the campaign, Obama's message stayed on point. American citizens learned what reclaiming the meaning of citizenship meant—including creating a digital citizen who did not have to leave their home to support their candidate of choice. Most importantly, the Internet provided a gateway to the political process no one had previously utilized. Obama's announcement reinvented presidential campaigns with a sign of the change ahead—BarackObama.com.

Obama's campaign created a user-friendly website, which allowed supporters to organize fundraising events. One significant influence in the online Obama campaign was Chris Hughes, co-founder of Facebook. Hughes helped design a campaign website that helped "like-minded supporters across the country come together to generate new financial support, share ideas and ways of volunteering."[3] The website's donation page looked "like the checkout page on Amazon.com. About a quarter of Mr. Obama's $25 million first-quarter haul came via the Internet from more than 50,000 donors."[4] The campaign team organized My.BarackObama.com for active social media users who were familiar with the Facebook format. The website allowed supporters to create a profile, limited to one personal photograph and a small biography. David Talbot explained,

> The Obama team put such technologies at the center of its campaign—among other things recruiting 24-year-old Chris Hughes, co-founder of Facebook, to help develop them. And it managed those tools well. Supporters had considerable discretion to use MyBO to organize on their own; the campaign did not micromanage but struck a balance between top-down control and anarchy. In short, Obama, the former Chicago community organizer, created the ultimate online political machine.[5]

The website contained campaign tools that allowed supporters to help with fundraising. Instead of the campaign doing all the work, the website encouraged supporters to become a channel to inform their followers. This motivational campaign tool allowed Obama's campaign message to spread organically.

2008 PRESIDENTIAL CAMPAIGN

"Change" became the mantra for how Americans experienced presidential elections. Thanks to Howard Dean, the campaign blog became an integral part of the campaign process, which Obama's team used to create a strong presence. As social media started to bud, blogging was still popular. The blog connected the reader to the candidate and the candidate to the reader. This new type of relationship created valuable action plans over the Internet, which became key to growing the grassroots campaign Obama needed to keep his campaign thriving.

Obama's campaign used both traditional and new mass communication methods. The Internet, especially new social networking sites, allowed the Obama campaign to organize and recruit volunteers to walk door-to-door or make phone calls to support their campaign. Rasmus Nielsen reported, "In political campaigns, new technologies have not replaced older forms of communication as much as they have revived them."[6] Nielsen argues that modern political campaigns use "people as media."[7] Daniel Kreiss explains,

> On social media platforms, campaigns use data and analytics to identify their supporters, determine their influence, and track their engagement. Campaigns urge their supporters to share political content and make personal appeals to their friends on these platforms.[8]

Collecting data and analytics from social media users allowed the campaign to craft shareable messages to identify with the electorate's collective ideas and goals. Elizabeth A. Petre writes, "Identification is a helpful concept to use when exploring political campaign communication, as candidates attempt to get the public to identify and connect with their message (and ultimately, vote for them)."[9]

Andrew Bleeker and Nathaniel Lubin both worked on digital marketing for the 2008 Obama campaign. After the Iowa primary, they said, they had a particularly busy night:

> We remember just hitting the computer screen, hoping it would refresh and not crash anything. In one night, both the Obama and Hillary campaigns made more money through online ads than any campaign before me.[10]

Bleeker and Lubin write that digital marketing was expensive, but the campaign had to do something different. They both said digital campaigns are more targeted and "ramped up on short notice to capture the peak of a target audience's interest."[11]

Obama's social media team created a website that engaged supporters to move to action. Obama's website created an online community to raise money and organize groups of people to canvas and make phone calls. Consequently, Obama's online campaign strategy created a way for Obama's campaign to quickly respond to opponents' attacks. Instantly, Obama's campaign could respond to attack advertisements from his opponents. For example, when Hillary Clinton asked, "It's 3 a.m. and your children are safe and asleep. Who do you want answering the phone?"[12] Obama had a response advertisement within a few hours. The quickness of the response "highlighted the speed with which campaigns now believe they must react to attacks."[13] By contrast, when Lyndon B. Johnson's "Daisy" commercial aired in 1964, Barry Goldwater's rebuttal took weeks.[14] Obama's team had a rebuttal advertisement within the same day, and the ad was shareable.

Moreover, the Internet is also a place to expand and explain rogue sound bites. YouTube videos "have been called the death of the TV sound bite, for the way voters can experience lengthen realities without the filters of a news show constrained by time-limits and commercials."[15] What made the most impact was Facebook—where people could comment and share candidate information.

John McCain

President Herbert Hoover's opponent, Al Smith, did not use radio effectively in the 1928 campaign because he avoided speaking into the microphone. The same concept applied to Senator John McCain's presidential campaign. McCain failed to use digital media for his campaign's rhetorical advantage. John McCain was qualified to become president, but his campaign could not grasp the same kind of grassroots movement that Obama's digital campaign created. Daniel Kreiss writes, "staffers on both sides of the aisle cited the ways the Obama campaign in 2008 helped create impassioned supporters through design, messaging, and rhetoric across multiple platforms."[16] McCain's campaign message did not reach across multiple platforms to create the excitement Obama's campaign created. McCain's campaign was more traditional and did not focus on the digital citizen because "the e-Campaign team had little autonomy on the campaign, was generally undervalued, and was not in a position to win battles for resources."[17] Furthermore, the campaign's digital media struggles showed because McCain's website lacked content and consistency.

Although McCain was the first politician to use the Internet for fundraising, his website did not engage readers as well as Obama's. McCain's website did not have a "Web 2.0" feel and instead felt static. McCain tried to create a social network called "McCainSpace" housed on his campaign website, JohnMcCain.com, but supporters did not use the space.[18] In October 2008, before the national election, McCain's blog was nonexistent. Jennifer Stromer-Galley explains, "In the thick of the general election, McCain focused more on traditional, mass-media campaigning, spending precious resources on television ads."[19] The staff had visions of digital applications to entice voters, but "they did not contemplate effective but inexpensive ways to innovate with (digital communication technologies) to mount a super-supporter-driven-campaign."[20] Overall, the visual rhetoric of McCain's campaign website's design helped prove Obama's message that McCain was out of touch and too old. The overall look of Obama's campaign offline and online created a youthful and fresh image—a vision for Change.

Obama, who was forty-six years old to McCain's seventy-two, was noticeably younger. The media kept reminding citizens about McCain's age. The media mentioned McCain's age 1,390 times during the campaign season; the media mentioned Obama's age 898 times in print, broadcast, and cable transcripts from June 1 to November 4, 2008.[21] The repetition and the comparison of McCain's and Obama's ages became a rhetorical strategy to convince voters McCain was too old to become president. Obama's campaign knew how to tell a compelling story about their opponent: "in the course of campaigns, narratives don't just exist, they're created. Candidates must discern what the public's looking for and how to step into that role."[22]

McCain's campaign tried to promote him as a war hero, telling the story of how, in 1967, McCain's plane was shot down, and he spent five years in a North Vietnam prison as a prisoner of war.[23] McCain's campaign labeled him as a "maverick" who would do anything for his country. During America's economic downward slide during the election, Obama's "Change" message resonated more than McCain's maverick, war hero status. Obama's message of change permeated his campaign:

> Obama's very face showed the radical break his election would be with the past. He's black. In a country, not quite 150 years past slavery and just 40 years past the assassination of the Rev. Dr. Martin Luther King, Jr., hope wasn't just the message, it was the visage. If voters wondered (and some surely hoped it might) whether electing John McCain would just be giving Bush four more years, they knew that electing Barack Obama would not.[24]

McCain's lack of an online presence during the last month of his campaign reinforced Obama's argument that he was out of touch. Moreover, McCain's rhetorical strategy concentrated on the "I" am a war hero instead of identifying with the "We."

ONLINE POLITICAL RHETORIC

New media's ability to create a two-way communication venue was still new for campaigns. In *The Rise of the Blogosphere,* Aaron Barlow explains, "Over the intervening century and a half, the pressures of commercialism and professionalism constrained the public sphere, limiting the ability of the people—the amateurs—to participate directly in the discussions."[25] Through new media, the audience can hear a candidate's message and give feedback to the campaign, and the candidate can then respond. Campaigns post and, hopefully, citizens respond to post their support and concerns. This interaction is helpful to both the voter and the candidate: the candidate learns which messages are clear and which messages need clarifying; the voter learns about the candidate without the influence of mainstream media.

According to Andrew W. Robertson in *The Language of Democracy,* not only did technology enrich the relationship between the electorate and a candidate, but technology also changed the language of politics.[26] The American people are participants in the electoral process, and technology encourages participation beyond voting. Andrew W. Robertson argues:

> A participatory political culture, in which the voters take more than an acquiescent role in politics, requires a form of rhetoric that intersects with their moral sensibilities, informs them of their obligations, and elicits their interest. In oral, printed, and visual appeals, a language had to be discovered, which provided voters the means for determining the suitability of a candidate or a course of action. Voters cannot judge measures in the same way they do men; voters required a new language for appraising policy in the same way they had earlier evaluated personality.[27]

Robertson adds that the mass-circular presses and the communication revolution during the 1830s allowed for a rhetorical innovation by the leaders.[28] He writes:

> A mark of the transforming leader is a speaker or writer who can create a new pattern of resonant appeal from familiar theorems at his disposal. . . . The rhetorical innovators exploited old themes, new technology, and market orientation to recreate new rhetorical opportunities for themselves and those that followed.[29]

Barack Obama's campaign knew they needed to use new media to their advantage. The Internet allowed for a new way to craft messages for micro audiences. New media made it easy for Obama's campaign to build online communities. The campaign strategy was to identify as a "We." The Internet allowed Obama's campaign to reinforce what they emphasized offline. Elizabeth Petre explains, "The grassroots organizing efforts of Barack Obama's 2008 presidential campaign offered an effective model for national political campaigns that emphasized the power of the Internet and social media with direct actions on the ground."[30]

The Rhetoric of Sound Bites

Unlike print, radio, and television, the Internet allows for argumentative language. Kathleen Hall Jamieson believes media has omitted what she considers an integral element—argument. In "Discourse and the Democratic Ideal," Jamieson argues:

> Moreselized ads and news items consistent instead of statement alone, a move that invites us to judge the merit of the claim on the ethos of the speaker or

the emotional appeals (pathos)-unwrapping the claim. In the process, appeal to reason (logos)—one of Aristotle's prime means of persuasion—is lost. With it goes some of the audience's ability to judge.[31]

Candidate blogs allowed the candidates to expand and explain sound bites that audiences misinterpreted when published through television, radio, and print.

Moreover, blogs allowed candidates to manipulate the rhetorical situation by expanding sound bites into rich, persuasive messages. On April 13, 2008, Kate Albright-Hanna posted:

> In the age of constant media chatter about sound bites and poll numbers, what does it really mean when Barack says that he thinks that "change happens not from the top-down, but from the bottom up?"
>
> It means that the people you rarely see in the spotlight are the ones who are actually driving this campaign: our field organizers and unpaid volunteers.

The campaign blog highlighted these field organizers. The expanded sound bite and explanation allow for the campaign to expand on Obama's ideas. Jamieson writes, "The shifts in how our leaders communicate affect their ability to lead as well."[32]

Obama's campaign blog allowed the campaign to expand sound bites lost in translation. The Obama campaign's explanations only enhanced the candidate's persuasive message because of the timeliness. On October 4, 2008, Christopher Hass posted a response from campaign spokesperson Bill Burton about John McCain's campaign strategy to distract from the fallen economy:

> On a day after we learned that American lost three-quarters of a million jobs this year and a week after our financial system teetered on the brink of collapse, John McCain and his campaign have announced they want to "turn the page" on the economic crisis facing working families and spend the last month of this election launching dishonest, dishonorable character attacks against Barack Obama. We understand that it's not easy for John McCain to defend the worst economic record of our lifetime, but he will have to explain to the people struggling to pay their bills and stay in their homes why he would rather spend his time tearing down Barack Obama than laying out a plan to build up our economy.

Burton refuted McCain's character attacks. The rhetorical figure, *apodioxis*, which is refusing absurd and false claims, helped Burton argue McCain tried to deflect from the more significant issue—the economy. This post also united the "We" through identification through antithesis. George Cheney explains this is "the act of uniting against a common 'enemy.'"[33]

What Is an Author?

Deborah Tannen explains, "Technology also exacerbates the culture of critique by making it much easier for politicians or journalists to ferret out inconsistencies in a public person's statements over time."[34] The 2008 campaign showed citizens that social networking sites allowed the audience to analyze and compare the candidates' arguments without media involvement. The public can scrutinize, support, and gather information quickly.

The online posts for the candidate are to reflect their voice and their campaign. Campaign staff members or volunteers craft the blog and social media posts. Michel Foucault called this "author function." In his essay "What Is an Author?,"[35] Foucault explains that an author's "precedence is functional in that it serves as a means of classification."[36] Additionally, "The function of an author is to characterize the existence, circulation, and operation of certain discourses within a society."[37] Therefore, the campaign blogs function as a tool for building a discourse community for the candidate and not for the actual author who posts.

Of course, Obama and other campaign officials participate and assist the blog's author(s) by sending individual messages to post on the blog. The campaign organizers' posts help identify common grounds with the audience. George Cheney explains the common ground technique is "where the rhetor equates or links himself or herself with others in an overt manner."[38] The collection of individual blog posts then becomes a polyphonic, persuasive text to explain why people should vote for a candidate. The universal message "We" are fighting for the same "Change."

Polyphony of Voices

Mikhail Bakhtin, a twentieth-century literary theorist from Russia, studied language and discourse in the novel. Bakhtin believes that through language, humans reveal more about themselves. For example, the nature of language may reveal the character of a presidential candidate. In *The Dialogical Imagination,* Bakhtin explains how language creates a dialogical interaction through the novel. However, scholars can apply Bakhtin's theories to other texts, such as online political rhetoric.

Bakhtin explains that the dialogical aspect and dynamics of language are about the intention of the speaker. In his book *The Dialogical Imagination,* Bakhtin writes:

> Language, for the individual consciousness, lies on the borderline between oneself and the other. The word in language is half someone else's. It becomes "one's own" only within the speaker populates it with his own intention, his

own accent when he appropriates the word, adapting it to his own semantic and expressive intention.[39]

For language to work, both a speaker and an audience must exist. If one or the other is missing, the message within the utterance is lost. To understand the dialogic nature of human thought is to understand the dialogic understanding of the idea. Bakhtin argues:

> The idea *lives* not in one person's *isolated* individual consciousness—if it remains there only, it degenerates and dies. The idea begins to live, that is, to take shape, to develop, to find and renew its verbal expression, to give birth to new ideas, only when it enters into genuine dialogic relationships with other ideas, with the ideas of *others*.[40]

The critical point Bakhtin makes is that a communicator is always aware of their audience. The communicator and audience are creating a dialogue. Bakhtin scholar Michael Holquist writes, "Dialogically conceived authorship is a form of governance, for both are implicated in the architectonics of responsibility, each is a way to adjudicate center/non-center relations between subjects."[41] In other words, authors can bring the audience closer to the candidate or pull the audience away from an issue through language. The author uses language to provoke a response from the audience. If that response is not what they intended, the author may want to revise and rewrite the message to provoke the appropriate (re)action from their audience.

Barack Obama's campaign team needed to understand their audience's ideas or opinions to have a genuine dialogical interaction. Kenneth Burke explains, "You persuade a man only insofar as you can talk his language by speech, gesture, tonality, order, image, attitude, idea, identifying your ways with his."[42] Words form from ideas, and those words then result in back-and-forth interchanges, which usually result in the form of persuasion. In other words, Bakhtin's idea that more diverse speech, which blends people's experiences, in turn, creates a more intense and thought-provoking dialogue than a monologic dialogue that does not consider the "We" but only the "I." For example, on April 16, 2008, Christopher Hass posted "Matching Donations: 'Together We Can Make a Difference'":

> All-day long, we've seen more and more people join in our matching donor program, taking advantage of the opportunity to share their personal message with a fellow donor and to double their impact. One by one (or two by two), they are taking this campaign into their own hands, and showing the power of millions of people coming together to work for change.

From Roger in Virginia:

I just wanna say that I, "the little guy," finally feel like I can make a difference. It is amazing how all of us are coming together to make a difference.

From Pamela in Texas:

I'm glad I'm in a position to match your contribution! The fact that it's people like you and me giving to Obama, making him beholden to the American people and NOT corporate lobby interests, is one of the primary reasons I'm so enthusiastic about his candidacy. . .

From Peggy in Oregon:

I feel like for the 1st time in my life that I can actually make a difference because I believe so much in Barack's ability to inspire everyday people like me.

The campaign organizers concentrated on the "We." The "We" identifies the common grounds to achieve the common goal.

THE THREE APPEALS

Aristotle believed that a powerful, persuasive message should include three appeals: *logos* (arguments of logic), *ethos* (argument of credibility), and *pathos* (argument of emotion). To expand these three appeals, Aristotle wrote that a person must be able:

(1) to reason logically, (2) to understand human character and goodness in their various forms, and (3) to understand the emotions—that is, to name them and describe them, to know their causes and the way in which they are excited.[43]

M. Jimmie Killingsworth, who wrote the article "Rhetorical Appeals: A Revision," argues that these "terms fail to cover the variety of uses and the full suggestiveness of the concept."[44] Killingsworth believes that the relationship of all three elements should be considered triangularly.[45] He suggests that the triangle becomes the positions of the author, audience, and value.[46]

Most importantly, Killingsworth's model is about community: "The author's position represents a particular communal outlook that points toward agreed-upon values and invites the audience to join (or return to) the community."[47] This communal outlook leads the rhetor to find new ways to identify with the audience. Robert L. Heath explains:

Rhetoric, in sum, works its symbolic magic through identification. It can bring people together by emphasizing the "margin of overlap" between the rhetor's and the audience's experiences, and even lead to consubstantiation. If people find that old identifications are unacceptable, they can be persuaded, and even persuade themselves, to abandon them and adopt new ones.[48]

The Internet can nurture and organically grow a communal outlook. Killingsworth also notes that the movement usually occurs through a medium.[49] The ideas and values of both candidate and audience are at the forefront, which allows for a new Aristotelian-style techno-persuasive dialogue.

Digital *Ethos*

Building Barack Obama's *ethos* was one of the most important aspects of his campaign. Many American citizens were not familiar with Barack Obama. Obama was young and still a novice in politics as a freshman U.S. senator.

All candidates make mistakes during their campaigns; Obama is not an exception. Mayhill Fowler reported in *The Huffington Post* that Obama made a controversial statement at a fundraiser:

> Obama made a problematic judgment call in trying to explain working class culture to a much wealthier audience. He described blue-collar Pennsylvanians with a series of what in the eyes of Californians might be considered pure negatives: guns, clinging to religion, antipathy, xenophobia.[50]

The Huffington Post posted the audio of the comment. Obama explained his comment because "the digital communication technologies his campaign had been using so effectively had also been used against him."[51] Campaigns learned, "The hybrid media environment made the challenge of image construction even greater for candidates."[52] On April 14, 2008, Christopher Hass posted "Social Networking Update":

> More and more responses from Pennsylvania residents continue to pour in, sharing their stories and their frustrations at a government that they feel no longer listens or speaks to them. In addition, supporters from all over the country have left comments on Barack's *MySpace* and *Facebook* pages, often echoing these same concerns.
>
> From Ehtermind:
> *Barack you are not out of touch my friend. You are the leader that understands the massive issues this country is facing.*
>
> From They call me "B":
> *Senator Obama, you hit the nail on the head! Voters are bitter . . . Americans, such as myself, are bitter their voices are not being heard.*

These social networking sites are just one of the many ways that you can reach out and connect with each other with the campaign and a presidency that listens, and that understands that millions of voices cannot be ignored.

The campaign showed examples of Pennsylvanians who agreed with the issues Obama discussed in his controversial speech. Obama did not establish his *ethos* through experience—he established his *ethos* through language by showing how supporters identified with his words. It was also the language of others that validated his. This validation increased his ethos and dismissed Hillary Clinton's accusation that Obama was "out of touch."

In "Ethos Dwells Pervasively: A Hermeneutic Reading of Aristotle on Credibility," Craig Smith explains that the orator must adapt to the audience.[53] The audience in presidential campaigns is the community. In fact, in Aristotle's *Nicomachean Ethics*, the community is about a common advantage.[54] Aristotle explains,

> Now all forms of community are like parts of the political community; for men journey together with a view to some particular advantage, and to provide something that they need for the purposes of life; and it is for the sake of advantage that the political community too seems both to have come together originally and to endure, for this is what legislators aim at, and they call just that which is to the common advantage.[55]

Obama's campaign identified a common goal with the audience—winning the presidential election. The Obama campaign showed their candidate's advantages by presenting examples (*exemplum*) on their blog, which allows the electorate to follow endorsements and volunteer activities.

Orators use *exemplum* to generalize, such as "I am the best candidate to become president."[56] Through *exemplum*, the orator proves his or her point with evidence. Aristotle writes, "The use of persuasive speech is to lead to decisions."[57] On May 14, 2008, Sam Graham-Felsen posted "John Edwards Endorses Barack Obama for President." Within the blog post, Graham-Felsen also posted an email from Barack Obama:

Friend—

I have some exciting news.

My good friend John Edwards is endorsing our campaign and joining our movement for change.

Let's welcome John Edwards to the campaign with an outpouring of the kind of grassroots support that is bringing our political process back to the people.

Barack Obama's message creates a feeling of unity when he says, "Let's welcome John Edwards to the campaign." These endorsement examples help persuade readers to reach an informed decision and feel as if they are a part of the process.

During the presidential campaign, the campaign announced super delegate endorsements as well as those of city officials, newspapers, and congressional representatives. These endorsements helped present Obama as a credible, viable candidate. These people acted independently from the campaign to recognize Obama as their candidate. One such organization, the American Postal Workers Union (APWU), released a statement that Obama highlighted on my.barackobama.com. Campaigner Sam Graham-Felsen posted on April 9, 2008, the news of the endorsement, followed by the press release:

> The American Postal Workers Union has endorsed Barack Obama for president. The APWU is the world's largest postal union, representing over 330,00 USPS employees and retirees, as well as nearly 2,000 private-sector mail workers.

The blog post highlighted the press release sent out by the APWU, which elevated the endorsement and Obama's credibility with government workers. Obama's campaign team built his reputation one blog post and endorsement at a time.

Kenneth L. Hacker explains, "winning presidential candidates find the weaknesses in their public images and use persuasive messages to change those perceptions."[58] Obama's campaign identified his weakness—his lack of experience—and countered that information by posting endorsement announcements.

As for John McCain and Hillary Clinton, both were already well known and had the advantage of mentioning their past accomplishments. McCain was labeled a "maverick" for his time spent in the military and as a seasoned Arizona senator. Clinton is a former first lady who transitioned into a successful New York senator. Unfortunately, their online presence was lacking at a time when an audience expected a presidential candidate to have an online presence. Obama's campaign understood that in 2008 Americans' news consumption was changing. Obama's campaign posted transcripts and videos of his speeches and highlighted volunteers' reasons for their campaign support. The grassroots efforts, both online and offline, built Obama's *ethos* through narratives.

To keep the feeling of unity, Obama's campaign organizers highlighted volunteers' narratives. One example from the Pennsylvania state update blog highlighted the reason why Cathie supports Obama:

> Less than a hundred miles from Cathie's home in southern Pennsylvania, Barack Obama gave a compelling speech in mid-March addressing the role

of race in America entitled "A More Perfect Union." The speech, given at the National Constitution Center in Philadelphia, amazed her and inspired her to follow the campaign intently.

"His approach to the issues of the race and diversity is so incredibly real, honest, and compassionate," she said.

The idea of citizens taking a greater role in the political process resonates with Cathie. She studied mass communications in graduate school and knows broadly supported movements are wholly effective. Through our involvement, and Barack's leadership, we can create this change. (August 7, 2008)

These personal narratives identified with the types of support Obama was gaining.

After the first presidential debate between Barack Obama and John McCain, Amanda Scott posted "Early Reviews Are In: Obama 'Terrific,' Honest,' 'Direct Hit'" on September 26, 2008:

Philadelphia Inquirer: McCain Uncertain, "McCain has been uncertain— Obama not."
The Atlantic: McCain sounds angry and passionate; Obama seems cool.
Talking Points Memo: Obama seems to have come into the debate with a much clearer strategy.
New Republic: Obama tells it like it is on economics: Obama just gave a terrific, honest explanation of his economic agenda.

A persuasive argument has proof. The newspaper headlines above were proof people supported Obama's political stances. Obama, through his blog, gave his readers proof. Sharing examples is a simple and successful rhetorical strategy to build one's credibility. Online means of communication allow candidates to expand their arguments to provide as much information as the electorate needs to decide on Election Day. The persuasive powers increased.

Digital *Pathos*

Aristotle defines *pathos* as, "the emotions are all those feelings that so change men as to affect their judgments, and that are also attended by pain or pleasure."[59] Jeanne Fahnstock explains that to achieve the emotional connection, figures of speech should "'add distinction' or other virtues in the sense that the text with appropriate figures has used the most effective linguistic means possible to do its work."[60] Obama wanted to create a feeling for a need for change

One rhetorical figure that Obama's campaign—and most all other political campaigns—relied upon to persuade citizens to move to action is the rhetorical figure *protrope*. *Protrope* encourages independent action. Henry Peacham, in his 1593 text *The Garden of Eloquence*, explains:

> The use of this figure is great, and often necessaries and needfull to be used, the virtue and power whereof is worthie of high praise and commendation, for when commanding cannot force, nor promises allure, nor combination terrifie, as alone by themselves working in their single strengthes: yet Adhoratation having al these conjoined with it, and also sundry reasons of mightie power, as helping hands to force and move the mind forward, to a willing consent, doth prevailed in his purpose.[61]

Peacham says *protrope* can move a person's mind forward and spark an independent action within the audience. For example, Obama's campaign applied *protrope* when, on his blog, he asked readers if they want "change," and then asks for donations; Obama used *protrope* to persuade readers through urgency the need to donate to bring about "change." The theory is to promise or threaten the reader with a premise that encourages them to take action. On August 25, 2008, Amanda Scott posted an email from Barack Obama. Here are some excerpts:

> The Democratic convention starts today, and my new running mate Joe Biden and I recorded a message about what we all need to do next.
>
> When we started this campaign, very few people thought we would make it this far.
>
> But we put our faith in the power of ordinary supporters like you coming together and building a movement for change from the bottom up. And that's why we're here . . .
>
> With only 10 weeks to go, now is the time to give again to support this campaign.
>
> You joined this campaign because you're ready for real change in this country . . .
>
> But make no mistake about what we're up against. John McCain has embraced the same old politics of fear.

Obama encourages his blog's readers to donate $25 or more. Toward the end of each month, Obama's campaign staff also posted requests from Obama or his campaign manager, David Plouffe, to ask supporters to donate immediately to increase that month's donation amount. The campaign wanted readers to take immediate action.

Obama's campaign blog instructed people on how to support the campaign. For example, on October 22, 2008, Christopher Haas posted "Talk to your grandparents about Obama":

When it comes to your family, you are Barack's most effective advocate. There are less than two weeks left in this election. If you haven't already talked to your family, now is the time.

If you've already talked to your parents and grandparents about Barack and what's at stake in this election, let us know how it went, and what advice you would offer fellow supporters who are thinking about having the talk themselves.

Obama's campaign helped readers organize their thoughts about how to best support Obama's candidacy. Obama created an emotional appeal to create the urgency to act NOW: "There are less than two weeks left in this election. If you haven't already talked to your family, now is the time." The urgency and the importance of the rhetorical structure are highlighted in this next example, when Christopher Hass on October 18, 2008, blogged:

We learned on Thursday that voters in key battleground states are receiving automated phone calls from John McCain's campaign, spreading some of the most vile smears of this election. But these desperate "robocalls" say more about John McCain and his campaign than they do about Barack.

It was McCain himself who denounced these underhanded and cowardly tactics as "hate calls" after a rash of them helped sink his primary campaign in 2000. The perpetrator behind those attacks: George W. Bush.

Haas is persuading voters that McCain is a threat. His tactics are "underhanded," and he is just like George W. Bush. Haas insinuates if McCain wins, he will act just like President Bush. Whether this is true or not, this appeals to people's fears and enhances the campaign's core message for change. Again, this blog post is another example of identification through antithesis—where the campaign wants to persuade readers to feel united to fight the common enemy, which is Obama's Republican opponent, Senator John McCain.

Robert Heath explains, "Rhetoric is a contest of identifies and loyalties, the courtship of coming together and separating." Obama's campaign blog had a courtship of coming together to gain loyal supporters. New media allowed loyalty to grow organically and develop identities and communities through the online grassroots organization. During the 2008 election, the economy took a downward spiral, and conversations about the message change increased. The open exchange of communication and responses to topics on Obama's campaign blog helped clarify the campaign's persuasive stance. Obama's blog helped guide the community interactions through donation buttons, links to volunteer, and comment. As the world was in flux, the campaign's open exchanges of communication helped to identify people's hardships of why a change was needed.

Digital *Logos*

Obama's campaign sought to provide the electorate with justifiable conclusions that supported each of his arguments that he was the best candidate. In *The Uses of Argument*, Stephen Toulmin writes:

> For logic is concerned not with the manner of our inferring, or with questions of technique: its primary business is a retrospective, justificatory one—with the arguments we can put forward afterwards to make good our claim that the conclusions arrived at are acceptable, because justifiable, conclusions.[62]

Obama's blog used recaps and summaries (*dinumeratio*) and examples (*exemplum*) to prove their positions in their campaign blogs. These figures of speech apply examples for proof, a method that Aristotle addresses. Aristotle points out, "Argument by 'example' is highly suitable for political oratory, argument by '*enthymeme*' better suits forensic."[63] As discussed earlier, "argument by example" helped Obama show readers that other credible sources believed he was capable of the presidency. As for an *Enthymeme*, it is a persuasive tool that "uses a commonplace—something in the audience's mind—to support a choice."[64] Whereas, example "leads to either a premise or a conclusion. . . . If they think it works, you probably will too."[65] Rhetors use *exemplum* to provide concrete proof to the audience, whereas rhetors use *enthymeme* to allow the audience to fill in the blank. Obama's campaign blog left little for the audience to fill in the blanks. The campaign staff posted examples of people who volunteered and who endorsed him to help the audience identify with the campaign message for change.

Obama's campaign blog summarized speeches and campaign stops. The figure *dinumeratio* is useful to inform, list, and explain, as well as summarize; Aristotle uses *dinumeratio* as the ninth line of argument.[66] In Aristotle's *Rhetoric*, *dinumeratio* is referred to as division.[67] However, in Richard Lanham's *A Handlist of Rhetorical Terms*, the figure *dinumeratio* is defined as a recapitulation or summary.[68] In this interpretation, the speaker or writer uses *dinumeratio* in lists and divisions to retell events, which a campaign blog should effectively do. For example, through blog posts, Obama summarized or listed the most important news stories about his campaign. Amanda Scott on October 22, 2008, posted "15,000 Doors in Two Days":

> Three weeks ago, almost 80 Utah residents and Obama supporters drove to Colorado to knock on doors. In the cities of Fort Collins and Grand Junction, they knocked on nearly 15,000 doors. That's 15,000 households in two days where volunteers reached out to undecided voters.

Again, *exemplum* became a way for Obama's campaign to explain to voters the deeper meaning behind the campaign's core messages. In Edward P.J. Corbett's *The Classical Rhetoric for the Modern Student*, Corbett explains how scientists must offer supporting evidence from experiments to convince other scientists "of the validity of their generalization."[69] In the same way, political candidates must provide evidence to prove their qualifications. Obama's campaign showcased volunteers' grassroots activities and provided examples through volunteer narratives. The Obama Road Blog posted "Road Blog: Joe Biden, Fired Up in Liberty":

> After Russell Tucker was laid off from his job at the BM plant in Kansas City this past summer, he was hanging around the house, watching T.V. when he found inspiration:
>
> "It was the middle of July when I got laid off. I was laying around the house when I saw the Democratic Convention on TV, and I recorded it. I was so taken by Barack Obama's speech, I watched it twice the next day. I had to find out some way to get involved . . . . This is the first election in which I've done any volunteering."
>
> Now the Steel Metal Workers Union member works for the campaign full time, on a volunteer basis.

Russell Tucker's narrative is a persuasive text. The post is to help others identify with Tucker's story. The persuasive goal is to show how people with different experiences and backgrounds share in the common goal of helping Obama win the election.

Obama made his readers feel more confident in their decisions because his campaign created websites that presumably were fact-checking venues. The fact-checking websites motivated potential voters, encouraging them to seek more information about Obama and his opponents. On October 20. 2008, Molly Claflin posted "Fight Back with the Truth":

> Heard any ugly, false rumors about Barack? Well, you don't have to sit back and let the rumors fly—you can fight back with the truth. We've created a special website, FightTheSmears.com, to combat smear campaigns and give you all the information you need to spread the truth.

The campaign created the fact-checking website to provide evidence and to instill trust. In *Un-Spun: Finding Facts in a World of [Disinformation]*, Brooks Jackson and Kathleen Hall Jamieson explain:

> When it comes to politics, you can have the satisfaction of knowing you chose your candidate based on facts, not just TV-spot fantasies. It might not change

the way you vote, but then again, it might. Either way, you can be more confident you've made the right choice.[70]

FighttheSmears.com engaged supporters to help debunk myths about Barack Obama and to unite in the fight against the common enemy—Obama's political opponent. The campaign encouraged supporters to forward the facts to their followers to help them fight the smears and fake news.

OBAMA'S CAMPAIGN IMPACT

The 2008 presidential campaign set the standard for future online campaign blogs and how influential social media is to a presidential campaign. The campaign blogs, especially Obama's, posted updates, information, speeches, and events, which created a reason for readers to visit candidates' websites and gave readers the sense that they were a part of the campaign. In the end, Obama's campaign blog succeeded in applying Bakhtin's definition of political rhetoric discourse.

> In political rhetoric . . . discourse can support some candidacy, represent the personality of a candidate, present and defend his point of view, his verbal statements, or in other cases protest against some decree, law, order, announcement, occasion—that is, protest against the specific verbal utterances toward which it is dialogically aimed.[71]

The campaign blog represented Obama, presented and defended his points of view, and refuted arguments and claims from his opponents.

Obama's campaign created a successful online campaign strategy. Listed are three of the essential parts of Obama's online campaign strategy.

1. The blog created *ethos* by being able to highlight endorsement and share volunteers and supporters. Obama's campaign allowed other voices to build Obama's credibility.
2. The campaign staff created emotional connections with the audience through blog posts to share stories and create urgency for support through canvassing, calling, and fundraising. The online grassroots movement urged supporters to move to action to not lose the momentum of Obama's message for change. Obama may not have directly engaged, but he sent emails and created personal posts to address his online audience.

3. The campaign staff and organizers would keep the electorate informed through informational posts. The blog created a space to summarize speeches, share positive news stories about Obama, and prove the grassroots efforts kept building momentum.

An essential aspect of Obama's campaign was the inclusivity of the language through the blog that connected the reader and writer. Such persuasion helps readers identify with the core message. The blog posts highlighting Pennsylvanians' support of Obama's Pennsylvania comments to a California audience, which Hillary Clinton labeled as out of touch, was an example of persuading by "identifying your ways with his."

The campaign built a community by personalizing blog posts showcasing volunteer efforts and the volunteers' reasons for supporting Obama. Additionally, the blog praised everyday citizens for their grassroots efforts and financial support—reminding supporters that they were part of the "change." The reader—"You"—became an essential character in Obama's "We" campaign blog. The rhetorical significance from volunteer stories and even highlights on the blog resulted in more grassroots efforts because blog posts became examples and reasons why citizens passionately supported Obama's campaign. As a result, the website allowed citizens to participate easily. Each citizen could create a small campaign headquarters to make phone calls, fundraise, and talk to other supporters via Obama's website. The website also allowed volunteers to organize to walk door-to-door. New media, such as campaign websites and social media, creates an opportunity to organize groups easily. Obama's rhetorical impact on the Internet and social media proved that engaging multiple voices into the voice of "change" was how a candidate's campaign could create momentum through persuasive language that unites.

Not all of Obama's rhetorical techniques and motives inspired people to act positively. His campaign tackled naysayers and controversial topics that other presidential candidates have not endured, especially remarks regarding racial issues. Seth Stephens-Davidowitz studied Google Trends during Obama's first election night. He found one in every hundred Google searches included racial slurs, and "there was a darkness and hatred that was hidden from the traditional sources but was quite apparent in the searches that people made."[72] With this type of data in mind, Obama's campaign fought to establish and maintain Obama's credibility. Obama's campaign motivated his supporters to help him combat the rumors. The campaign website provided the campaign's side of the story and pre-written emails people could forward to their friends to help Obama spread his message for change.

People did help spread the campaign message for change. David Plouffe said this about the 2008 presidential campaign he ran for Obama:

Technology played a key role in our success. Reaching an audience involves more than just figuring out who your audience is; it also means knowing how to find them. Part of the reason our campaign was so successful is that we were able to identify early that many people we wanted to reach were spending more of their time on the Internet . . . they were already immersed in the world of technology and would be more likely to encounter us there.[73]

Since 1996, campaigns had slowly embraced the use of the Internet. As the Internet's usage increased, campaigns had to follow and strategize for the new media. Obama's campaign message and his use of technology created a possible change in campaign rhetoric ideology. Obama's campaign created a "We" campaign instead of the "I" campaign. Together Obama and the electorate could create Change. Obama's campaign strategy was about the inclusivity of new political ideologies that excluded only past political ideologies. Obama's campaign used people as information vessels. In 2008, the Internet became a way for campaigns to empower voters and identify with audiences through narrative. In the end, as David Plouffe says, "The one thing I'm sure of is that in this swiftly changing world we find ourselves in, staying in the same place is the surest route to defeat."[74]

NOTES

1. David Plouffe, *The Audacity to Win* (New York: Penguin Books, 2010), 42.
2. "Barack Obama's Presidential Announcement," *YouTube video*, 22:03, Uploaded on December 10, 2007, by *BarackObama.com*. https://m.youtube.com/watch?v=gdJ7Ad15WCA.
3. Amy Schatz, "BO, UR so Gr8: How a Young Tech Entrepreneur Translated Barack Obama into the Idiom of Facebook," *Wall Street Journal*, May 26, 2007.
4. Ibid.
5. Talbot, "How Obama *Really* Did It."
6. Rasmus Kleis Nielsen, *Ground Wars: Personalized Communication in Political Campaigns* (Princeton, NJ: Princeton University Press, 2012), 6.
7. Ibid., 7.
8. Daniel Kreiss, *Prototype Politics: Technology-Intensive Campaigning and the Data of Democracy* (Oxford: Oxford University Press, 2016), 217.
9. Elizabeth A. Petre, "Encouraging Identification with the Larger Campaign Narrative: Grassroots Organizing Texts in Barack Obama's 2008 Presidential Campaign," *Communication Quarterly*, 66 no. 3 (2018): 284.
10. Andrew Bleeker and Nathaniel Lubin, "Growing Power: Digital Marketing in Politics," in *Margin of Victory: How Technologists Help Politicians Win Elections*, ed. Nathaniel G. Pearlman (Santa Barbara, CA: Praeger, 2012), 53.
11. Ibid., 54.

12. Ariel Alexovich, "Clinton's National Security Ad," *The New York Times*, February 29, 2008, https://thecaucus.blogs.nytimes.com/2008/02/29/clintons-national-security-ad/.

13. Brian Stelter, "Candidates Responding Almost as Fast as they can Attack," *The New York Times*, March 4, 2008.

14. Ibid.

15. Lee Gomes, "Does the Web Deserve the Power it Gained to Influence Politics?," *Wall Street Journal*, March 26, 2008.

16. Kreiss, *Prototype Politics,* 77.

17. Ibid., 78.

18. Brian Stelter, "The Facebooker Who Friended Obama," *The New York Times*, July 7, 2008, https://www.nytimes.com/2008/07/07/technology/07hughes.html.

19. Jennifer Stromer-Galley, *Presidential Campaigning in The Internet Age* (Oxford: Oxford University Press, 2014), 133.

20. Ibid.

21. Kate Kenski, Bruce W. Hardy, and Kathleen Hall Jamieson, *The Obama Victory: How Media, Money, and Message Shaped the 2008 Election* (Oxford: Oxford University Press, 2010), 57.

22. Jeffrey C. Alexander, "Heroes, Presidents, and Politics," *Contexts* 9, no. 4 (Fall 2010): 17.

23. Senator John McCain knew his time spent as a POW benefited his career: "But, I did not want my experiences in Vietnam to be the leitmotif of the rest of my life. I am a public figure now, and my public profile is inextricably linked to my POW experiences. Whenever I am introduced at an appearance, the speaker always refers to my war record first. Obviously, such recognition has benefited my public career, and I am grateful for that." John McCain and Mark Salter, *Faith of My Fathers* (New York: Random House, 1999), 346.

24. Ibid., 19.

25. Barlow, *The Rise of the Blogosphere*, 183.

26. Andrew W. Robertson, *The Language of Democracy* (Charlottesville: University of Virginia Press, 1995), 69.

27. Ibid., 212–213.

28. Ibid., 216.

29. Ibid., 216.

30. Petre, "Encouraging Identification with the Larger," 302.

31. Kathleen Hall Jamieson, "Discourse and the Democratic Ideal," *Proceedings of the American Philosophical Society* 137, no. 3 (1993): 336.

32. Ibid., 332.

33. George Cheney, "The Rhetoric of Identification and the Study of Organizational Communication," *Quarterly Journal of Speech* 69, no. 2 (May 1, 1983): 148.

34. Deborah Tannen, *The Argument Culture* (New York: Random House, 1998), 244.

35. Michel Foucault, "What is an Author?" in *Language, Contemporary, Practices: Selected Essays and Interviews by Michel Foucault,* ed. Donald F. Bouchard (Ithaca, NY: Cornell University Press, 1977), 124.

36. Ibid., 123.

37. Ibid., 124.

38. Cheney, "The Rhetoric of Identification," 148.

39. M. M. Bakhtin, *The Dialogic Imagination: Four Essays*, ed. Michael Holquist, trans. Caryl Emerson and Michael Holquist (Austin: University of Texas Press, 1981), 293.

40. Mikhail Bakhtin, *Problems of Dostoevsky's Poetics*, ed. and trans. Caryl Emerson (Minneapolis: University of Minnesota Press, 1984), 87–88.

41. Michael Holquist, *Dialogism* (New York: Routledge: 1990), 34.

42. Kenneth Burke, *Rhetoric of Motives* (Berkley: University of California Press, 1969), 55.

43. Aristotle, "Rhetoric," 1356a.

44. M. Jimmie Killingsworth, "Rhetorical Appeals: A Revision," *Rhetoric Review* 24, no. 3 (2005): 249.

45. Ibid.

46. Ibid., 251.

47. Ibid., 252.

48. Robert L. Heath, "Identification," in *Encyclopedia of Rhetoric*, ed. Thomas Sloan (Oxford: Oxford University Press, 2001), 377.

49. Ibid., 262.

50. Mayhill Fowler, "Obama: No Surprise That Hard-Pressed Pennsylvanians Turn Bitter," *HuffPost*, April 11, 2008, https://www.huffingtonpost.com/mayhill-f owler/obama-no-surprise-that-ha_b_96188.html.

51. Chapter 5 in Jennifer Stromer-Galley's book examines the 2008 networked campaign. Stromer-Galley, *Presidential Campaigning in the Internet Age*, 127.

52. Ibid., 128.

53. Craig Smith, "*Ethos* Dwells Pervasively: A Hermeneutic Reading of Aristotle on Credibility," in *The Ethos of Rhetoric*, ed. Michael J. Hyde (Columbia: University of South Carolina, 2004), 13.

54. Aristotle, "Nicomachean Ethics," in *The Basic Works of Aristotle*, ed. Richard McKeon (New York: The Modern Library, 2001), 1160a.

55. Ibid.

56. See. Edward P.J. Corbett, *Classical Rhetoric for the Modern Student*, (Oxford: Oxford University Press, 1990), 68–70.

57. Aristotle, "Rhetoric," in *The Basic Works of Aristotle*, ed. Richard McKeon (New York: The Modern Library, 2001), 1391b.

58. Kenneth L. Hacker, "Introduction: The Continued Importance of the Candidate Image Construct," in *Presidential Candidate Images*, ed. Kenneth L. Hacker (New York: Rowan & Littlefield Publishers, 2004), 11.

59. Aristotle, "Rhetoric," 1378a.

60. Jeanne Fahnstock, *Rhetorical Figures in Science* (Oxford: Oxford University Press, 1999), 23.

61. Henry Peachum, *The Garden of Eloquence (1593): A Facsimile Reproduction* (Gainesville, Florida: Scholars' Facsimiles & Reprints, 1954), 77.

62. Stephen Toulmin, *The Uses of Argument* (Cambridge: Cambridge University Press, 2003), 6.

63. Aristotle, "Rhetoric," 1418a.

64. Jay Heinrichs, *Thank You for Arguing: What Aristotle, Lincoln, and Homer Simpson Can Teach Us About the Art of Persuasion* (New York: Three Rivers Press, 2007), 125.

65. Ibid., 127.

66. Aristotle, "Rhetoric," 1398a. Aristotle ninth line states, "Another line is based upon logical division."

67. Ibid., 1398a.

68. Richard Lanham, *A Handlist of Rhetorical Terms* (Berkley: University of California Press, 1991), 192.

69. Edward P. J. Corbett, *Classical Rhetoric for the Modern Student* (Oxford: Oxford, 1990), 69.

70. Brooks Jackson and Kathleen Hall Jamieson, *Un-Spun: Finding Facts in a World of [Disinformation]* (New York: Random House, 2007), 185.

71. Bakhtin, *The Dialogic Imagination*, 353. See "Discourse in the Novel."

72. Stephens-Davidowitz, *Everybody Lies*.

73. Plouffe, *The Audacity to Win*, 378.

74. Ibid., 411.

Chapter 4

Twitter and Mitt Romney's Rhetoric

"Rhetoric" is a word that news media haphazardly uses in political coverage during campaign season. More often than not, when political pundits discuss the rhetoric that a candidate uses, the candidate is perceived as negatively persuading the electorate. Most people, if asked their perceptions of the term "rhetoric," might describe rhetoric as deceptive, manipulative, and persuasive—all negative modifiers. The word "rhetoric" has a negative connotation, which is unfortunate because few people consider the history behind the rhetoric that humans use every day to create persuasive messages. Rhetoric is simply persuasion through communication.

Presidential candidates who want to develop relationships and effectively communicate with the electorate use social media to persuade and inform their audiences. Twitter, Facebook, and other mobile media applications are all within a campaign's media strategy. Social media channels are rhetorical tools to develop relationships between presidential candidates and voters. The use of new media applications such as Twitter in the 2008 U.S. presidential election changed how campaigns disseminated information and how candidates interacted with voters.[1]

Candidate Barack Obama effectively used social networks and his campaign blog to enlist volunteers, communicate with supporters, and gather donations to support his campaign. As a result, seasoned social media campaigners made up President Obama's 2012 campaign team. Governor Mitt Romney's campaign had to try to seize an opportunity to create an online campaign as active and as savvy as Obama's. Obama established his grassroots organization in 2008 and called upon his supporters to keep the momentum rolling for four more years.

This chapter could go in many different rhetorical analysis directions to explain Romney's failure in winning the 2012 presidential campaign.[2]

Romney's struggle with *Kairos*, embracing the opportune moment, and the right rhetorical situation to look presidential created many constraints throughout his campaign. In 2008, President Obama created a strategic Internet campaign that motivated a grassroots movement. President Obama's administration also created official White House social media accounts. Mitt Romney's campaign did not have the backdrop of the White House to make speeches and address the country. Unfortunately, Mitt Romney's campaign failed at promoting his campaign slogan to "Believe in America" to Obama's simple message of "Forward." Kenneth Burke, in *The Grammar of Motives*, says, "When confronting such issues, one has a great variety of circumferences to select as characterizations of a given agent's scene."[3] In 2012, President Obama's campaign cast a larger circumference than Romney's campaign.

BACKGROUND

In 2008, Obama employed a team of social networking specialists to create and maintain his online campaign. With that success in his past, President Obama, as the incumbent, then repeated that strategy in the 2012 presidential campaign to persuade the American electorate to reelect him. Therefore, Republican nominee Romney needed to create a social media campaign that could rival Obama's to attract young voters, entice new volunteers, encourage donors, and highlight established supporters. Both Obama and Romney needed to use the rhetorical tools within this rhetorical medium. Twitter was one of those rhetorical tools. Obama's administration had hesitations, and "White House officials were leery of it, in no small part because of concerns about how the freewheeling environment of social media would mesh with the requirements of the Presidential Records Act, which mandates that all the traffic end up in the National Archives."[4]

Twitter limits the amount of text a "tweet" can contain. In 2012, a person could send only 140 characters in each message. Through Twitter, newsmakers are creating their sound bites, and within those Twitter bites of 140 characters, they are providing links to expand the included message. The limited characters create a constant stream of information in a follower's Twitter feed. Another unique feature of Twitter is that a person can subscribe to another person's Twitter messages, or tweets, without being "accepted" as a follower or friend, as with Facebook. What friends are to Facebook, followers are to Twitter, but Twitter allows anyone who is not blocked from an account to access a Twitter feed.

Obama's 2008 Republican opponent, Senator John McCain, did not actively tweet while running for U.S. president but decided to tweet after the 2008 presidential campaign. According to ABC News, "474 out of 535 Congressional legislators [are] active on Twitter. The Republican Party dominates with 261 tweeting members while Democrats trail with 211 members."[5] These numbers show how the 2008 Obama campaign, which actively used Twitter, in turn, influenced the Republican Party to take advantage of their rhetorical situation in new ways.[6]

Modern-day candidates need to adapt to these types of media technology demands. Obama's team observed the White House reporters on Twitter and decided they were missing an opportunity.[7] Even Mitt Romney's campaign learned the value of Twitter. The Romney campaign responded to a Democratic pundit who accused Ann Romney of never working a day in her life. Ann Romney sent out her first tweet on April 11, 2012:

@AnnDRomney: I made a choice to stay home and raise five boys. Believe me, it was hard work.

On April 12, 2012, Mitt Romney tweeted:

@MittRomney: Just watched @AnnDRomney on @FoxNews. Her work raising our boys was tougher than any job I had [Link to video]

Twitter allowed Ann Romney to respond quickly and Mitt Romney to respond to support his wife.

Twitter has changed the concept of how people receive and respond to media events. With an estimated 500 million users in 2012, Twitter is a medium of immediacy, information, and interactivity.[8] Tyler Cowen explains that the Internet is ever-present: "Culture is there all the time, and you can receive more of it, pretty much whenever you want."[9] Twitter is also ever-present, and the audience knows that they can consume information at any time—or block out any information they do not need.[10]

Many researchers are studying Twitter by measuring tweet sentiments, that is, the intentions of the individuals who are tweeting.[11] Carnegie Mellon University researchers found that monitoring Twitter sentiments is an inexpensive and fast way to analyze public opinion.[12] Additionally, Andranik Tumasjan and colleagues concluded that Twitter is a valid source for measuring the political landscape offline. Their research found, "The mere number of tweets reflects voters' preferences and comes close to traditional election polls, while the sentiment of political Twitter messages closely corresponds to the electorate's sentiment and evidence from the media coverage of the campaign trail."[13] Political candidates and policymakers must recognize that Twitter is a powerful tool to which they should pay attention. Neil Savage explains that sometimes the sentiment behind a tweet cannot be correctly measured because words' double meanings can be either positive or negative, and the writer has not considered the ambiguity to ensure that the message relayed is clear and accurate.[14] This type of data analysis does not consider the ambiguity of language or allow the campaign to learn to create more persuasive messages. Campaign staffers who are creating these bite-sized messages must ensure their messages are accurate and persuasive and that readers understand the campaign's tweets' sentiments. Gina Chen reports that "Twitter is not just virtual noise of people talking at each other, as some critics contend, but that it is a medium that people actively seek out to gratify a need to connect with others."[15] Although Twitter is a useful tool to organize and rally people, it is also a useful persuasive tool, and political candidates do not consistently rely on it for this benefit.[16]

Daniel Kreiss studied the 2012 presidential campaigns' use of Twitter. Kreiss examined the differences between both Obama's and Romney's campaigns. Kreiss says Obama's digital team had "significantly more autonomy," which allowed them to respond to political events the moment they happened.[17] Romney's team had sixteen staffers compared to Obama's four staffers. Romney's team "had to go through multiple layers of vetting and approvals that not only made it difficult to respond to events as they unfolded, it resulted in content on Twitter that was often repackaged press releases."[18]

Political candidates must learn to use rhetoric in the digital world.[19] When a person learns to communicate a clear, concise, and persuasive message at the appropriate time and direct that message to a specific audience about a particular situation, that person creates leverage. By creating "rhetorical leverage," political candidates communicate messages effectively with the electorate to create an advantage.

DEATH OF THE SOUND BITE

The use of social media, especially social media sites like Twitter, allows the reader to experience firsthand a candidate's activities. Citizens cannot attend every campaign event. Instead of allowing the media to control what citizens know about them through selected sound bites from the candidates' speeches, today's candidates can control what parts of their public presence are released. Candidates can now expand the sound bite to create a compelling argument to fit the context for which the sound bite was initially intended. Kathleen Hall Jamieson addressed this concern when she wrote, "Morselized ads and news bites consist instead of statement alone, a move that invites us to judge the merit of the claim on the *ethos* of the speaker or the emotional appeals (*pathos*)—enwrapping the claim. In the process, appeal to reason (*logos*), one of Aristotle's prime means of persuasion—is lost. With it goes some of the audience's ability to judge."[20] The sound bite is not a persuasive argument, and the audience loses the logic behind the bite of information because the sound bite is presented out of context.

New media allows for more immediacy to present information closer to the original context. The sound bite becomes more logical with all three proofs—*ethos* (credibility), *logos* (logic), and *pathos* (emotion)—because the candidate can publish complete and accurate messages and thus "speak" directly to the audience. The candidates who use Twitter, Facebook, and a blog can expand sound bites and ensure that the sound bites are accurate presentations of what the candidates want to present. Twitter is a powerful tool as campaigns can create their own "Twitter bites." For example:

@*MittRomney:* Video: [Link]. Despite @BarackObama's attempts to distract from his failed record, the American people remember. (May 23, 2012)

Romney's campaign tweeted links to a video that had people confirming Romney's argument about a failed economy and their disappointment in President Obama.

@*MittRomney:* We must make the tax code simpler and fairer. Read my @WSJ op-ed on reducing tax rates to promote economic growth. (February 23, 2012)

This tweet links to Romney's *Wall Street Journal* article that explains his plan on reducing tax rates to spark the economy. Twitter can guide readers to a story that has more details about Mitt Romney's proposed economic policy.

ROMNEY'S ONLINE RHETORICAL SITUATION

As mentioned above, rhetoric uses language to construct persuasive messages for an audience and a specific situation. When a person is creating a message online, the message has the ability to circulate quickly. For example, twenty years ago, when a newsworthy event happened, the media required time to gather coverage, edit the story, and share that story with the public. Television, as immediate as it can be, is still hindered by the time required to set up, to place reporters, and to broadcast. Television is a one-time broadcast, while online publishing creates a record and allows viewers to retrieve and reexperience the story.

For social media to be a rhetorical medium as part of a political campaign, the campaign must create persuasive messages. The message should motivate the audience to respond in some way. By using persuasive language to create a dialogical interactive campaign, a candidate must connect on a different level with the electorate. Through emerging media, the audience can read, watch, listen to a candidate's message, and give the campaign feedback. The candidate can immediately respond through independent action, which creates a rhetorically interactive community. *The New York Times* reported Romney's campaign team used Twitter as a tool to monitor reporter bias:

> Mr. Romney's aides say they can get a sense of where a story is headed before it is published simply by reading reporters' Twitter messages. If reporters have flagged a particular incident on Twitter—for instance, the woman who stood up at South Carolina event and asked Mr. Romney, a Mormon, if he believed "in the divine saving grace of Jesus Christ"—Mr. Romney's aides might pull him aside before a press conference and warn him that the topic is likely to come up.[21]

Twitter can also act as a focus group for ideas. The likes, retweets, and comments can act as data to construct more poignant and engaging messages, both online and offline.

Candidates' Twitter accounts are one of many social media channels, which candidates can convince voters to vote for them. Twitter provides a place to react with an immediate and brief message. Twitter can reinforce the candidates' messages and link readers to the candidates' blogs and websites, which, in contrast to tweets, provide an expanded version of the story. Mitt Romney promoted his campaign app for people to hear campaign news first:

@MittRomney: Soon, I'll be announcing my choice for VP. Download the app and be the first to hear the news. [Link] (August 7, 2012)

Candidates could announce political events to the press and the electorate simultaneously. Any political event discussed online could create a viral moment to reach the intended audience and an unintended audience.

Lloyd Bitzer explains three elements make up the rhetorical situation: exigence, audience, and constraints.[22] The first element, exigence, is "the precipitating event for the rhetorical act."[23] The second element, audience, "produces change by influencing the decision and action of persons who function as mediators of change . . . a rhetorical audience consists only of those persons who are capable of being influenced by discourse and of being mediators of change."[24] The third element is constraints. According to Bitzer, constraints "have the power to constrain decision and action needed to modify the exigence."[25] He describes the standard sources for constraints as beliefs, attitudes, documents, facts, traditions, images, interests, and motives.[26]

Some researchers scrutinize Bitzer's rhetorical situation as being too simplistic.[27] Often, as Richard Vatz explains, "Except for those situations which directly confront our own empirical reality, we learn of facts and events through someone's communicating them to us."[28] Until a situation is presented to the public, that situation has no given meaning.[29] However, as soon as the situation is presented to the public, the public defines that situation. Donna Gorrell argues, "Reality may have a whole new exigence and constraints, and the way both rhetor and audience perceive it changes inexorably too."[30] Gorrell observes, "When the audience responds and becomes the rhetor, reality again is changed."[31] This role reversal happens on Twitter when someone retweets a message or adds to the original tweet. In social media, users are communicating an overabundance of messages. It is foreseeable that rhetoricians may want to rethink the rhetorical situational structure of Twitter and other social media messages where messages are repeated, added to, and changed.

While analyzing through situational theory, Kathleen Farrell and Marilyn Young say that the theory "allows us to view rhetoric as an organic phenomenon," and suggests that Bitzer's theory may seem mechanistic because the critic may "overlook elements that are not part of the situation."[32] Thus, a political campaign should determine if the tweet will enhance a candidate's credibility, expand understanding of an issue, or create an emotional tie to the audience. The more powerful the message created through emerging media, the more a campaign can control the release of information, silence the competition, and influence or silence the media sound bites. As Joan Leach says, "Once discourse enters a communication arena, it is no longer under full control of those who produced it."[33] For example, Mitt Romney, during a presidential debate on October 26, 2012, described how he hired women into his administration as governor:

> We took a concerted effort to go out and find women who had backgrounds that could be qualified to become members of our cabinet. I went to a number of women's groups and said can you help us find folks, and they brought us binders full of women.[34]

After Romney said, "Binders full of women," Twitter responded with #binderfullofwomen. Even though the response was about workplace equality, his response to the question went viral. Unfortunately, the audience misunderstood.

@DavidCornDC: I think Romney could have avoided all the trouble if he had said a "floppy disk full of women." #binderfullofwomen (October 17, 2012)
@alex_ruiz: I hope the #binderfullofwomen is a Lisa Frank Trapper Keeper. (October 16, 2012)

@*articpenguin:* I don't want to be in a #binderfullofwomen because of my gender. I should be in a binder because I'm awesome. (October 16, 2012)

@*TheBindersFull:* How is it that in 25 years as a professional & businessman from Harvard that he didn't know ANY WOMEN on his own? #binderfullofwomen (October 17, 2012)

Romney's campaign lost control of the intent behind the message by not anticipating the response from social media users. During presidential campaigns, "rhetoric is more than 'mere rhetoric.'"[35]

@MITTROMNEY

Kathleen Hall Jamieson suggests "that perception of the proper response to an unprecedented rhetorical situation grows not merely from the situation but also from the antecedent rhetorical forms."[36] Jamieson's observations seem accurate concerning Romney's use of Twitter because Romney focused mostly on overcoming the constraints and trying to use his message to identify with the electorate. During the primary, Romney's motivation was to influence the audience to vote for him:

@*MittRomney:* I will make government simpler, smaller, & smarter. This is not only good for the economy, it is a moral imperative. (November 14, 2011)

@*MittRomney:* Iowa can help put an end to @BarackObama's failed leadership. Take action today & join the GOTV from home team [Link] (January 2, 2012)

Romney's team wants to motivate and identify with the audience to take action to change what he calls "failed leadership." Romney's campaign also tweets, "It is a moral imperative." Romney's campaign tries to move his audience by pathos. He wants to urge voters that if they agree with his political ideology, they are voting for what is morally right. The precipitating event of the economy is a concern in every election, especially in years when the economy has failed to show an upward swing. Romney's persuasive argument is to create motivation for the audience to want to vote for him. The audience is the mediator for change, and Romney faces the constraints of changing people's political beliefs and political motives.

Bitzer explains, "Since rhetorical discourse produces change by influencing the decision and action of a person who functions as mediators of change, it follows that rhetoric always requires an audience—even in those cases when a person engages himself or ideal mind as audience."[37] Of course, as Bitzer notes, "A rhetorical audience consists only of those persons who are capable of being influenced by discourse and of being mediators of change."[38] The motivation behind Romney's tweets that ask questions, express thanks to supporters, and guide readers to donation pages within a tweet creates opportunities for social media users to participate in the conversation. For example, on February 1, 2012, Romney tweeted,

> *@MittRomney:* Thanks everyone for helping the #OneTermFund raise over 600k so far. Continue to hold the President accountable onetermfund.com.

The tweet was to encourage the reader to donate, which is why most candidates use Twitter and other social media channels.[39]

Mitt Romney's campaign also asked questions about how people felt about the economy.

> *@MittRomney:* Millions of Americans aren't better off in the @BarackObama economy. Is it an "incomplete" or a failing grade? #AreYouBetterOff (September 4, 2012)

Romney's campaign tweet posted a common ground issue concerning the economy. Romney's question was a rhetorical question, with hashtag #AreYouBetterOff. Romney wants the audience to answer NO! Jeanne Fahnestock explains, "Rhetors put themselves into their texts to interact with their audiences, calling on them, telling them who they are, asking them questions, acting on them, and trying to elicit a response."[40]

Romney moved from the Republican "hopeful" to the Republican candidate. He started tweeting about more events and more issues that people may have wanted to change. Romney's campaign kept the economy at the forefront of his argument against Obama's presidency:

> *@MittRomney:* A lot of Americans are having hard times & the unemployment report is not good news. This is not progress; it is very disappointing. (May 4, 2012)
> *@MittRomney:* @BarackObama says private sector is #doingfine. Is he really that out of touch? 23m Americans struggling for work [Link] (June 8, 2012)
> *@MittRomney:* Economic freedom is the only force in history that has consistently lifted people out of poverty—and kept people out of poverty. (September 25, 2012)

Romney kept planting common ground issues within his tweets, which would show he identified with the struggles with an economy that was still struggling after President Barack Obama took office in 2008. The campaign's tweets criticized Obama's actions:

@*MittRomney:* @BarackObama is moving us away from our Founders' vision. Instead of limited government, he is leading us toward limited freedom. (April 13, 2012)

@*MittRomney:* How can @BarackObama fix our economy if he doesn't understand it's broken? We are not "doing fine." [Link] (June 14, 2012)

This tweet's motivation was to remind American citizens of our country's traditions and to contrast those with Obama's actions. Moreover, as Jamieson points out, "Establishment and maintenance of definable institutional forms of rhetoric serve to define the institution itself."[41] This tweet maintained the patriotic spirit that U.S. citizens have established and done so by using the artistic proof *pathos* (emotion) as a persuasive tool to guide citizens to modify the situation and keep the United States as the founders envisioned.

Romney's campaign tried to set their agenda because "the rhetor is responsible for what he chooses to make salient."[42] The news articles found through the search engine Google during the same time Romney tweeted rarely linked to news events. Instead, news articles linked to Romney's online conversation with voters about his vision. The motivation behind a majority of Romney's tweets was to establish logical connections and to build credibility. Romney's campaign created a second Twitter account @RomneyResponse. Here, the campaign announced endorsements:

@*RomneyResponse:* ENDORSEMENT-Florida Times-Union: "Romney's Turnaround Skills Are Right For America" [Link] #RomneyRyan2012 #tcot (October 28, 2012)

The Twitter account was Romney's campaign's solution to "quickly point out online what it views as false information promoted by President Obama and his campaign team, along with inaccuracies made in reports from mainstream news media organizations."[43] On August 1, 2012, the campaign tweeted,

@*RomneyResponse:* Follow @RomneyResponse for the latest on @BarackObama's failed record, his campaign's false attacks, and our response.

The New York Times reported, "The Romney campaign's beefed-up Twitter presence comes after some supporters complained that Mr. Romney did not do enough to push back on criticism of his recent trip to Europe and Israel or fight hard enough against a Newsweek magazine cover calling him a 'wimp.'"[44] The @RomneyResponse account lacked engagement. The likes and retweet numbers were low for these tweets, which means the rhetorical language did not motivate people to take action, which was to retweet and like @RomneyResponse tweets.

At moments, Romney's campaign tried to engage the audience by asking them to take action. These two tweets asked for an immediate reaction:

@MittRomney: If you agree it's time to stop the spending and pass a permanent ban on earmarks, stand with me and sign the petition mi.tt/yuU5Xk (February 9, 2012)

@MittRomney: Welcome to Ohio @BarackObama. I have a simple question for you: Where are the jobs? RT if you agree http://mi.tt/IApn44 #Mitt2012 (May 4, 2012)

Regarding the second tweet, Twitter reported 50+ retweets and 50+ favorites.

Romney's tweets show that he shifted from concentrating on winning the Republican nomination to acting like the Republican nominee. His tweets became more topical and driven to remind people how to modify the situation. In 2008, President Obama did this with his blog posts by reminding voters about their current situation to make them modify their situation by voting.[45] This motivation can be situational but explains what types of information the audience needs and wants to become motivated, which is why one must go beyond just looking at the situation and look at the motivation and the rhetor's understanding of their audience. The rhetorical key is that Romney kept reminding the audience of their situation because, in the end, as much as Bitzer wants us to believe that three ideals make a situation rhetorically valuable, the audience has to decide if a situation exists as well as give meaning to it.[46]

Mary Garret and Xiaosui Xiao argue that "no rhetor can completely break free of the fundamental values and presuppositions of his or her discourse community and tradition."[47] Understanding one's audience is key to creating persuasive messages that promote action, create interest, and show that the rhetor understands the audience's problems. Through situational analysis—content analysis to note any artistic proofs—tweets can show what the candidate's agenda becomes. Because of Twitter's community-building nature, Twitter is situational and rhetorical, and Romney tried to take advantage of this nature to compete with his media-savvy opponent, President Obama. In the end, Romney's rhetorical strategy failed due to a hurricane.

Because of Obama's use of social media as a presidential candidate in 2008, the election was a campaign game-changer. Through Twitter, Romney kept responding and reminding readers of the situation while also guiding his readers to his specific policy plans and stances on social issues. What Romney could not have foreseen is a hurricane days before the election. Hurricane Sandy hit at the end of October 2012 and created an opportunity for President Obama. President Obama looked presidential handling the East Coast crisis, especially touring the area with New Jersey Republican governor Chris Christie. President Obama's social media team tweeted about Hurricane Sandy:

@BarackObama: President Obama on Hurricane Sandy: "The great thing about America is that during tough times like this, we pull together." (October 29, 2012)

Mitt Romney could only lend his support to victims and tweeted a link to the Red Cross. The rhetorical situation favored President Obama because it boosted his ethos, and he could lend support to the country that Mitt Romney could not. Both candidates canceled some campaign events. President Obama had to lead the hurricane relief efforts as Romney waited out the storm. Mitt Romney's campaign organized for the campaign bus to deliver supplies.[48]

President Obama and Mitt Romney both made speeches about the hurricane. They both had different rhetorical approaches because both of their situations were different. President Obama said,

> I am not worried at this point about the impact on the election . . . I am worried about the impact on families. . . . Right now, our No. 1 priority is to make sure that we are saving lives. . . . That people are going to get the food, the shelter, the water they need in case of emergency. And that we respond as quickly to get the economy back on track.[49]

The visual of President Obama speaking in the White House press room gave him a boost in credibility and a common ground goal of connecting to the emotions and worries a hurricane brings to a community. As President of the United States, he spoke for the country—not a party.

As for Mitt Romney, he gave his speech in Ohio in a high school gym.

> I want to mention that our hearts and prayers are with all the people in the storm's path. . . . And so if you have the capacity to make a donation to the American Red Cross, you can go online and do that . . . and the people in Ohio have big hearts, so we're expecting you to follow through and help out.[50]

Mitt Romney could speak only to the crowd in Ohio and not to the entire country. His rhetorical reach was limited. As President Obama tweeted through official White House media, Mitt Romney had his campaign websites and social media accounts to encourage people to donate to hurricane relief efforts. At this time, Mitt Romney's rhetorical situation constraints were too many to react in a presidential way as President Obama could. President Obama could take action, and Mitt Romney could only encourage people to donate to help Hurricane Sandy victims.

CONCLUSION

Without the use of social media, the candidates on both sides would have to rely directly on traditional media. Both sides used social media heavily in the 2012 election. Their communication through social media gave voters a firsthand experience of the political process, which television, radio, and print could not accomplish in past elections.

U.S. citizens do not need the mainstream news media—what Thomas Patterson calls the "day-to-day window on the world of politics."[51] Social media "audiences filter the news through their personal needs, interests, prejudices, attitudes, and beliefs. Yet the media supply most of the raw material that goes into people's thinking about their political leaders and institutions."[52] Politics is no longer a "secondhand experience, lived through the stories of journalists."[53] Instead, politics are experienced firsthand. The electorate is interacting directly with political candidates. The electorate catches glimpses of a politician's private life, such as when Romney watched the Superbowl, or when he acknowledged his wife in many of his tweets. The essential aspect of tweets is the interaction that occurs between author and reader. Campaigns' social media followers act as informers, and the term "word of mouth" evolves into a "retweet."

Andrew Robertson believes technology enriches the relationship between the electorate and a candidate and the language of politics.[54] The intimacy that new media creates allows the electorate access to candidates and allows candidates to access voters directly. Campaign staffers should always post with intention and to take advantage of the online rhetorical situation. Tweets are rhetorical. Thus, an online campaign aims to expand the sound bite so the campaign, not the media, controls the rhetorical situation. Unfortunately, Mitt Romney did not have the visual rhetorical impact the White House could supply for President Obama, who could also respond at the opportune moment in the most profound rhetorical setting during a crisis.

NOTES

1. See John Allen Hendricks and Robert E. Denton Jr., *Communicator-in-Chief: How Barack Obama Used New Media Technology to Win the White House* (New York: Lexington Books, 2010).

2. This chapter is an article I wrote in 2012 for *The Journal of Contemporary Rhetoric*, who gave me permission to reuse and edit my article for this book. I wrote this journal article in 2012 to show how Republicans started to embrace social media in their presidential campaigns.

3. Kenneth Burke, *A Grammar of Motives* (Berkley: University of California Press, 1969), 84.

4. Karen Tumulty, "Twitter becomes a Key Real-Time Tool for Campaigns," *The Washington Post*, April 26, 2012, https://www.washingtonpost.com/politics/ twitter-becomes-a-key-real-time-tool-for-campaigns/2012/04/26/gIQARf1TjT_story .html.

5. Jilian Fama, "Twitter has Become a Favorite of Republicans in Congress," *ABC News*, June 21, 2012, http://abcnews.go.com/Politics/republicans-tweet-democr ats-congress/story?id=16619963#.T-PfF44yCI4.

6. Ibid.

7. Tumulty, "Twitter becomes a Key Real-Time."

8. Joann Pan, "Will You be Twitter's 500 Millionth User?" *Mashable*, February 22, 2012, http://mashable .com/2012/02/22/twitters-500-million-user/.

9. Tyler Cowen, "Three Tweets for the Web," *The Wilson Quarterly* 33, no. 4 (2009): 58.

10. As of October 25, 2018, *New York Times* reported Twitter said it had 326 million monthly active users. Kate Conger reports, "Twitter has cracked down on fake and misleading accounts this year which the social media company said [. . .] was partly responsible for its decline in users." Kate Conger, "Twitter Posts Another Profit as User Numbers Drop," *New York Times*, October 25, 2018, https://www.nytimes. com/2018/10/25/technology/twitter-quarterly-earnings.html.

11. "CMU Researchers Analyze Twitter Sentiments," *Communications of the ACM* 53, no. 7, (2010): 18.

12. Ibid.

13. Andranik Tumasjan, Timm O. Sprenger, Philipp G. Sandner and Isabell M. Welpe, "Election Forecasts with Twitter: How 140 Characters Reflect the Political Landscape," *Social Science Computer Review* 29, no. 4 (2010): 414.

14. Neil Savage, "Twitter as Medium and Message," *Communications of the ACM* 54, no. 3, (2011): 18.

15. Gina Masullo Chen, "Tweet this: A Uses and Gratifications Perspective on How Active Twitter Use Grati-fies a Need to Connect with Others," *Computers in Human Behavior* 27 (2011): 760.

16. Kyle Leighton and David Taintor, "Hashtags are the New Lawn Signs: Why Twitter won't Predict Political Success in the 2012 Cycle," *Neiman Journalism Lab*, March 23, 2012, http://www.niemanlab.org /2012/03/hashtags-are-the-new-lawn-signs-why-twitter-wont-predict-political-success-in-the-2012-cycle/.

17. Daniel Kreiss, "Seizing the Moment: The Presidential Campaigns' Use of Twitter during the 2012 Electoral Cycle," *New Media & Society* 18, no. 8 (2014): 1475.

18. Ibid.

19. This is a consequence of any change in the media environment. For more on this, see Kathleen Hall Jamieson, *Eloquence in an Electronic Age: The Transformation of Political Speechmaking* (New York: Oxford University Press, 1988).

20. Jamieson, "Discourse and the Democratic Ideal," 336.

21. Ashley Parker, "In Nonstop Whirlwind of Campaigns, Twitter is a Critical Tool," January 28, 2012, https://www.nytimes.com/2012/01/29/us/politics/twitter-is -a-critical-tool-in-republican-campaigns.html.

22. Lloyd F. Bitzer, "The Rhetorical Situation," *Philosophy and Rhetoric* 1 (1968): 6.

23. Troy B. Cooper, "The Impromptu Rhetorical Situation," *Communication Teacher* 33, no. 4 (2019): 263.

24. Ibid., 8.

25. Ibid.

26. Ibid.

27. See Barbara A. Biesecker, "Rethinking the Rhetorical Situation from Within the Thematic of Différeance," *Philosophy & Rhetoric* 22, no. 2 (1989): 110–130; Donna Gorrell, "The Rhetorical Situation Again: Linked Components in a Venn Diagram," *Philosophy & Rhetoric* 30, no. 4 (1997): 395–412; Richard L. Larson, "Lloyd Bitzer's 'Rhetorical Situation' and the Classification of Discourse: Problems and Implications," *Philosophy & Rhetoric* 3, no 3 (1970): 165–168.

28. Richard E. Vatz, "The Myth of the Rhetorical Situation," *Philosophy & Rhetoric* 6, no. 3 (1973): 156.

29. Ibid.

30. Gorrell, "The Rhetorical Situation Again," 407.

31. Ibid.

32. Kathleen Farrell and Marilyn J. Young, "The Rhetorical Situation," in *Rhetorical Criticism: Perspectives in Action*, ed. by Jim A. Kuypers (Lanham, MD: Lexington Books, 2009), 35.

33. Leach, "Rhetorical Analysis," 2002, 224.

34. "Election 2012: Romney on Pay Equity for Women: 'Binders Full of Women,'" Posted October 16, 2012, by *New York Times* on *YouTube*, https://www .youtube.com/watch?v=wfXgpem78kQ.

35. Ibid., 225.

36. Kathleen M. Hall Jamieson, "Generic Constraints and the Rhetorical Situation," *Philosophy & Rhetoric* 6, no. 3 (1973): 163.

37. Ibid., 7.

38. Ibid.

39. Janet Lynn Johnson, "Blogs and Dialogism in the 2008 United States Presidential Campaign," (PhD diss, Texas Woman's University, 2010).

40. Jeanne Fahnestock, *Rhetorical Style: The Uses of Language in Persuasion* (Oxford: Oxford University Press, 2011), 303.

41. Jamieson, "Generic Constraints," 165.

42. Vatz, "Myth of the Rhetorical Situation," 158.

43. Jennifer Preston, "Campaigns Rapid Response Efforts Get a Little More Rapid," *New York Times*, August 1, 2012, https://thecaucus.blogs.nytimes.com/2012 /08/01/campaigns-rapid-response-efforts-get-a-little-more-rapid/.

44. Ibid.

45. Johnson, "Blogs and Dialogism."

46. Mary Garret and Xiaosui Xiao, "The Rhetorical Situation Revisited," *Rhetoric Society Quarterly* 23, no. 2 (1993): 39.

47. Ibid., 38.

48. Frank James, "Obama and Romney Respond to Sandy with Election (And Katrina) in Mind," *NPR*, October 29, 2012, https://www.npr.org/sections/itsallpolit ics/2012/10/29/163862168/obama-and-romney-respond-to-sandy-with-election-and -katrina-in-mind.

49. Ibid.

50. Ibid.

51. Thomas E. Patterson, *The Vanishing Voter: Public Involvement in an Age of Uncertainty* (New York: Vintage, 2003), 65.

52. Ibid.

53. Ibid.

54. Robertson, *The Language of Democracy*, 69.

Chapter 5

2016 Presidential Campaign Narrative

Presidential elections are one of the oldest American rituals in the United States. Every four years, American citizens vote for president of the United States. Political campaigns follow a traditional story pattern. The characters change, but "we understand our lives and our world through story."[1] Through these stories, American citizens develop a sense of each candidate's agenda, an agenda the media spews into the world and is amplified by social media users' messages. Through media, the campaigns "tell stories of what they believe and what they do not believe."[2] Once the candidates establish their stories, traditional story archetypes start to develop. Mark McKinnon writes:

> How do you tell a story? Identify a threat and/or opportunity. Establish victims of the threat or denied opportunity. Suggest villains that impose the threat or deny the opportunity. Propose solutions. Reveal the hero.[3]

These archetype stories are the crux of our society and the manifestation of how news is American's storytime because "news, of all things, has become the inheritor of humanity's essential stories."[4] The story of a presidential campaign becomes the story of a country's existence.

The 2016 campaign story had all the dramatic elements; the story had heroes, villains, threats, solutions, and a surprise ending. Donald J. Trump beat out sixteen Republican opponents and won the nomination. The top Democratic candidate was Hillary Clinton.

The 2016 campaign did not succumb to the traditional campaign narrative. The campaign's two nominees were opposites. Democratic nominee, Hillary Clinton, is a traditional, seasoned politician (former first lady, senator, and secretary of state), and Republican nominee, Donald Trump, is a businessman and a reality show celebrity who lacked political experience. Trump was media savvy, and Clinton shunned the media spotlight. Several important events made the story of Campaign 2016 unique.

CRAFTING THE CAMPAIGN STORY

Every campaign has a unique narrative, which then becomes the story of our nation. Gil Troy says,

> As Americans grumble, in what has become a quadrennial ritual, that the presidential campaign is too long, too nasty, and too frivolous, they should consider whether they would really prefer a return to the nineteenth-century rules of the game that are so often held up as an alternative.[5]

The alternative might not work in today's culture. Each campaign since George Washington has built upon our nation's changes—both technologically and ideologically. Campaigns change because America and Americans change—both by new inventions and by new ideological, cultural shifts. Communication standards change. During Washington's campaign, he stood for election. Washington feared Americans would believe he wanted to be their king. Eugene Vasilew explains the president "was supposed to represent all the people, not merely his party, and was chosen to head a nation, not a political ticket. This was true of Washington but has not been true since."[6] During Washington's campaign, newspapers disseminated information, and word-of-mouth stories moved across the land. A presidential candidate could not tweet and make news within five minutes of that tweet. Information took weeks, if not months, to reach every American.

Candidates did not publicly address Americans until as late as 1840. The first candidate to break tradition and speak directly to the people was William Harrison, who tried to defeat President Martin Van Buren.[7] This campaign defined our modern-day campaign structure as a two-party system. The 1840 campaign also established and reiterated the myth of the presidency within our culture.

First, a candidate must create an image. What changed presidential campaign rhetoric started in 1840; the Whig party recruited seventy-seven-year-old William Henry Harrison to defeat Democrat incumbent Martin Van Buren. The Whigs created a character after President Van Buren said in *Baltimore Republican* that if Harrison collected a pension, he would sit in a log cabin and drink hard cider.[8] The Whigs then took Van Buren's comments and created an image of Harrison as the common man. In this way, "Capitalizing their candidate's new image, the Whigs held great parades with log cabins and rolled hard-cider barrels down the streets."[9] The Whigs also held rallies all the while serving hard cider, "as thousands of individuals attended these rallies."[10] Harrison's campaign concentrated on his war hero status and less on issues. Campaigns changed from policies to personalities when "the Whig campaign ignored all issues, except those relating to the personality of their candidate."[11] The campaign also wrote songs to already existing tunes so that "people were able to learn the songs quickly."[12] The songs either celebrated Harrison or mocked "Little Van."[13] The 1840 campaign was the beginning of selling an image, and a story, to the American electorate—that campaign defined identity politics.

The American citizen might not sing campaign songs about Hillary Clinton or Donald Trump. However, Republican nominee Donald Trump created nicknames for his opponents, such as "Little Marco," "Lying Ted," and "Crooked Hillary."

The list of 2016 presidential candidates is long. The following list contains each candidate's party affiliation—Republican (R) or Democrat (D)—and the date the candidate dropped out of the presidential race.

- Rick Perry (R, September 11, 2015)
- Scott Walker (R, September 21, 2015)
- Jim Webb (D, October 2015)
- Lincoln Chafee (D, October 23, 2015)
- Lawrence Lessig (D, November 2, 2015)
- Bobby Jindal (R, November 17, 2015)
- Lindsey Graham (R, December 21, 2015)
- George Pataki (R, December 29, 2015)
- Mike Huckabee (R, February 1, 2016)
- Martin O'Malley (D, February 1, 2016)
- Rand Paul (R, February 2, 2016)
- Rick Santorum (R, February 3, 2016)
- Carly Fiorina (R, February 10, 2016)
- Chris Christie (R, February 10, 2016)
- Jim Gilmore (R, February 12, 2016)
- Jeb Bush (R, February 20, 2016)
- Ben Carson (R, March 4, 2016)
- Marco Rubio (R, March 15, 2016)
- Ted Cruz (R, May 3, 2016)
- John Kasich (R, May 4, 2016)
- Bernie Sanders (D, July 12, 2016)

The two nominees for president were Republican nominee, businessman Donald J. Trump, and the Democrat nominee, former first lady, senator, and secretary of state Hillary Clinton.

Donald Trump defeated his opponents by labeling them, much like Harrison did to Van Buren. Donald Trump's name-calling, such as "Little Marco," "Low Energy Jeb," and "Lying Ted," created a negative connotation toward those candidates. Trump created characters out of his opponents' weaknesses and stuck with those labels until he won the nomination. The media started showing sound bites of Donald Trump's name-calling, which soon trickled down into identifying the candidates by Trump's given nicknames.

As the number of candidates grows each election cycle, a candidate must stand out. Trump stood out from his opponents with an engaging and unique storyline. Donald Trump's narrative resonated with citizens. Walter Fisher, in "Narration as a Human Communication Paradigm," explains, "Some stories are better than others, more coherent, more "true" to the way people and the world are—in fact and in value."[14] Moreover, if people feel like "meaningless spectators rather than co-authors," they are more apt to not participate in the narrative.[15] Trump engaged his audience through his online accounts. Trump liked to retweet members of the public.[16] Tweets from members of the public contributed to 78 percent of Trump's retweets.[17] Clinton retweeted no members of the public. Donald Trump had the most social media responses to his posts and averaged almost 6,000 retweets per Twitter post compared to Hillary Clinton's average of about 1,500 retweets per Twitter post.[18]

THE 2016 NOMINATING CONVENTIONS

Today's parties' nominating conventions are not pragmatic but ritualistic.[19] In 1832, the Democratic Party held its first convention to nominate the vice president because President Andrew Jackson sought a second term.[20] The nominees never attended the nominating convention but corresponded by letter. In 1835, the Democratic convention notified Martin Van Buren by letter.[21] The nominees then wrote an acceptance letter back to the party. Also, "during the period of 1892 to 1928, notification ceremonies were staged, including band music, parades, and speeches."[22] It was not until 1932 that the convention evolved to include the nominee when President Franklin D. Roosevelt spoke to the convention in person.[23] As media technology changed, so did the nominating conventions.

The ritual of the nominating convention signals the official start of the nominees' campaign. At first, radio allowed Americans to listen to politicians, and then the rise of television changed the way Americans viewed politicians. Both radio and television changed the nominating convention, moving it from a political process to a compelling storyline. Broadcasters turn nominating conventions into television events that they spin into a story to keep American viewers' interest.

The primary season is when the candidates for each party introduced themselves to the public. At this time, candidates need to concentrate on becoming a household name. When television first became popular during the 1950s, politicians had to learn to become not only politicians but also a "name."[24] In William G. Carleton's 1957 article in the *Political Science Quarterly*, Carleton predicted:

The days when the political lightning in a nominating convention would strike an unknown or a comparative unknown are over. If politicians do not find the ways to make themselves household names, real national celebrities, presidential nominations will go to celebrities in other fields.[25]

The 2016 primary season turned out the way Carleton predicted. Celebrities in other fields were nominated president if the career politicians could not transform into political celebrities. Donald Trump's reality show, celebrity status proved that his name recognition could turn into a political victory without his being a career politician. Trump's campaign strategy proved that he knew media well enough to rely on free media exposure for his rallies and tweets. Additionally, Trump made himself accessible for quick over-the-phone news interviews rather than implementing traditional political advertising.

Not only did the politicians have to change to garner attention on television, but journalists also had to cover the nominating conventions differently. Nominating conventions were not exciting; broadcasters had to create a storyline to keep audiences interested. The carefully prepared script leads to the highlight of the nominating convention, the presidential nominee's acceptance speech. Thomas B. Farrell explains,

The optimal convenient ritual begins with the statement and demonstration of theme, progresses to the clustering of roles and generic personae, and culminates in the annointing of the person who condenses, symbolizes, and enacts the theme.[26]

The candidate then campaigns with that theme, and the people can then decide to either adopt that candidate's agenda or not. The nominating conventions are where the candidate solidifies their agenda or theme to the American public. The nominating convention also establishes the political characters, who help establish the archetype to the storyline.[27]

Farrell also researched the 1976 conventions and noted,

What cannot be denied, however, is that party structures historically have evolved into a crude dialectical arrangement where combat reigns supreme. This strangely reversible battle of good and evil requires that each party falsify itself

Table 5.1   The Republican (RNC) and the Democratic (DNC) Nominating Convention daily themes.

Day	RNC Themes	DNC Themes
Monday	Make America Safe Again	United Together
Tuesday	Make America Work Again	A Lifetime of Fighting for Children and Families
Wednesday	Make America First Again	Working Together
Thursday	Make America One Again	Stronger Together

and the other—not quite acknowledging, not quite dismissing its own responsibility for social problems.[28]

Farrell's assessment of the 1976 nominating conventions is what happened in the 2016 conventions. Both conventions in 2016 created a storyline of "Us vs. Them."

The themes, shown in table 5.1, for the parties' national conventions were also very different. One convention instilled hope and unity, while the other convention invoked fear and divisiveness. Each campaign's message is evident when comparing the themes side by side.

The daily themes in table 5.1 offer a way to see the differences in each convention's rhetorical choices. Each convention's themes helped to create the overall narrative that led to the final Thursday night event—the ritualistic act of the presidential nominee officially accepting the party's nomination.

Republican Nominating Convention

The Republican National Convention (RNC) showcased lots of political characters and plotlines. On the first night, Donald Trump's wife, Melania Trump, delivered her speech. Before the speech was over, social media buzzed with accusations that Melania's speech sounded much like Michelle Obama's 2008 Democratic National Convention speech. MSNBC reported on the ways that social media users took to fact-checking Melania's speech. Rachel Maddow reported:

This started on social media. People on Twitter first started circulating sort of eyebrow-raising claims about Melania Trump's speech this evening. That led us, because it started to pick up a lot of speed online, it led us to go dig up the archival material and check these claims. And it does appear that there are some unusual similarities, some unusual, very tight parallels between Melania Trump's speech tonight and Michelle Obama's speech in a similar position in the 2008 Democratic nominating convention for her husband, Barack Obama.[29]

Before Melania finished her speech, social media had discredited her speech, which led the mainstream media to verify the claims made on social media. With the attention on the possible plagiarism, Melania missed an opportunity to "humanize Donald Trump."[30] The plagiarized speech also created a loss of *ethos* for the Trump campaign and the convention. Social media changed the story, and instead of Melania creating a moment in history with an invaluable speech made by a nominee's spouse, the moment became a plot twist.

The mainstream media compared first lady Michelle Obama's 2008 speech to Melania Trump's speech.[31] Without the influence of social media, people may have overlooked the apparent similarities in the two speeches. Twitter responded:

@*KateDahls:* I have a dream. #FamousMelaniaTrumpQuotes (July 18, 2016)

@*Jonfavs Sarah Hurwitz:* Michelle's head speechwriterused to be Hillary's. So the Trump campaign plagiarized from a Hillary speechwriter. (July 18, 2016)

@*JarrettHill:* OMG. Melania. That was literally a whole line from Michelle Obama 2012. ". . .their willingness to work hard for them." #GOPConvention (July 18, 2016)

Jarrett Hill, a freelance journalist, was the first to tweet that Melania's speech had lines lifted from first lady Michelle Obama's 2008 Democratic Convention speech.[32] Donald Trump responded:

@*realDonaldTrump:* The media is spending more time doing a forensic analysis of Melania's speech than the FBI spent on Hillary's emails. (July 20, 2016)

A former chief speechwriter for President George W. Bush Michael Gerson said, "An error like Melania Trump committed last night tells us that the Trump campaign lacks seriousness and structure."[33]

As Melania emerged as the victim of the Republican National Convention, Senator Ted Cruz emerged as the villain. Senator Cruz's speech elicited boos from the crowd. Cruz told the audience to "vote your conscience" and did not publicly endorse Donald Trump during his convention speech. In the *New York Times*, Michael Paulson's story, "The Drama of Ted Cruz: A Little Bit of Shakespeare in That Speech?" shows how mainstream media acknowledged the dramatic storyline. Paulson explains,

In Cleveland, of course, Mr. Cruz accepted an invitation from Mr. Trump to speak at the nominating convention, but then surprised the crowd and upended the night by withholding his support. In Ancient Rome, at least as described by Shakespeare in "Julius Caesar," Antony accepts an invitation from Brutus to speak at Caesar's funeral, but then undermines Brutus with a speech that superficially praises Brutus but is understood by listeners to do the reverse.[34]

Cruz's speech was critically received. Donald Trump tweeted his response to Cruz's speech:

@*realdonaldtrump:* Wow, Ted Cruz got booed off the stage, didn't honor the pledge! I saw his speech two hours early but let him speak anyway. No big deal! (July 20, 2016)

Donald Trump's tweet received 10,000 responses, 21,000 retweets, and 70,000 likes.

Cruz, who did not endorse Trump at the convention, motivated a response from the Republican nominee. Donald Trump's social media helped the convention's narrative structure. Twitter allowed Trump to talk directly to the audience with no filter. Trump's interaction with the audience created a polyphony of responses in both support and criticism. Trump took advantage of the scene and knew how to cast a large circumference to attract audiences to motivate ordinary citizens to take action.

On the final night of the Republican National Convention, Donald Trump delivered the final speech to accept the Republican Party's nomination. Trump spoke about how America is in crisis. Some of the lines in Trump's speech:

Our convention occurs at a moment of crisis for our nation . . .
    The attacks on our police, and the terrorism in our cities, threaten our very way of life.
    Many have witnessed this violence personally; some may have been victims.
    Our roads and bridges are falling apart, our airports are Third World condition . . .
    The problems we face now—poverty and violence at home, war, and destruction abroad—will last only as long as we continue relying on the same politicians who created them.
    There can be no prosperity without law and order.[35]

The content and delivery created the illusion that America is doomed. In the speech, he says, "I alone can fix it."[36] The ending to the national convention story, as told by Donald Trump, was, "I am your voice."[37] Trump's use of

I "broke with two centuries of American political tradition, in which candidates for office—and above all, for the nation's highest office—acknowledge their fallibility and limitations, asking for the help of their fellow Americans, and of God, to accomplish what they cannot do on their own."[38] At the Republican National Convention, Donald Trump defied the traditional story and told Americans "that he, alone, could solve their problems."[39] Donald Trump's speech identified with people's fears and worries. The use of *I* was to instill confidence that he could solve the country's problems.

Democratic Nominating Convention

A long list of notable A-list celebrities spoke during television's prime time hours of the Democratic National Convention, including Sarah Silverman, Meryl Streep, Elizabeth Banks, America Ferrera, Lena Dunham, Eva Longoria, Katy Perry, and Bradley Cooper. The Democratic National Convention produced a well-thought-out prime time event every night. Unlike the Republican National Convention, the Democratic National Convention showed videos and speakers who had name recognition. Celebrity endorsements are meant to influence citizens' opinions: "with a multitude of information descending on citizens at any one point in time, citizens take cues from celebrities, just as they do from other elites, helping citizens determine both what to pay attention to and also influencing what to think about an issue."[40] The celebrities gave the DNC a polished Hollywood production look rather than the RNC's low-budget reality show. A high-profile celebrity presence at the RNC was nonexistent. Instead, the RNC featured D-list celebrities such as former *Happy Days* actor Scott Baio, reality show *Duck Dynasty*'s Willie Robertson, and former *General Hospital* actor Antonio Sabato, Jr.

The DNC did not escape a dramatic convention storyline. Before the DNC began, WikiLeaks released 20,000 hacked emails containing information that DNC officials had wanted to thwart the Bernie Sanders's campaign.[41] *The Washington Post* reported one email "suggests that the party could help Clinton by raising questions about Sanders's faith."[42] These emails revealed that the Democratic Party did not support the Sanders's campaign. As a result of the DNC email hack, the DNC chairwoman, Debbie Wasserman Schultz, resigned. To add to the narrative, intelligence agencies revealed Russia might have been behind the hacking.[43] *The New York Times* reported in August 2016, "American intelligence agencies have said they have 'high confidence' that the attack was the work of Russian intelligence agencies."[44] The intrigue and mystery added to the campaign narrative.

The convention reminded voters of the weakness of Hillary Clinton. Her reputation as a less-than-dynamic speaker made her reliant on her husband, former President Bill Clinton, President Barack Obama, and first lady Michelle Obama. They all delivered dynamic speeches that spoke about Hillary Clinton as a wife, mom and how she was the most qualified person to run for president. As *The New York Times* reported,

> Mrs. Clinton will have to win this election herself. She has long been polarizing, but the F.B.I.'s investigation into her email and server may have done irreversible damage to her credibility, as Mr. Trump clearly hopes given his nickname for her, Crooked Hillary. Mrs. Clinton did not tackle that head on, instead seeming to try for a workaround: Take me as I am. Or, perhaps: Better me than him.[45]

Hillary Clinton's speech was the opposite of Trump's speech. She presented her audience with the message of hope and presented the argument on why people should not vote for Trump. Hillary, unlike Trump, stated her qualifications. She clarified statements such as, "I'm not here to take away your gun . . . I just don't want you to be shot by someone who shouldn't have a gun in the first place."[46] She also pointed out Trump's bombastic rhetoric:

> For the past year, many people made the mistake of laughing off Donald Trump's comments—excusing him as an entertainer just putting on a show. They think he couldn't possibly mean all the horrible things he says—like when he called women "pigs." Or said that an American judge couldn't be fair because of his Mexican heritage. Or when he mocks and mimics a reporter with a disability. Or insults prisoners of war like John McCain—a true hero and patriot who deserves our respect. At first, I admit, I couldn't believe he meant it either.[47]

Trump's speech instilled emotions, such as fear. He spoke about change, whereas Clinton's speech was about why Americans should not vote for Trump. Her speech was more organized and sounded more hopeful about America's future, but she did not address change as well as Trump did. Trump's speech discussed change, such as reforming tax laws:

> Next comes the reform of our tax laws, regulations, and energy rules. While Hillary Clinton plans a massive tax increase, I have proposed the largest tax reduction of any candidate who has declared for the presidential race this year—Democrat or Republican. Middle-income Americans will experience profound relief, and taxes will be simplified for everyone.[48]

Clinton avoided discussing the controversies surrounding her about her email server and what happened in Benghazi during her time as secretary of state. Clinton missed an opportunity to have a heart-to-heart with the American people to gain their trust. Clinton's speech spoke mostly about Trump's rhetoric:

Now you didn't hear any of this from Donald Trump at his convention.

He spoke for 70-odd minutes—and I do mean odd.

And he offered zero solutions. But we already know he doesn't believe these things.

No wonder he doesn't like talking about his plans.

You might have noticed; I love talking about mine.

But here's the sad truth: There is no other Donald Trump. . . . This is it.

And in the end, it comes down to what Donald Trump doesn't get: that America is great because America is good.

So enough with the bigotry and bombast. Donald Trump's not offering real change.[49]

Clinton participated in the ritual of the convention in hopes that she would "gather the like-minded around [her] and affirm [her] common worth. Because social rituals—including political rituals—offer a society protection, predictability, and self-identification, they are extremely important devices for cohesion."[50]

DEBATES

By the time the final presidential debates occur in October before Election Day, debates help confirm voters' preexisting beliefs about a candidate. Debates either confirm decisions or help undecided voters decide.

Historically, debates did not frequently happen between candidates. On Saturday, August 21, 1858, Lincoln and Douglas debated for the Illinois Senate seat. Newspapers at the time seem to have reported two different debates.[51] Ronald C. White, Jr., in his book *A. Lincoln: A Biography*, explains that different newspapers told different stories of the debates:

The reader, searching for the truth between such politically biased reporting, might wish to turn to the text of the debate. Reporter Horace White and stenographer Robert R. Hit covered the debates for the pro-Lincoln *Chicago Press & Tribune*, while Henry Binmore and James B. Sheridan, two shorthand reporters, wrote on the debates for the pro-Douglas *Chicago Times*. The difficulty was that the texts in the two newspapers sometimes varied on crucial words or phrases.[52]

The drama brought out the audience to witness the seven Lincoln-Douglas debates. White said these "debates became the Fourth of July picnic, summer revival meeting, county fair, visiting circus and visiting lecturer all rolled into one grand pageant."[53] The ritualistic act of gathering to listen to two politicians became part of the election process that would not be revisited for many years after.

Throughout the nineteenth century, politicians enlisted surrogates to debate for them.[54] Politicians wanted to uphold their image and did not want to speak to the voters directly.[55] At that time, most candidates refrained from formal campaigns—it was not until the 1896 race that voters started to see the beginnings of what has evolved into modern presidential campaign practices. Technological advances were the catalyst for modern presidential debates. For example, radio helped promote the idea that political debates could be entertaining and brief, unlike traditional non-broadcasted debates. Kathleen Hall Jamieson and David S. Birdsell explain, "Nineteenth-century political debates did not vie for audience attention with circuses, drama, music, sitcoms, and first-run movies. Contemporary debates do."[56] Radio became a venue for debates after William Harkness, vice president of AT&T, testified before Congress in 1924 to propose a debate between the Democrat, Republican, and Progressive presidential candidates.[57] Broadcast regulations required equal time for all candidates—even the lesser-known candidate, who had a small following. By the end of the 1950s, television was ready to broadcast a debate in time for the 1960 election cycle. Newton Minow and Lee Mitchell explain, "Presidential television debates originated in the 1960 contest between John Kennedy and Richard Nixon when Congress suspended the equal-time law to relieve broadcasters of the need to give corresponding time to other candidates."[58]

There is no doubt the first televised debate in 1960 influenced voters. Presidential candidates in debates:

> function as glorified television characters, regulars in a long-running series. By the time they reach the general election debates, these individuals are known commodities to most of the audience, albeit within a carefully arranged context. Debates remove these characters from their predictable, controlled *mise-en-scene* and throw them into a much more stimulating setting.[59]

John F. Kennedy's campaign staff prepared him aesthetically for television. Kennedy studied and prepared himself before the broadcast and used what his campaign called the "'Nixopedia' crammed with data about his opponent's past positions and statements."[60] Presidential candidates had to learn how to talk to the television audience. Kennedy was not only a good-looking man, but he was also well prepared for the debate.

People who watched the debate on television believed Kennedy won; those who listened to the debate on the radio believed Nixon won. Television proved a candidate's image was just as important as his words. The goal of a televised debate is to "directly persuade voters but also to create a political buzz that stimulates voter information-seeking and communication."[61]

It was not until 1976 that Congress lifted the section 315 equal-time provision, allowing television channels to broadcast debates hosted by an outside organization. If an organization asked political candidates to debate, the excuse against not to debate would not lie on the broadcasters but the candidates.

When seasoned movie and television actor Ronald Reagan campaigned, he knew the power of television. Reagan knew when and how to deliver a sound bite. During a debate against then-president Jimmy Carter, he responded with the famous line, "There you go again."[62] Reagan's delivery is a reminder that "all the great orators in history have been great 'hams.'"[63]

The media started to frame the debates around those sound bite moments. Broadcast networks "set up a 'must-win' scenario because that was the most exciting, the most consistent with their role as an entertainment medium."[64] Both the media and the public watch the political debates simultaneously and can assess the situation together. Voters use debates to confirm their already-held beliefs about the candidate.[65] Audiences can react and "decide who controlled the agenda, who ducked the questions, and who was confrontational or aggressive."[66] Now, audiences, through social media, can instantly set the media's agenda about the debates' hot topics. One example is the October 16, 2012 debate between Republican nominee Mitt Romney and President Barack Obama. Mitt Romney mentioned "binders full of women."[67] Instantly, Internet users created websites and tweeted memes spoofing "binders full of women." *Google Politics* reported the phrase became the third top-trending query that night.[68]

2016 Republican Primary Debates

Presidential debates help reinforce the frames, which "are mental structures that characterize ideas."[69] Erving Goffman writes,

Frame, however, organizes more than meaning; it also organizes involvement. During any spate of activity, participants will ordinarily not only obtain a sense of what is going on but will also (in some degree) become spontaneously engrossed, caught up, enthralled.[70]

Americans are familiar with a debate's structure: candidates stand at podiums, answering moderator's questions about policy and issues. Americans expect a civil conversation between the candidates to help them confirm their already-held beliefs about a candidate. However, what if a candidate changes that frame and reorganizes the mental structure people are used to experiencing? That is what Donald Trump did. He wrote his own story, and he started breaking the familiar political frame during his first Republican debate.

On August 6, 2015, Fox News aired the first Republican primary debate. Moderator Megyn Kelly asked Donald Trump a question about his verbal attacks on women:

Kelly: Your Twitter account has several disparaging comments about women's looks. You once told a contestant on Celebrity Apprentice it would be a pretty picture to see her on her knees. Does that sound to you like the temperament of a man we should elect as president, and how will you answer the charge from Hillary Clinton, who was likely to be the Democratic nominee, that you are part of the war on women?

Trump: I think the big problem this country has is being politically correct.

(APPLAUSE)

I've been challenged by so many people, and I don't frankly have time for total political correctness. And to be honest with you, this country doesn't have time either. This country is in big trouble. We don't win anymore. We lose to China. We lose to Mexico both in trade and at the border. We lose to everybody.

And frankly, what I say, and oftentimes it's fun, it's kidding. We have a good time. What I say is what I say. And honestly, Megyn, If you don't like it, I'm sorry. I've been very nice to you, although I could probably maybe not be, based on the way you have treated me. But I wouldn't do that.[71]

Trump's red herring fallacy, "If you don't like it, I'm sorry. I've been very nice to you, although I could probably maybe not be, based on the way you have treated me. But I wouldn't do that" is distracting the audience to make them forget what was asked. Trump offers no proof of how Megyn Kelly has treated him poorly. He never answered the question Megyn Kelly asked, which was about disparaging remarks about women and if he is contributing to the war on women. Trump gives proof to Megyn Kelly's claim about his disparaging remarks toward women. Trump offers Kelly proof when he says, "I've been very nice to you, although I could probably not be."

Trump fills his post-debate late-night tweets with hyperboles and logical fallacies about the debate. His tweets after each debate became a ritual act. Notice the colloquial language he uses to describe Megyn Kelly's performance.

@realDonaldTrump: Wow, @megynkelly **really bombed** tonight. People are going wild on twitter! Funny to watch. (August 7, 2015, 2:40 AM)

@realDonaldTrump: "@FrankLuntz: I'm getting a lot of @MegynKelly hate mail tonight #GOPDebate" She is **totally** overrated and angry. She **really bombed** tonight. (August 7, 2015, 2:31 AM)

@realDonaldTrump: @timjcam: @megynkelly @FrankLuntz @realdDonaldTrump Fox viewers give low marks to **bimbo** @MegynKelly will consider other programs!" (August 7, 2015, 2:24 AM)

@realDonaldTrump: "@RubenMMoreno: @realDonaldTrump **The biggest loser** in the debate was @megynkelly. You can't out trump Donald Trump. **You will lose!** (August 7, 2015, 2:23 AM)

All of Donald Trump's tweets and retweets include many logical fallacies, which are errors in reasoning usually because the argument lacks logic and proof. Trump's favorite logical fallacy is the ad hominem argument, which attacks a person's character. Trump started framing his Twitter responses as character insults when he felt like a person betrayed him as Megyn Kelly did during the debate. Trump tried to project a self-image of restraint, but he kept breaking out of the familiar political campaign narrative frame. No other candidate tweeted as candidly as Trump, which set him apart from ordinary citizens. His tweets became breaking news. His logical fallacies and use of repetition defined his debate style. In the ninth Republican primary debate, Trump's rhetorical strategy was repetition:

> I want everybody taken care of, but we have to take care of our people in this country. We're not taking care of our people. We have no border. We have no control. People are flooding across. We can't have it. We either have a border, and I'm very strongly, I'm not proposing. I will build a wall. I will build a wall.[72]

Trump repeated "taken care of" and "wall." Fahnstock says, "When listeners hear, or readers see that a succession of clauses (or of other text segments) opens with repeated phrasing, they will tend to group those segments in their minds."[73] He framed his story, set the mental structures for his ideas, and kept repeating his claims.

On February 26, 2016, Donald Trump tweeted:

@realdonaldtrump: Lightweight checker Marco Rubio looks like a little boy on stage. Not presidential material!

These types of tweets from Trump created a catalyst for Trump's opponents to argue back. The week before the eleventh Republican debate became memorable when Senator Marco Rubio insinuated that Donald Trump had small hands. Rubio's comment led to an altercation between him and Trump during the debate.

RUBIO: Let's talk about Donald Trump's strategy and my strategy and Ted's strategy and John Kasich's strategy when it comes to ISIS. And on healthcare and on the important issues facing this country.

But let's be honest about all this. The media has given these personal attacks that Donald Trump has made an incredible amount of coverage. Let's start talking again about the issues that matter to this country. I'm ready to do that starting right here right now tonight.

BAIER: Mr. Trump, your response?

TRUMP: Well, I also happened to call him a lightweight, OK? And I have said that. So, I would like to take that back. He is really not much of a lightweight. And as far as—and I have to say this, I have to say this. He hit my hands. Nobody has ever hit my hands. I have never heard of this. Look at those hands. Are they small hands?

(LAUGHTER)

TRUMP: And he referred to my hands, if they are small, something else must be small. I guarantee you there is no problem. I guarantee.[74]

The debates were less about the tradition of revealing the candidates' policy and issue stances and more about the repetition of insults and name-calling. The repetition created a mental structure for audiences to identify, consciously or unconsciously, Trump's opponents.

These types of distractions are not new in campaigns. Kathleen Hall Jamieson visited such political antics in her book *Dirty Politics: Deception, Distraction, and Democracy.* Jamieson found that the 1960 and 1964 campaigns did not concentrate on the issues of the day but concentrated on distractions:

Kennedy and Johnson entranced the public with a shell game. As our attention focused on their mesmerizing stories and anxiety-producing attacks, central issues slipped out of sight. The lesson is that campaigns can engage without necessarily engaging central issues of biography and policy.[75]

The 2016 campaign borrowed many strategies from some of the hardest fought campaign stories throughout history.

Trump's main competitors were Senator Marco Rubio and Senator Ted Cruz. Trump framed Cruz as a liar and Rubio as inexperienced and too young. The traditional story frame of policy and issue conversation slowly dissolved during the Republican primary debates. In the end, the career politicians did not have the showmanship to match Trump. The senators' delivery of their message fell "on deaf ears."[76] Trump, like Ronald Reagan and John F. Kennedy, knew how to deliver to the audience through the media. Kennedy had the looks for television, Reagan knew how to deliver a line, and Trump knew how to create an engaging storyline. Trump engaged the audience by engaging and including ordinary citizens in his tweets and retweets.

2016 Democratic Primary Debates

The Democratic primary debates were more subdued than the Republican primary debates. Hillary Clinton did not expect Senator Bernie Sanders to become a fierce contender with a rapidly growing social media following. Bernie Sanders gave the best sound bite when he wanted to talk about the issues rather than Hillary Clinton's emails:

CLINTON: But I'll be there. I'll answer their questions. But tonight, I want to talk not about my emails, but about what the American people want from the next president of the United States.
(APPLAUSE)
COOPER: Senator Sanders?
SANDERS: Let me say this.
(APPLAUSE)
Let me say—let me say something that may not be great politics. But I think the secretary is right, and that is that the American people are sick and tired of hearing about your damn emails.
(APPLAUSE)
CLINTON: Thank you. Me, too. Me, too.
SANDERS: You know? The middle class—Anderson, and let me say something about the media, as well. I go around the country, talk to a whole lot of people. Middle class in this country is collapsing. We have 27 million people living in poverty. We have massive wealth and income inequality. Our trade policies have cost us millions of decent jobs. The American people want to know whether we're going to have a democracy or an oligarchy as a result of Citizens Union. Enough of the emails. Let's talk about the real issues facing America.
(APPLAUSE)
CLINTON: Thank you, Bernie. Thank you.[77]

The Democratic candidates did not deflect from the issues. Sanders said it might not have been great politics to say that Americans were sick and tired of Hillary Clinton's email scandal, but Sanders turned the discussion back to policy issues.

2016 Presidential Debates

After Donald Trump and Hillary Clinton became the final two nominees, the debates became less about issues and more about the horserace and the surprises. The electorate became familiar with stories about the Trump bus tape scandal, Russian ties, and James Comey's announcement about Clinton's emails.[78]

The first debate set a precedent for Trump's and Clinton's debate styles. *The Atlantic* reported, "[Clinton] remained calm and often smiling as Trump repeatedly attacked her and interrupted her answers—doing it so often that moderator Lester Holt, often a spectral presence at the debate, finally cut in twice in short order to chide him."[79] An example of the back-and-forth fighting shows how Trump and Clinton were both challenging each other's *ethos* while Lester Holt, the moderator, tried to move the conversation to a more productive tone:

Holt: Please just take 30 seconds, and then we're going to go on.

Clinton: I kind of assumed that there would be a lot of these charges and claims, and so

Trump: Facts [Interruption]

Clinton: So we have taken the home page of my website, HillaryClinton.com, and we've turned it into a fact-checker. So if you want to see in real-time what the facts are, please go and take a look. Because what I have proposed . . .

Trump: And take a look at mine, also, and you'll see. [Interruption]

Clinton: would not add a penny to the debt, and your plans would add $5 trillion to the debt. What I have proposed would cut regulations and streamline them for businesses. What I have proposed would be paid for by raising taxes on the wealthy, because they have made all the gains in the economy. And I think it's time that the wealthy and corporations paid their fair share to support this country.

Holt: Well, you just opened the next segment.

Trump: Well, could I finish—I think I [Interruption]

(CrossTalk)

Holt: I'm going to give you a chance right here . . .

Trump: I think I should—you go to her website, and you take a look at her website.

Holt: with a new 15-minute segment . . .

Trump: She's going to raise taxes $1.3 trillion.

Holt: Mr. Trump, I'm going to . . .

Trump: and look at her website. You know what? It's no difference than this. She's telling us how to fight ISIS. Just go to her website. She tells you how to fight ISIS on her website. I don't think General Douglass MacArthur would like that too much.

Holt: The next segment, we're continuing . . .

Clinton: Well, at least I have a plan to fight ISIS . . . [Interruption]

Holt: achieving prosperity . . .

Trump: No, no, you're telling the enemy everything you want to do. [Interruption]

Clinton: No, we're not. No, we're not.

Trump: See, you're telling the enemy everything you want to do. No wonder you've been fighting—no wonder you've been fighting ISIS your entire adult life. [Interruption]

Clinton: That's a—that's—go to the—please, fact-checkers, get to work.[80]

The Internet allows everyone to fact-check information. Hillary Clinton's fact-checking website offered real-time proof to the audience to support her debate arguments.

In the 2008 election and in 2012, President Obama had his own fact-checking website. As for fact-checking in real-time, the social media conversation is too fast to check every tweet by the campaigns as they happen. Political reporters have realized the narrative keeps rapidly changing:

> That speed would have seemed unthinkable 10 years ago, when "twitter" was merely something birds did. For political reporters today however, it's an information highway with no speed limits. Prolificacy and humors are rewarded, especially during live events. And fact-checking—by nature a reactive aspect of journalism—isn't well-suited for such a fast-paced environment.[81]

That is why Clinton used her website as a portal to clarify any statements she made and retaliate claims made by Trump. As we can see from the above transcript from the first presidential debate, the narrative changed quite often, and the claims made by each candidate grew to a point where moderator Lester Holt could not keep up. He tried to slow them down and said, "OK, you are unpacking a lot here."[82]

CNN reported, "the Twitter hashtag #debatenight cropped up more than 5.7 million times in 24 hours."[83] This debate also resulted in tweets discussing Trump's constant sniffling during the debate and Clinton's shoulder shimmy, which turned into an Internet meme that people shared through social media channels. The body language of the candidates was becoming a part of the campaign's and candidate's story.

The news cycle drove the second and third presidential debates. Each week in October, surprising news about each candidate created the most debate moments. Social media became the gathering place to discuss and talk about each campaign's controversies—as well as how each candidate's campaigns handled their crisis. Daniel Kreiss researched how candidates use Twitter to seize the moment. Kreiss said, "Campaigns . . . now pay close attention to shaping commentary on social media platforms such as Twitter during the debates themselves, in large part to influence journalistic perceptions of public opinion about the event."[84]

A day before the second debate, a 2005 tape emerged of Donald Trump bragging about "kissing, groping and trying to have sex with women" to *Access Hollywood* host Billy Bush.[85] That same night, Trump's campaign aired a taped apology. Trump said, "I said it, I was wrong, and I apologize."[86] The next day, Trump held a news conference before the debate with three women who had accused Hillary Clinton's husband and former president Bill Clinton of sexual assault, as well as a woman "who was raped by a man

Hillary Clinton defended at trial in 1975."[87] Trump's campaign broadcasted the news conference via Facebook Live. This strategic move allowed social media followers to see the press conference on devices other than their televisions. Trump's tactics were to offer proof of his opponent's fallacies by comparison examples.

One debate strategy is to create an overall theme within the first few minutes.[88] The debate was a town hall setting moderated by Anderson Cooper and Martha Raddatz. Patrice Brock asked Clinton the first question, "Knowing that educators assign viewing the presidential debates as students' homework, do you feel you are modeling appropriate and positive behavior for today's youth?"[89] Hillary Clinton made sure she created a moment to relate the question to her campaign slogan, "Stronger Together." Clinton answered:

> Yes, I think that's a very good question because I heard from lots of teachers and parents about some of our concerns about some of the things being said and done in their campaign. And I think it is very important for us to make clear to our children that our country really is great because we are good . . . . That's why the slogan of my campaign is stronger together.[90]

Clinton continued to discuss her plan to work with everyone. Clinton never answered the audience member's question; instead, she summarized her campaign's theme and took on common ground topics. Clinton repeats, "We are" several times. Using "We" creates a feeling of unity, mostly when she repeats her slogan, "Stronger Together." She wants the audience to feel a part of the solution to fix the political divisiveness. Anderson Cooper then asked Donald Trump to answer the question, and again, Trump summarized his campaign's theme:

> Well, I'll actually agree with that. I agree with everything she said. I began this campaign because I was so tired of seeing such foolish things happen to our country. This is a great country. This is a great land. I have gotten to know the people of the country over the last year and a half that I have been doing this as a politician. I cannot believe I'm saying that about myself, but I guess I have been a politician. And my whole concept was to make America great again.[91]

Notice that Trump does not use "We" but "I" throughout his answer. Trump discusses his experience. Trump, like Clinton, did not answer the question, which Anderson Cooper repeated:

> Thank you, Mr. Trump. The question from Patrice was about, "Are you both modeling positive and appropriate behaviors for today's youth?" We received a lot of questions online, Mr. Trump, about the tape that was released on

Friday, as you can imagine. You called what you said "locker room banter." You described kissing women without consent, grabbing their genitals. That is sexual assault. You bragged that you have sexually assaulted women. Do you understand that?[92]

Cooper's question allowed Trump to discuss what he meant by "locker room banter," but Trump decided to deflect answering locker room talk and discuss how he would destroy ISIS:

Yes, I am very embarrassed by it, and I hate it, but it's locker room talk, and it's one of those things. I will knock the hell out of ISIS. We are going to defeat ISIS.[93]

Cooper was not satisfied with Trump's answer and repeated the question.

Trump: I have great respect for women. Nobody has more respect for women than I do.
Cooper: So, for the record, you're saying you never did that?
Trump: Frankly, you hear these things. They are said. And I was embarrassed by it. But I have respect for women.
Cooper: Have you ever done those things?
Trump: And they have respect for me. And I will tell you, no, I have not. And I will tell you that I'm going to make our country safe and we're going to have borders, which we don't have now.[94]

Trump kept repeating the word "respect." He starts to deflect from Cooper's question to talk about the borders.

Anderson Cooper asked Clinton if she wanted to respond to Trump's statements. She took this opportunity to tell Americans that Donald Trump was not "fit to be president and commander in chief."[95] Clinton continued to say that he berated women, and targeted minority groups, such as African Americans, Latinos, people with disabilities, POWs, and Muslims. Clinton took advantage of the question to restate that she would work for all Americans. She kept listing proof of Trump's past comments and tweets. Trump's response:

It's just words folks. It's just words . . . I'm going to help the African Americans, I'm going to help the Latinos, Hispanics. I am going to help the inner cities. She has done a terrible job for the African Americans. She wants their vote and she does nothing.[96]

Trump dismisses what he says by repeating that his words do not matter. Trump also goes back to "I am," which he tries to persuade people to understand that he is the solution. Unlike Clinton, who uses the word "We," which creates a more unified connection with her audience.

Moderator Martha Raddatz interrupted Trump and went back to the bus tape and mentions that millions of people on social media were discussing the bus tape. This debate moment showed that social media users' posts would drive the presidential debate content. Jessica T. Feezell researched social media and agenda-setting and found:

> as people can easily tailor their individual media diets to suit their wants and needs, traditional agenda-setting effects might be expected to disappear. However, with the increasing prevalence of social media as a source of news, mass media agenda setting may persist to some extent through incidental information shared by sources within our social networks.[97]

The media was now a vessel to deliver the messages sent by digital citizens.

During the third presidential debate, Donald Trump made comments claiming he would not accept election results and called Clinton a "nasty woman." *The Wall Street Journal* reported five takeaways from the third debate:

(1) Mrs. Clinton attacked her opponent's character. Mr. Trump challenged his opponent's effectiveness.
(2) Mr. Trump is still not a traditional Republican.
(3) Mrs. Clinton laid out a message of unity, Mr. Trump of revival.
(4) Mr. Trump returned to his strongest issues: Change and the economy.
(5) Mr. Trump made the biggest news of the night.[98]

Additionally, during the debate, Trump alluded to not accepting the results of the elections if he lost. The Fox News debate moderator, Chris Wallace, asked a question regarding information that came from WikiLeaks.

Wallace: Secretary Clinton, I want to clear up your position on this issue, because in a speech you gave to a Brazilian bank for which you were paid $225,000, we've learned from *WikiLeaks*, that you said this. And I want to quote. "My dream is a hemispheric common market with open trade and open borders."
Trump: Thank you.
Wallace: That's the question. Please, quiet, everybody. Is that your dream? Open borders?
Clinton: If you went on to read the rest of the sentence, I was talking about energy. We trade more energy with our neighbors than we trade with the rest of the world combined. And I do want us to have an electric grid, an energy system, that crosses borders. I think that would be a great benefit to us. But you are very clearly quoting from *WikiLeaks*. What is really important about *WikiLeaks* is that

the Russian government has engaged in espionage against Americans. They have hacked American websites, American accounts of private people, of institutions. Then they have given that information to *WikiLeaks* for the purpose of putting it on the Internet. This has come from the highest levels of the Russian government. Clearly, from Putin himself, in an effort, as 17 of our intelligence agencies have confirmed, to influence our election. So, I actually think the most important question of this evening, Chris, is finally, will Donald Trump admit and condemn that the Russians are doing this, and make it clear that he will not have the help of Putin in this election? That he rejects Russian espionage against Americans, which he encouraged in the past. Those are the questions we need answered. We've never had anything like this happen in any of our elections before.

Trump: That was a great pivot off the fact that she wants open borders. Okay? How did we get on to Putin?[99]

Clinton did pivot from the question to clarify the question was based on information gathered from WikiLeaks, the website that illegally posted emails with the help of Russian hackers. The Internet is shown to have influenced and changed the political process. The information asked during debates now included hacked information that was put out by WikiLeaks during the Democratic National Convention.

Ten years before the 2016 election, Julian Assange, on December 3, 2006, published a post on his website iq.org, titled "Conspiracy as Governance." Assange wrote:

Literacy and the communications revolution have empowered conspirators with new means to conspire, increasing the speed of accuracy of their interactions and thereby the maximum size a conspiracy may achieve before it breaks down.[100]

The speed of information makes it harder to pinpoint the source of information. Regarding the two-party system in the United States, Assange said:

Consider what would happen if one of these parties gave up their mobile phones, fix and email correspondence—let alone the computer systems, which manage their subscribes, donors, budgets, polling, call centers, and direct mail campaigns? They would immediately fall into an organizational stupor and lose to the other.[101]

Wired magazine reported in October about Assange's 2006 predictions:

Of course, Assange's claim that a political party leaks in direct proportion to its dishonesty looks almost laughable after the last several months. WikiLeaks has published leaks exclusively damaging to Clinton and the Democratic Party while publishing nothing from Donald Trump or his campaign. (Trump has, of course, faced leaks of his 1995 tax returns and a damning video where he brags about sexual assault. But mainstream newspapers published both, and neither came from the sort of internal communicates Assange wrote about. Trump himself also famously doesn't use email, as good a security measure as anyone could hope for.)[102]

Assange's WikiLeaks affected the election enough that Chris Wallace quoted an email posted on the WikiLeaks website.

CONCLUSION

The Internet created a gateway for websites like WikiLeaks to emerge and infiltrate the news cycle. American campaigns had to worry about information leaks, hacked information, and candidates who had no fear of communicating through new media venues. Clinton's campaign struggled to respond to these controversial rhetorical situations generated through traditional and new media. All the while, Trump's campaign showed no fear of technology, especially engaging ordinary citizens in his tweets.

By isolating Hillary Clinton's and Donald Trump's campaign narratives, we can tell the untraditional narrative won over the traditional, familiar narrative frame. Trump solidified his overall message to voters about change and identified with the audience through commonplace topics and repeated themes despite logical errors. Trump also made himself accessible to media. He created a rhetorical style that did not shift from the style he used on his reality show, *The Celebrity Apprentice.* His style and delivery were familiar to audiences. The 2016 campaign reminded the electorate that media is powerful—and social media is even more powerful in creating a campaign's narrative.

NOTES

    1. Jack Lule, *Daily News, Eternal Stories: The Mythological Role of Journalism* (New York: The Guilford Press, 2001), 3.

    2. Ibid., 33.

    3. Mark McKinnon, "It's Storytelling, Stupid: What Made Donald Trump Smarter than Hillary Clinton," *The Daily Beast*, November 24, 2016, http://www.thedailybeast.com/articles/2016/11/24/what-made-donald-trump-smarter-than-hillary-clinton.html.

    4. Ibid., 20.

5. Gil Troy, "The Campaign Triumph," *Wilson Quarterly* 36 no. 3 (Summer 2012): 20.

6. Eugene Vasilew, "The Real vs. The Mythical Campaign," *Today's Speech* 8, no. 4 (1960): 25.

7. Ibid.

8. Kevin M. Brady, "Presidential Election 1840," in *Encyclopedia of American Political Parties and Elections,* ed. Larry J. Sabato and Howard R. Ernst. (New York: Checkmark Books, 2007), 312–313.

9. Ibid.

10. Ibid., 313.

11. Judith S. Trent, Robert V. Friedenberg and Robert E. Denton Jr, *Political Campaign Communication* (New York: Rowman & Littlefield, 2011), 71.

12. Leslie L. Hunter, "The Role of Music in the 1840 Campaign of William Henry Harrison," *The Bulletin of Historical Research in Music Education* 10, no. 2 (July 1989): 110.

13. Ibid., 108–109.

14. Walter Fisher, "Narration as a Human Communication Paradigm," in *Contemporary Rhetorical Theory*, ed. John Louis Lucaites, Celeste Michelle Condit and Sally Caudill (New York: The Guilford Press, 1999), 274.

15. Ibid.

16. Pew Research Center: Journalism and Media Staff, "Election 2016: Campaigns as a direct Source of News," *Pew Research Center*, July 18, 2016, https://www.jou rnalism.org/2016/07/18/election-2016-campaigns-as-a-direct-source-of-news/.

17. Ibid.

18. Ibid.

19. Trent, Friedenberg and Denton, *Political Campaign Communication*, 50.

20. David B. Valley, "Significant Characteristics of Democratic Presidential Nomination Acceptance Speeches," *Central States Speech Journal* 25, no. 1 (1974): 56.

21. Ibid.

22. Ibid., 58.

23. Ibid., 58.

24. William G. Carleton, "The Revolution in the Presidential Nominating Convention," *Political Science Quarterly* 72, no. 2 (June 1957): 234.

25. Ibid.

26. Thomas B. Farrell, "Political Conventions as Legitimation Ritual," *Communication Monographs* 45, no. 4 (1978): 293.

27. Ibid., 297.

28. Ibid., 304.

29. Media Matters Staff, "MSNBC Panel on Melania Trump's Plagiarized Speech: "This Turns this Night into a Catastrophe,"" *Media Matters for America* video of MSNBC's *The Place for Politics*, July 19, 2016. http://mediamatters.org/v ideo/2016/07/19/msnbc-panel-melania-trump-s-plagiarized-speech-turns-night-catas trophe/211677.

30. David Frum, "Ten Reasons Why Melania Trump's Speech Will Have a Lasting Impact," *The Atlantic*, July 19, 2016, http://www.theatlantic.com/politics/archive/2016/07/melania-trumps-speech-matters/492038/.

31. Jenny Starrs, "Melania Trump's 2016 Speech vs. Michelle Obama's 2008 Speech," *The Washington Post* video, July 19, 2016, https://www.washingtonpost.com/video/c/embed/ce608edc-4d71-11e6-bf27-405106836f96. This video shows side-by-side comparison of the passages that Trump's campaign speech writers allegedly plagiarized from Michelle Obama's speech.

32. Elisha Brown, "How a Freelance Journalist Broke the Melania Trump Plagiarism Story in 3 Tweets," *Vox*, July 21, 2016, https://www.vox.com/2016/7/21/12247504/jarrett-hill-melania-trump-plagiarism.

33. Chris Cillizza, "What George W. Bush's Chief Speechwriter Thinks of the Melania Trump Mess," July 19, 2016, https://www.washingtonpost.com/news/the-fix/wp/2016/07/19/what-george-w-bushs-chief-speechwriter-thinks-of-the-melania-trump-mess/?utm_term=.0ab54b06a69e.

34. Michael Paulson, "The Drama of Ted Cruz: A Little Bit of Shakespeare in That Speech?" *New York Times,* July 21, 2016, http://www.nytimes.com/2016/07/22/theater/ted-cruz-speech-rnc-shakespeare.html.

35. Los Angeles Times Staff, "Donald Trump's Complete Convention Speech, Annotated," *Los Angeles Times,* July 21, 2016, http://www.latimes.com/politics/la-na-pol-donald-trump-convention-speech-transcript-20160721-snap-htmlstory.html.

36. Ibid.

37. Ibid.

38. Yoni Applebaum, "I Alone Can Fix It," *The Atlantic*, July 21, 2016, http://www.theatlantic.com/politics/archive/2016/07/trump-rnc-speech-alone-fix-it/492557/.

39. Ibid.

40. Craig Grizzell, "Public Opinion and Foreign Policy: The Effects of Celebrity Endorsements," *The Social Science Journal* 28 (2011): 315.

41. Tom Hamburger and Karen Tumulty, "Hacked Emails are Posted Online as Democrat's convention nears," *Washington Post,* July 22, 2016, https://www.washingtonpost.com/politics/2016/07/22/117f0574-504f-11e6-a422-83ab49ed5e6a_story.html.

42. Ibid.

43. Special Counsel Robert S. Mueller's investigation found, "WikiLeaks's first release came in July 2016. Around the same time, candidate Trump announced that he hoped Russia would recover emails described as missing from a private server used by Clinton when she was Secretary of State (he later said that he was speaking sarcastically)." See Robert S. Mueller, III, "Report on the Investigation into Russian interference in the 2016 Presidential Election," *U.S. Department of Justice*, March 2019, https://www.justice.gov/storage/report.pdf.

44. Eric Lichtblau and Eric Schmitt, "Hack of Democrats' Accounts was Wider Than Believed, Officials Say," *New York Times*, August 10, 2016, http://www.nytimes.com/2016/08/11/us/politics/democratic-party-russia-hack-cyberattack.html.

45. Adam Nagourney, "With Conventions Behind Us, Our Takeaways," *New York Times*, July 29, 2016, http://www.nytimes.com/2016/07/30/us/politics/convention-highlights.html.

46. Hillary Clinton, "Transcript: Hillary Clinton's Speech at the Democratic Convention," *New York Times,* July 28, 2016, http://www.nytimes.com/2016/07/29/u s/politics/hillary-clinton-dnc-transcript.html?_r=0.

47. Ibid.

48. *Politico* Staff, "Full Text Donald Trump 2016 RNC draft speech transcript," *Politico,* July 21, 2016, https://www.journalism.org/2016/07/18/election-2016-cam paigns-as-a-direct-source-of-news/.

49. *Politico* Staff, "Full Text Hillary Clinton's DNC speech," *Politico,* July 28, 2016, https://www.politico.com/story/2016/07/full-text-hillary-clintons-dnc-speech -226410.

50. Bruce E. Gronbeck, "The Presidential Campaign Dramas of 1984," *Presidential Studies Quarterly,* 15, no. 2 (1985): 391.

51. White, *A. Lincoln,* 268.

52. Ibid.

53. Ibid., 264.

54. Kathleen Hall Jamieson and David S. Birdsell, *Presidential Debates the Challenge of Creating an Informed Electorate* (New York: Oxford University Press, 1988), 84.

55. Ibid., 86.

56. Ibid., 93.

57. Michael X. Delhi Carpini, Scott Keeter and Sharon Webb, "The Impact of Presidential Debates," in *Politics and Press: The News Media and Their Influence,* ed. Pippa Norris. (Boulder, CO: Lynne Reiner Publishers, 1997), 145.

58. Newton N. Minow and Lee Mitchell, "Putting on the Candidates: The Use of Television in Presidential Elections," *The Annals of the American Academy of Political and Social Science* 486 (July 1986): 150.

59. Alan Schroeder, "Watching between the Lines: Presidential Debates as Television," *Press/Politics* 1, no. 4 (1996): 59.

60. Ibid.

61. Jaeho Cho and Syng Pom Choy, "From Podium to Living Room: Elite Debates as an Emotional Catalyst for Citizen Communicative Engagements," *Communication Research* 38 no. 6 (2011): 794.

62. Schroeder, "Watching between the Lines," 62–63.

63. Corbett, *Classical Rhetoric for the Modern Student,* 28.

64. Kathleen E. Kendall, "Presidential Debates through Media Eyes," *American Behavioral Scientist* 40, no. 8 (1997): 1205.

65. Benjamin R. Warner, Diana B. Carlin, Kelly Winfrey, James Schnoebelen, and Marko Trosanovski, "Will the "Real" Candidates for President and Vice President Please Stand Up? 2008 Pre-and Post-Debate Viewer Perceptions of Candidate Image," *American Behavioral Scientist* 55 no. 3 (2011): 249.

66. Yaris Tsfati, "Debating the Debate: The Impact of Exposure to Debate News Coverage and Its Interaction with Exposure to the Actual Debate," *Press/Politics* 8, no. 3 (2003): 70–86.

67. Mitt Romney said, "And—so we—we took a concerted effort to go out and find women who had backgrounds that could be qualified to become members of our

cabinet. I went to a number of women's groups and said, 'can you help us find folks,' and they brought us whole binders full of women. I was proud of the fact that after I staffed my Cabinet and senior staff, the University of New York in Albany did a survey of all 50 states, and concluded that mine had more women in senior leadership positions than any other state in America."

"October 16, 2012 Debate Transcript," *Commission on Presidential Debates*, http://www.debates.org/index.php?page=october-16-2012-the-second-obama-romney-presidential-debate.

68. Padmananda Rama, "Want Thousands of Twitter Followers? Put A Meme On It," *NPR*, October 17, 2012, https://www.npr.org/sections/itsallpolitics/2012/10/16/163054345/want-thousands-of-twitter-followers-put-a-meme-on-it.

69. Jeffrey Feldman and George Lakoff, *Framing the Debate: Famous Presidential Speeches and How Progressives Can Use Them to Change the Conversation (And Win Elections)* (Brooklyn, NY: IG Publishing, 2007), xi.

70. Erving Goffman, *Frame Analysis: An Essay on the Organization of Experience* (Boston, MA: Northeastern University Press, 1974), 345.

71. *Washington Post* Staff, "Annotated Transcript: The Aug. 6 GOP Debate," *The Washington Post*, August 6, 2015, https://www.washingtonpost.com/news/post-politics/wp/2015/08/06/annotated-transcript-the-aug-6-gop-debate/?utm_term=.74ef6d077a90.

72. Federal News Service, "Transcript of the Republican Presidential Debate," *New York Times,* February 14, 2016, https://www.nytimes.com/2016/02/14/us/politics/transcript-of-the-republican-presidential-debate.html.

73. Jeanne Fahnstock, *Rhetorical Style: The Uses of Language in Persuasion* (Oxford: Oxford University Press, 2011), 231.

74. Team Fix, "The Fox News GOP Debate Transcript, Annotated," *Washington Post*, March 3, 2016, https://www.washingtonpost.com/news/the-fix/wp/2016/03/03/the-fox-news-gop-debate-transcript-annotated/?utm_term=.e20044394246.

75. Kathleen Hall Jamieson, *Dirty Politics: Deception, Distraction, and Democracy* (Oxford: Oxford University Press, 1992), 249–250.

76. Corbett, *Classical Rhetoric for the Modern Student*, 28.

77. Ryan Teague Beckwith, "Transcript: Read the Full Text of the Primetime Democratic Debate," *Time*, October 26, 2015, http://time.com/4072553/democratic-debate-transcript-primetime-cnn/?iid=sr-link1.

78. *The Washington Post* reported Trump was bragging "in vulgar terms about kissing, groping and trying to have sex with women" while waiting to do an interview with *Access Hollywood's* host Billy Bush. See David A. Fahrenthold, "Trump Recorded Having Extremely Lewd Conversation about Women in 2005," *The Washington Post*, October 8, 2016, https://www.washingtonpost.com/politics/trump-recorded-having-extremely-lewd-conversation-about-women-in-2005/2016/10/07/3b9ce776-8cb4-11e6-bf8a-3d26847eeed4_story.html?utm_term=.a56993af3cdb.

79. David Graham, "Clinton Keeps Her Cool," *The Atlantic*, September 26, 2016, https://www.theatlantic.com/liveblogs/2016/09/first-presidential-debate-clinton-trump-2016/501647/.

80. *Politico* Staff, "Full Transcript: First 2016 Presidential Debate," *Politico,* September 27, 2016, http://www.politico.com/story/2016/09/full-transcript-first-2016-presidential-debate-228761.

81. David Uberti, "Twitter and Factchecking don't Mix During Debates," *Columbia Journal Review*, July 21, 2014, http://archives.cjr.org/behind_the_news/twitter_and_fact-checking_dont.php.

82. *Politico* Staff, "Full Transcript."

83. Alison Daye, "Shimmying and Sniffling: Social Reaction to the Presidential Debate," *CNN*, September 27, 2016, http://www.cnn.com/2016/09/27/politics/presidential-debates-social-media-reaction/.

84. Kreiss, "Seizing the Moment," 1482.

85. Fahrenthold, "Trump Recorded Having Extremely Leased."

86. Ibid.

87. Liam Stack, "Donald Trump Featured Paula Jones and 2 Other Women Who Accused Bill Clinton of Sexual Assault," *New York Times,* https://www.nytimes.com/2016/10/10/us/politics/bill-clinton-accusers.html?_r=0.

88. Trent, Friedenberg and Denton Jr, *Political Campaign Communication*, 273.

89. *Politico* Staff, "Full Transcript: Second 2016 Presidential Debate," *Politico,* October 10, 2016, http://www.politico.com/story/2016/10/2016-presidential-debate-transcript-229519.

90. Ibid.

91. Ibid.

92. Ibid.

93. Ibid.

94. Ibid.

95. Ibid.

96. Ibid.

97. Jessica T. Feezell, "Agenda Setting through Social Media: The Importance of Incidental News Exposure and Social Filtering in the Digital Era," *Political Research Quarterly* 7, no. 2 (2018): 491.

98. Aaron Zitner, "5 Takeaways from Final Donald Trump, Hillary Clinton Debate; Presidential Nominees Trade Barbs Over Character, Effectiveness; a Question Over Election Results," *Wall Street Journal*, October 20, 2016.

99. *Politico* Staff, "Full Transcript: Third 2016 Presidential Debate," *Politico,* October 20, 2016, http://www.politico.com/story/2016/10/full-transcript-third-2016-presidential-debate-230063.

100. Julian Assange, "Conspiracy as Governance," *iq.org*, December 3, 2006, http://web.archive.org/web/20070129125831/http://iq.org/conspiracies.pdf.

101. Ibid.

102. Andy Greenberg, "Want to Know Julian Assange's Endgame? He Told You a Decade Ago," *Wired*, October 14, 2016, https://www.wired.com/2016/10/want-know-julian-assanges-endgame-told-decade-ago/.

Chapter 6

Hillary Clinton, the Cyborg Candidate

In April 2015, Hillary Clinton announced her second run for the presidency, and she made her announcement via social media:

> I'm getting ready to do something too, I'm running for president. . . . Everyday Americans need a champion. And I want to be that champion. So, I'm hitting the road to earn your vote—because it's your time. And I hope you'll join me on this journey.[1]

On July 26, 2016, the Democratic National Convention nominated Hillary Clinton for president, the first woman presidential nominee for a major political party. In 2008, Barack Obama defeated Hillary Clinton as the Democratic nominee. In 2016, Senator Bernie Sanders would become a social media sensation and run a campaign of his own to try to defeat Clinton as the Democratic nominee. In what should have been an easy road to become president of the United States, Hillary Clinton lost to Republican nominee Donald Trump. Many blame her loss to gender bias, Russian interference, fake news, and FBI director James Comey's investigation into Clinton's emails while serving as secretary of state. In Hillary Clinton's campaign narrative, her *ethos* was always challenged. Clinton's failure was shaped by a social media campaign that did not target the America Donald Trump spoke to and the lack of a well-defined message that resonated with the American public. Clinton's campaign story was about playing it safe against a man who never played by the rules. Clinton told the same story as every other career politician against a new narrative from a businessman and reality star with little to no political experience. For Hillary Clinton, gender bias played a large part in her political failure. However, her lack of dialogical interaction with her audience is one of the significant reasons Hillary Clinton lost to a candidate whose Twitter account made news not only daily but hourly.

BROKEN GENDER FRAME

Hillary Clinton's reputation has always centered on challenging her gender role. Her gender "plays a powerful role in rhetorical action and the rhetor's *ethos*."[2] She also changed the story of the first lady's image. Hillary Clinton's *60 Minutes* interview she did with her husband, then–presidential candidate Bill Clinton, in 1992, introduced Americans to the Clintons. The interview focused on the rumors of an affair Bill Clinton allegedly had with Gennifer Flowers. Hillary Clinton, in her Arkansas twang, said:

> I'm not sittin' here, some little woman, sittin' by my man like Tammy Wynette. I'm sitting here because I love him and I respect him and I honor what he's been through and what we've been through together and if that's not enough for people—heck, don't vote for him.[3]

Hillary and Bill Clinton managed to present their marriage as an equal partnership. She has never "stood by her man" in terms defined by society.

Clinton, in her autobiography, *Living History,* said recognizing that she was a national symbol was a new experience:

> There is no training manual for first ladies. You get the job because the man you married becomes president. Each of my predecessors brought to the White House her own attitudes and expectations, likes and dislikes, dreams and doubts. Each carved out a role that reflected her own interests and style and that balanced the needs of her husband, family and country. So would I. Like all First ladies before me, I had to decide what I wanted to do with the opportunities and responsibilities I had inherited.[4]

Hillary Clinton wanted to follow her own path, as did the first ladies before her. Take, for example, Eleanor Roosevelt, who was a strong and unconventional first lady. She wrote a newspaper column and had her own radio show. She held all-women press conferences, which meant media had to hire female reporters to cover the first lady.[5] Eleanor Roosevelt loved the media, and they loved her, but she also suffered from the double bind.[6] Roosevelt "was criticized for being an activist, too independent, too political, and a champion for equal rights."[7] She was known to speak her mind and did not fall into the category of what many people believed should be the role of the first lady. Sandra L. Combs, in her article "FLOTUS: Media Darling or Monster," lists the unwritten job qualifications for the job of FLOTUS, or first lady of the United States:

- Unpaid;
- The presidential escort;
- Leader of social protocol;
- Publicly visible;
- Unelected;
- The nation's hostess who is to be seen but not heard;
- Nonpolitical;
- Fashionable but at her best if she is a little understated; and
- A cross between a queen and a commoner.[8]

During the 1992 election, the media made sure to show the ways that Hillary did not fit into any of these job qualifications, and she seemed uncomfortable about changing her image for America. At the height of Bill Clinton's infidelity scandal, Bill Clinton's campaign rebranded Hillary Clinton. Instead of featuring her marriage, the campaign highlighted her accomplishments in Arkansas.[9] As Gwen Ifill pointed out in her 1992 *New York Times* article:

> Perhaps the most repeated story about Hillary Clinton is that she did not take her husband's name until others told her that her use of her maiden name may have contributed to his failure to win re-election as Governor in 1980. That detail is supposed to tell people something about Mrs. Clinton—that she is independent and knows her own mind.[10]

Hillary did not follow the traditional narrative of society's gender norms. The press continued to report on public opinion: "she is often seen as cold, guarded and supremely certain that hers is the right and only view."[11] Public opinions challenged Hillary Clinton's female *ethos*.

According to Karlyn Kohrs Campbell, even when Hillary Clinton softened her image after Bill Clinton's 1980 campaign, her rhetorical style did not change.[12] Hillary Clinton's stint as the first lady became controversial because,

> She had an office in the West Wing of the White House; she became head of the task force of healthcare reform; she met with members of Congress, testified before congressional committees, and spoke before audiences all around the country, seeking agreement about the goals that a healthcare should meet.[13]

Because Hillary Clinton violated gender norms, she was not a typical first lady.[14] Clinton may not have broken through any glass ceilings, but she slowly chipped away at the glass, redefining the first lady role.

Hillary Clinton's mistakes in the media during Bill Clinton's first campaign made her susceptible to scrutiny. The public, the media, and other politicians questioned her credibility, despite her political success. Her message stayed the same: Clinton changed only her outward appearance. She fabricated a softer physical image during her husband's political campaigns, but even then, her rhetoric did not soften with it.

CREDIBILITY

Aristotle identified three elements that establish the audience's confidence in an orator's character—"that induce us to believe a thing apart from any proof of it: good sense, good moral character, and goodwill."[15] The media, citizens, and other politicians frequently questioned Hillary Clinton's *ethos*. Although she changed her physical image as the first lady, the chance to boost her image as a good moral character has been harder to achieve. In 2008, Peggy Noonan, in the *Wall Street Journal*, wrote:

> Mrs. Clinton is transmitting, but people aren't receiving. She has been branded, tagged. She's been absorbed, understood and categorized. People have decided what they think, and it's not good.[16]

As the first lady, Clinton avoided the press. As a senator, Clinton avoided the press. As secretary of state, Clinton avoided the press. As a presidential candidate, Clinton tried to act friendly with the media but avoided press conferences. Her silence created a lack of dialogical interaction between herself and her audience. In the 2016 election, *The Wall Street Journal* compared Hillary Clinton to Nixon:

> Lately, Mrs. Clinton has shown some Nixonian tendencies to try to stonewall and cover-up. Her handling of the Clinton Foundation and email controversies is right out of the Nixon playbook. Treat every new revelation as old news, attack the messenger as biased, reveal only what you have to.[17]

The media reported instances where she forgot details such as lost files in Whitewater, memory lapses in visiting Bosnia, and lost emails as secretary of state.

Clinton's narrative of ambition dates back to the 1970s when she was building her career. In a 1998 *New York Times* article, Wendy Wasserstein writes, "Ask any Yale Law School graduate of that era, and he or she will remember the brilliance and ambition of Hillary Rodham. She was an activist, a student leader, someone with a great sense of civic responsibility. She was the hope for a new definition of professional women."[18] Wasserstein then adds, "She has flip-flopped on so many issues of image that her behavior can justifiably be called erratic."[19]

The media has not helped build Hillary Clinton's credibility. George Campbell, in *The Philosophy of Rhetoric*, writes, "When the opinion of the audience is unfavorable, the speaker hath need to be much more cautious in every step he takes, to show more modesty, and greater deference to the judgment of his hearers."[20] Clinton's record of inconsistent storytelling became a pattern over the years. Citizens, media, and opponents challenged her credibility and her overall character. During a speech at the George Washington University on March 17, 2008, Hillary Clinton recounted this story,

> Good morning. I want to thank Secretary West for his years of service, not only as secretary of the Army, but also the Veteran's Administration, to our men and women in uniform to our country. I certainly do remember that trip to Bosnia, and as Togo said, there was a saying around the White House that if a place was too small, too poor, or too dangerous, the president couldn't go, so send the first lady. That's where we went.
>
> I remember landing under sniper fire. There was supposed to be some kind of a greeting ceremony at the airport, but instead we just ran with our heads down to get into the vehicles to get to our base.[21]

The media found the footage of her trip and found no sniper fire, but instead a band playing. *The Washington Post* reported what Clinton said to the *Philadelphia Daily News* about her lapse in memory:

> Now let me tell you what I can remember, OK—because what I was told was that we had to land a certain way and move quickly because of the threat of sniper fire. So I misspoke—I did say that in my book or other times but if I said something that made it seem as though there was actual fire—that's not what I was told . . . I was told that the greeting ceremony had been moved away from the tarmac but that there was this 8-year-old girl and, I can't, I can't rush by her, I've got to at least greet her—so I greeted her, I took her stuff and then I left, now that's my memory of it.[22]

Her husband Bill Clinton quipped that his wife was in her sixties and that people that age sometimes forget details. Peggy Noonan explained that Clinton's lie about the sniper fire while stepping off a plane in Bosnia only solidified what people already thought about Clinton—she was, in their minds, manipulative.[23]

Hillary Clinton did not have the full support of women either because "they couldn't support her just because she was a woman."[24] Kathryn Kish Sklar found Hillary Clinton "'performed' especially well as a woman pretending to be a man."[25] Sklar calls this "the masculine mystique."[26] Hillary Clinton's feminine *ethos* was questioned when she:

> failed the gender question by allowing the masculine mystique to distort her political agenda and obscure the class agendas of Right-wing Republicans. She couldn't make a "gender" speech equivalent to Obama's "race" speech because she herself was playing a game of gender deception.[27]

Clinton failed to speak out about bias towards women in leadership roles. When a speaker speaks, it is the start of a chain of responses.[28] Hillary Clinton's credibility problems broke the chain of intended positive reactions about her gender because of her more masculine rhetorical style.

Rebecca S. Richards's article "Cyborgs on the World Stage: Hillary Clinton and the Rhetorical Performances of Iron Ladies" explains an "often-used successful strategy for women to secure the executive office, especially for the first time in a country, appears to be the rhetorical performance of the nickname 'iron lady,' a trope that began with Margaret Thatcher in England at the end of the 1970s."[29] Former Prime Minister of the United Kingdom Margaret Thatcher admits to being an Iron Lady in a speech she gave on February 6, 1976.

> I stand before you tonight in my Red Star chiffon evening gown. My face softly made up and my fair hair gently waved, the Iron Lady of the Western world. A cold war warrior, an amazon philistine, even a Peking plotter. Well, am I any of these things? (No!) . . . Yes, I am an iron lady, after all, it wasn't a bad thing to be an iron duke, yes if that's how they wish to interpret my defense of values and freedoms fundamental to our way of life.[30]

Margaret Thatcher owned the term Iron Lady that a Soviet Army newspaper gave to her that was supposed to be derogatory. Prime Minister Thatcher used the nickname to her rhetorical advantage. She blended her masculine rhetorical style with her feminine image of herself. Thatcher's rhetorical and visual dichotomy created her persuasive strategy. Clinton's lack of credibility with the audience in her political identity and female identity clouded her persuasive message.

Jennifer J. Jones has researched women in power, such as "Iron Lady" Margaret Thatcher, former prime minister of Britain, and "Iron Frau" Angela Merkel, the German chancellor. Jones explains the Iron Lady "label implies that treaties that are valued in leaders—strength, determination, and authority—are uncommon or anomalous in women."[31] When Jones studied Hillary

Clinton's linguistic styles from 1992 to 2013, she found that "Clinton's language grew increasingly masculine over time as her involvement and power in politics expanded."[32] As Hillary Clinton transitioned from White House hostess to New York senator, she had to shift her rhetorical strategy. Hillary Clinton "went from being viewed as a woman in her role as the first lady to being judged predominately as a candidate."[33] Furthermore, Clinton's political ambitions "challenges the stereotype of femininity, as she embraces roles not normally held by women."[34] Although, Keith V. Erickson and Stephanie Thomson applied seduction theory to analyze Hillary Clinton's U.S. senate run. They found:

> Hillary Rodham Clinton's articulation of a feminine grammar did not constitute an erasure of feminism, a turn to corporeal politics, or a rejection of either traditional or contemporary values. Hillary Rodham Clinton's displays of femininity held in balance her feminist idealism. Hillary Rodham Clinton's gender performance teased a feminine persona as it temporarily withheld/suspended her feminist identity.[35]

Clinton's political journey created a more obscure female rhetorical and political identity that resulted in Clinton failing to identify with her audience.[36]

CLINTON AND TECHNOLOGY

Clinton announced her run for the presidency over the Internet. Rebecca S. Richards explains, "This transparent manipulation of technology so as to be in multiple places at once is a type of becoming-imperceptible politics that Clinton would eventually suffer from."[37] A spoof video that reconfigured Clinton's presidential announcement appeared on YouTube soon after. The footage showed Clinton's head floating above men's as she spoke.[38] Her online presidential announcement failed "when Clinton tried to become imperceptible through her web-based materials, these texts were used against her as frightening, dehumanizing propaganda."[39] The Internet grew to become Hillary Clinton's opponent, where people posted anti–Hillary Clinton propaganda, which exacerbated her ongoing credibility problems.

Technology failed Hillary Clinton again when news circulated during the 2016 campaign that Clinton had a secret server at her house while she was secretary of state. The media reminded people of Clinton's inconsistency and how she had a habit of not keeping paper trails. *The Wall Street Journal* explains, "There are few politicians alive today who have a better understanding than the Clintons of the perils of papers trails—and the benefits of not having them."[40] New media's archival capabilities mean people can find inconsistencies in a politician's story quickly. Technology helped remind people of the discrepancies in Clinton's stories, and the Internet created viral moments to discredit her credibility.

Campaign 2008

In the 2008 campaign, Barack Obama became a social media campaign pioneer. His campaign went where his audience was located. Obama's campaign did not rely only on traditional media to spread his message. Kathleen Hall Jamieson, in an interview for the *National Journal*, said, "Obama and Clinton have different audiences, and if Hillary Clinton were just as smart about using the news media, it wouldn't do her much good because it's not her natural audience."[41]

Hillary has always encountered a hostile media. Joseph E. Usincski and Lilly J. Goren write,

> Beyond the gendered naming, the media covered Hillary Rodham Clinton's menstrual cycle, pantsuits, laugh, and her husband's infidelity. NBC's *The Chris Matthews Show* displayed a picture of Hillary Rodham Clinton with devil horns drawn on her forehead. Her male competitors were not treated this way.[42]

On her campaign blog, prestigious women wrote blog posts about their rise to success and encouraged people to vote for Clinton. Dr. Maya Angelou wrote a piece for Clinton's 2008 blog. Dr. Angelou started her blog post with a few lines of her poem *Still I Rise*. The word "rise" was the theme for Dr. Angelou's March 31, 2008, post "Celebrating Women: A Note from Dr. Maya Angelou":

> There is a world of difference between being a woman and being an old female. If you're born a girl, grow up, and live long enough, you can become an old female. But, to become a woman is a serious matter. A woman takes responsibility for the time she takes up and the space she occupies.
>
> Hillary Clinton is a woman. She has been there and done that and has still risen. She is in this race for the long haul. She intends to make a difference in our country . . .
>
> She declares she wants to see more smiles in the families, more courtesies between men and women, more honesty in the marketplace. Hillary Clinton intends to help our country to what it can become.
>
> She means to rise.
>
> She means to help our country rise. Don't give up on her, ever.

Dr. Angelou describes Hillary Clinton as not just a female, but a woman who has life experience. Dr. Angelou's post was lyrical and metaphorical to create the illusion that Clinton will rise to meet all Americans' needs. Clinton had to court the women's votes because "men are more likely to tell pollsters that they take issue with her politics and her personality."[43]

Hillary Clinton's 2008 campaign woes were plentiful. Barack Obama used new media to create a grassroots phenomenon using targeted messaging. Obama broke the conventional frame of political campaigning to create a new way to campaign and to spread political messages. But Clinton struggled. Frank Rich, in *The New York Times*, observed:

> The Clinton campaigns' cluelessness about the web has been apparent from the start, and not just in its lagging fundraising. Witness the canned Hillary web "chats" and "Hillcasts," the soupy web contest to choose a campaign song . . . and the little-watched electronic national town-hall meeting on the eve of Super Tuesday. Web surfers have rejected these stunts as the old-school infomercials they so blatantly are.[44]

Rich questioned Hillary Clinton's reasons why she kept insisting her Bosnia story was the truth after the news media provided proof that her story was false.[45] Debacles like this cost her the candidacy, but it was Obama's rhetoric that engaged an audience.

Hillary Clinton's use of new media was not as resourceful as Obama's website. Clinton's campaign did not take advantage of the potential rhetorical situation on the Internet. Her campaign posted only two or three posts a day, in contrast to Obama's daily twenty or more posts. Clinton also used her campaign blog to inform her readers of her views, but she did not openly write about strong support or argue against her competition. On May 14, 2008, Lindsay Levin posted "Why I'm In," a message Hillary Clinton sent out:

> Dear Friend,
>
> There are some people out there who want to declare this race over now, before all the ballots have been counted or even cast. There are some who say they don't know why I'm in this race. So let me tell you why I'm running.
>
> I'm in this race for everyone who needs a champion. For the hardworking families who are losing sleep over gas prices and grocery costs and mortgage payments and medical bills—but who never lose that American can-do spirit and optimism.
>
> I'm in this race for the more than 16 million people like you who have supported me—for the people who have put their hearts into winning this race. You never gave up on me, and I'll never give up on you.

I am in this race, and so are you, because we both know the stakes in this election are too high to stay on the sidelines.

So, let's keep going together, you and me. Let's keep driving our campaign forward, and let's keep winning.

May 14, 2008, is when John Edwards endorsed Barack Obama. Clinton kept repeating "I'm in this race" to start her sentences to create a rhythm to her words to resonate proof of why she is in this race. Clinton's message uses words to unite, such as, "So let's keep going together, you and me." The word "together" is uniting, but then she separates the group as individuals—"you and me." The pronouns You and Me create a personal connection to her listeners.

Clinton's mistake was not to use her blog to openly promote her political endorsements, as Obama did, but instead placed her endorsements in her posts behind a separate heading, "HUBdate." Clinton's campaign hid the best information in the news rundown that should have been individual blog posts. Communication director Howard Wolfson posted "HUBdate: Strongest at the Top of the Ticket" on May 10, 2008:

Strongest at the Top of the Ticket: Several members of Congress released a letter yesterday to other Democrats touting their support for Hillary, saying she is the strongest candidate to have at the top of the ticket in the fall.

Automatic Delegate Watch: Yesterday, Texas Congressman Ciro Rodriquez and Pennsylvania Congressman Chris Carney endorsed Hillary.

The post also lists two more endorsements. By placing Clinton's endorsements in a separately linked section, she enabled readers who were scanning her campaign blog to miss the *ethos*-building endorsements because readers might not click the link for more information. Barack Obama's campaign highlighted endorsements as separate posts. Obama's campaign created stories around his endorsements, whereas Hillary Clinton's campaign only provided a few lines of copy. The two opposing rhetorical and visual strategies show the impact of how a candidate builds credibility, especially if a candidate is not as well known. Clinton overestimated her *ethos,* whereas Senator Obama knew he had to build his *ethos.* While Obama promoted his support from private citizens, Clinton showcased endorsements from celebrities and high-profile women such as Dr. Maya Angelo. Therefore, as Clinton glorified the celebrity names, Obama highlighted ordinary citizens and organizations, which helped him motivate grassroots support.

In his article "Momentum in the 2008 Presidential Contests," R. Lawrence Butler discussed the showdown between Hillary Clinton and Barack

Obama. Butler identified *identity politics* as a factor in the 2008 campaign. Butler noted:

> The 2008 Democratic contest featured the first African-American and the first woman who had a legitimate shot at winning the nomination. Such racial and gender identity created intense loyalty among supporters that could never be shaken by campaign occurrences. Clinton's class-based appeals extended identity politics to an additional dimension, as did Obama's technologically sophisticated appeal to younger voters.[46]

Clinton and Obama defined new political identities. As the aggression toward Hillary Clinton intensified during 2008, she started to change her rhetorical style and delivery. Instead of the cold, stiff woman described in the press, Americans began to see a funny and feisty Hillary Clinton.[47] However, Clinton could not shake the stigma of her gender or her past rhetorical style. Tears formed in Clinton's eyes when asked about the stress she feels on the campaign trail—and at that moment, critics labeled her as weak.[48] Clinton answered:

> It's not easy, and I couldn't do it if I just didn't you know passionately believe it was the right thing to do. You know I have so many opportunities from this country. I just don't want to see us fall backwards. You know this is very personal for me. It's not just political. It's not just public. I see what's happening. We have to reverse it.
>
> So, as tired as I am—and I am—and as difficult as it is to kind of keep up what I try to do on the road like occasionally exercise and try to eat right, it's tough when the easiest food is pizza. I just believe so strongly in who we are as a nation.[49]

Clinton's tone is soft, engaging, and vulnerable. She admitted she is tired and struggles, but she keeps fighting for the nation. She uses uniting pronouns, but the visual image of tears is unexpected for a presidential candidate. During her husband's presidency, "clichés and stereotypes were tested, toyed with, fitted on her."[50] These stigmas placed on Clinton carried over into her candidacy for president.

2016 Presidential Campaign

Eight years later, the former first lady, senator, and now former secretary of state made a second bid to become the first woman president. She became the candidate to beat according to the media. Hillary Clinton's relationship with the press and the public has always been a bit rocky because she challenged gender stereotypes. For example, as first lady, Clinton took an office in the West Wing, which became controversial. As first lady the,

> Continuing negative publicity about the Whitewater affair and Hillary's role in it, and several scandals linked to her in the early days of the Clinton administration—most notably the travel office firings—led to a substantial decline in the general public's impressions of her and support for the job she was doing as first lady.[51]

As the 2016 Democratic presidential nominee, Hillary Clinton faced more controversy when she used a private email server during her time as secretary of state. The *Wall Street Journal* reported:

> The former Secretary of State wants voters to believe that her private email server scandal is old news, but every month brings new evidence that she put state secrets at risk in order to hide her emails from the public.[52]

Hillary Clinton's emails created doubt in voters' minds and reminded voters of her past.

Bernie Sanders

Vermont senator Bernie Sanders surprised Hillary Clinton's campaign. Before starting his campaign, Sanders knew Clinton's reputation would be hard to defeat. She had the money, the name, and the experience. She also had the support of senior citizens, but Sanders had the growing support of Millennials. Sanders, who adopted modern communications technology, explains,

> What an extraordinary and powerful organizing tool! We were able to live-stream many of the rallies and town meetings that we held. Almost every week we were sending out short videos on some of the most important issues facing the country, and millions of people viewed them and passed them on to their friends. Every single day, messages on issues of the day and events we were holding went out to millions.[53]

Sanders's campaign's social media presence helped grow his young voters' support.

Sanders's rhetorical style was candid, unpolished, truthful, and heartfelt. The media liked to describe him as "grumpy." He is a self-proclaimed socialist who wanted Democrats to get back to the issues and "pivot back to class politics."[54] His style and delivery carried his heartfelt message, which started resonating with the public. Senator Sanders expressed the desire to stop political gossip and to talk more about issues in the October 13, 2015 debate.

> Let me say something that may not be great politics. But I think the Secretary is right. And that is that the American people are sick and tired of hearing about your damn emails. And let me say something about the media as well . . . I go around the country, talk to a whole lot of people. The middle class of this country is collapsing. We have twenty-seven million people living in poverty. We have massive wealth and income inequality. Our trade policies have cost us millions of decent jobs. The American people want to know whether we're going to have a democracy or an oligarchy as a result of Citizens United. Enough of the emails. Let's talk about the real issues facing America.[55]

Sanders later noted the media chose not to air his quotes about the issues but only used his email remarks.[56] The media missed Sanders's most important argument—the middle class is suffering.

Bernie Sanders had a young social media team and borrowed some social media campaign veterans from Obama's social media success. His campaign understood that a candidate had to have a presence in more than one medium. Social media allowed Sanders to reach a new audience and allowed him to create viral messages. Scott Goodstein, who led Sanders's social media charge, credits Sanders himself for becoming a social media phenomenon.[57] The media did not initially give much coverage to Bernie Sanders's campaign. Social media was where Sanders's campaign could broadcast their campaign rallies and "talk directly to an entire generation about the most important issues facing their lives and start an online discussion about them."[58]

The Cyborg Candidate

Technology became an obstacle for Clinton's campaign. Henry Jenkins, in his book *Convergence Culture*, warned, "When people take media into their own hands, the results can be wonderfully creative; they can also be bad news for all involved."[59] Clinton's campaign converged into failure where "popular culture influenced the way that the campaigns courted their voters—but more importantly, it shaped how the public processed and acted upon political discourse."[60] Her technological failure throughout the 2016 election relates to what Rebecca S. Richards wrote: "This transparent manipulation of technology so as to be in multiple places at once is a type of becoming-imperceptible politics that Clinton would eventually suffer from."[61] Clinton's lack of extemporaneous rhetoric and her campaign's lack of connecting to voters through social media channels started to create a (mis)perception of who Clinton was trying to portray. Her campaign did not effectively merge technology and language. Clinton's campaign spent more than $200 million on television ads.[62] Trump concentrated on changing people's minds online.[63]

Using the Internet as a method to campaign means stepping into a crowded room where anyone can shout back to you and rearrange your words and your message even after you leave the room. Each member of that crowd can manipulate what they heard and what they witnessed. When Americans see candidates daily through social media channels such as Twitter and Facebook, the original message becomes murky and manipulated to the point of distortion. Most people will never meet Hillary Clinton, except through their computers and televisions, which constructs political candidates as if they are fictional characters.

Donna Haraway defined a cyborg as "a cybernetic organism, a hybrid of machine and organism, a creature of social reality as well as a creature of fiction."[64] As we look at Hillary Clinton as a cyborg through technology, she becomes a creature of fiction. She is a character with an already set fate in her story. She was the first first lady to run for public office and win a seat in the senate. The media tried to define Clinton, but Clinton resisted the traditional gender role of past first ladies.

A first lady is seen as a server, not as a worker. As Donna Haraway explains, "To be feminized means to be made extremely vulnerable; able to be disassembled, reassembled, exploited as a reserve labor force; seen less as workers than as servers."[65] Because she had been the first lady previously, Clinton struggled to be seen as a viable, credible candidate instead of the wife of President Bill Clinton. The press never knew how to tell her story because she was the first to challenge the first lady archetype, and Americans never knew how to process her many career transformations. Instead, Clinton's overall message became slanted through memes and viral videos. Haraway says, "The machine is us, our processes, an aspect of our embodiment. We can be responsible for machines; they do not dominate or threaten us."[66] Haraway is right— we control machines. We dominate machines; machines do not dominate us. For Hillary Clinton, "Cyborg politics is the struggle for language and is the struggle against perfect communication."[67] The "cyborg" struggles with what is real and what is an illusion. Hillary Clinton struggled with revealing her authenticity compared to the illusion painted by others in the media and online.

Clinton's 2016 campaign struggled with messages and failed to control what others released about her and the Democratic Party. Techniques that seemed to fit the traditional frame did not work for Clinton. She lacked a strong mass media presence during her email investigation. Moreover, hashtags that started such as #GirlIGuessImWithHer showed that Clinton was not an enthusiastic choice for voters because "women of all colors have pointed out that while they're excited to see a woman make history, for them, Clinton isn't necessarily the right woman."[68]

@_AvalonC_: #GirlIGuessImWithHer is the most accurate summation of my views of this election, unfortunate it's lesser of 2 evils, but no way I'm with him. (July 25, 2016)

@transoprah: if you can put your morals and beliefs aside and if you have the ability to then go vote for Hillary #girliguessimwithher (October 24, 2016)

@KianaBSqueeze: I get that this is big for women, or whatever, but did it have to be *that* woman? (June 8, 2016)

The hashtag shows how political support shifts even when the candidate is less than ideal.[69] Moreover, Clinton's legacy did not appeal to young people of color. PBS.org explains, "The hashtag first appeared as a way many young people of color shared their disappointment. Clinton's historical support of the 1994 crime bill—a policy that many argue harmed communities of color—has damaged her appeal among many minority voters."[70]

Viral Pneumonia

Donald Trump's campaign kept repeating how unhealthy Clinton looked, which added to her cyborg existence. A video of Clinton fainting after a 9/11 memorial ceremony circulated widely on social media. Social media users speculated about her health. The campaign said Clinton did not want to reveal her diagnosis and wanted to respect her privacy because:

> Political opponents on the right have spread a variety of conspiracy theories insinuating that she is physically unfit for the presidency, and Mr. Trump has fanned those theories, repeatedly questioning her "stamina."[71]

Her campaign did not reveal her diagnosis for two days until the video showed her fainting. Five hours after Clinton fainted, her doctor finally revealed her diagnosis. The repetition of the video clip when Clinton fainted solidified the "unhealthy Clinton" narrative offered by Trump's campaign. One YouTube video tried to find "proof" that Clinton wore leg braces.[72]

Additionally, videos of Clinton's coughing fits also surfaced, as well as the hashtag: #HackingHillary. According to the website *Know Your Meme*, the hashtag originated after a Cleveland, Ohio rally on September 5, 2016, when Clinton began coughing while giving her speech.[73] The hashtag started trending, with more video clips and memes of Hillary Clinton's coughing, which led to the assumption Clinton was not healthy. Social media posts blurred the lines between the truth and the illusion of Hillary's health.

When Clinton appeared in Greensboro, North Carolina, at a rally soon after, *Politico* reported that "she looked so refreshed, some of her detractors thought it had to be a body double."[74]

@jonathanweisman: @CNN now giving extensive attention to the theory that @HillaryClinton has a body double to hide her, what, death? Fun times. (September 13, 2016)

@BetteMidler: ALL DAY! Internet debating if Hillary has a body double. If she does, I think whoever it is would still make a better President than #Trump. (September 12, 2016)

@abshire_gary: It is my guess the Secret Service is ONLY AUTHORIZED to protect @HillaryClinton and not a body double! FAKE Hillary walks the streets alone. (September 12, 2016)

Twitter users created Clinton as a fantastical cyborg and a trickster character—someone who deceives others.

Wikileaks

In 2006, Julian Assange created WikiLeaks, a website that "specializes in the analysis and publication of large datasets of censored or otherwise restricted official materials involving war, spying, and corruption."[75] WikiLeaks may have helped sway the election results. The website twisted and manipulated the 2016 election outcome by sharing emails from the Democratic Nomination Committees, forcing DNC chair Debbie Wasserman Shultz to resign. Wikileaks also exposed emails from John Podesta, chairman of Clinton's campaign. Podesta's emails revealed unfavorable details about Hillary Clinton, but most of his emails were mundane election business. Again, Clinton was reduced to a digital persona. Chris Hables Gray explains,

> We live in a cyborg society, no matter how unmodified we are as individuals. So as humans continue to technologically transform ourselves, this process will play an increasingly important, eventually fundamental role in politics—and not always for the better.[76]

The 2016 campaign proved the Internet had become imperative in interfering with American presidential elections. Wikileaks's actions challenged journalism because truth and fiction became muddled. Donald Trump tweeted,

@realDonaldTrump: Very little pick-up by the dishonest media of incredible information provided by WikiLeaks. So dishonest! Rigged system! (October 12, 2016)

What WikiLeaks decided to reveal set the news agenda and framed the media's story. Donald Trump tweeted to challenge the media to report the content of the emails.

For Hillary Clinton, Wikileaks's role played in the election helped solidify in many people's minds that she could not be trusted. WikiLeaks crossed the boundaries that journalism cannot:

> WikiLeaks made it clear that traditional journalism is severely limited in its scope. It is constrained by commercial, technical, legal, and cultural boundaries that WikiLeaks was happy and able to cross. Wikileaks demonstrated that investigative journalism could go much further using new technologies, especially when combined with what some of its mainstream media collaborators have described as intellectual and ethical "recklessness."[77]

The hacked emails of Hillary Clinton and the Democratic National Committee resulted in proof to diminish Hillary Clinton's credibility. WikiLeaks released emails about the Democratic Party and Hillary Clinton that fed journalists more information, which in turn helped create Clinton's cyborg character—a persona made within the digital and media confines of modern communication technology.

Emails

While Clinton served as secretary of state, she had a private email server in her home without the State Department's approval. She endured special hearings and investigations. FBI director James Comey eventually said Clinton's email revealed no wrongdoings. However, one letter proved Hillary Clinton's FBI investigation had not yet ended—a letter which many believe was the product of Hillary Clinton's campaign loss. FBI director, James Comey, sent the letter on October 28, 2016, eleven days from Election Day. The letter stated:

> In previous congressional testimony, I referred to the fact that the Federal Bureau of Investigation (FBI) had completed its investigation of former Secretary Clinton's personal email server. Due to recent developments, I am writing to supplement my previous testimony.
>
> In connection with an unrelated case, the FBI has learned of the existence of emails that appear to be pertinent to the investigation. I am writing to inform you

that the investigative team briefed me on this yesterday, and I agreed that the
FBI should take appropriate investigative steps designed to allow investigators
to review these emails to determine whether they contain classified information,
as well as to assess their importance to our investigation.[78]

This letter provided more proof that damaged Hillary Clinton's credibility.
The letter served as a reminder of why people may not have trusted Hillary
Clinton's moral character.

FBI director James Comey's decision to start a new investigation over
Clinton's emails eleven days before the election created a setback for Hillary
Clinton. She could not recover and had little time to regain the trust of
American citizens. The Comey letter created doubt. A *Wall Street Journal*
article explains why people question her credibility:

It may be insane, but it's also vintage Hillary Clinton—her preoccupation
with secrecy, her recklessness, her lifelong conviction that she'll never be held
accountable.[79]

Hillary Clinton's damaged *ethos* legacy was amplified online. Clinton's
cyborg personality is a mesh of her truths and others' fiction. Clinton's
online persona made it hard for her to overcome her credibility problems
in the offline world. The offline world competes with the online world, and
the truth gets muddled along the way. Donna Haraway says, "The virtual
seems to be the counterfeit of the real; the virtual has effects by seeming,
not being."[80]

Social Media

Hillary Clinton had a strong social media campaign, but her presence became
pedestrian. Rarely would one of her tweets make the news. A good storyline
on social media entices potential supporters to anticipate the next post, video,
or tweet. A good storyline on social media creates viral moments for social
media users to share.

Overall, Hillary Clinton did not take full advantage of the rhetorical situation to build her credibility. Her tweets instead fit within the traditional campaign narrative frame. When a more radical version of a political campaign
story, like Donald Trump's, challenges the traditional frame, the ordinary is
lost to the extraordinary.

Hillary Clinton did not retweet unknown citizen's tweets but "preferred
sending out her or her staff's own campaign messages"[81] She kept to a strategy that rarely diverted from the norm of a campaign, unlike her opponent.[82]
Her significant themes in tweets included topics such as gun control, families,

people's rights, and working (American workers, working families, hard work, working people, etc.).

@HillaryClinton: Gun violence against Americans is all of our problem. We need to solve it together. (July 13, 2016)

@HillaryClinton: Whether you're a teacher, an executive, or a world-champion soccer player, you deserve equal pay. Red card, GOP. [link] (October 30, 2015)

@HillaryClinton: Proud to have the support of @SenWarren—a woman who is Trump's exact opposite: honest, decent, and deeply concerned for working families. —H (June 9, 2016)

Sometimes Clinton's campaign used Twitter to respond to Trump's Twitter attacks.

@HillaryClinton: "Nobody respects women more than me." –Donald Trump earlier tonight "Such a nasty woman." –Donald Trump just now #DebateNight (October 19, 2016)

@HillaryClinton: The presidency doesn't change who you are—it reveals who you are. And we've seen all we need to of Donald Trump. (November 4, 2016)

The most retweeted tweet of the Clinton campaign was a response to Donald Trump's tweet:

@RealDonaldTrump: Obama just endorsed Crooked Hillary. He wants four more years of Obama—but nobody else does! (June 9, 2016)

@HillaryClinton: Delete Your Account. (June 9, 2016)

Clinton's team responded quickly to the rhetorical situation. The "Delete your account" response is used when people respond to others who troll or disturb the flow of conversation.[83] Trump was trolling and disturbing the flow of conversation about President Obama's endorsement for Hillary Clinton.

The 2016 campaign tested Twitter's political role. Twitter proved to withstand the political parties' back-and-forth tweets, allowing conversations to emerge and essential topics to rise to the top. Clinton remained strategic with her online political rhetoric. *The New York Times* writes,

Mrs. Clinton's missive, most likely written and sent by her campaign staff, quickly became one of the most widely shared tweets of the 2016 campaign. It was precisely the kind of tweet that political junkies, and anyone else checking Twitter for a midday distraction, thirsts for in the middle of the afternoon when they'd prefer to think about something other than work.[84]

Clinton's Twitter account was active, but viral moments were lacking. Her offline persona crept into her online persona, whereas Bernie Sanders and Donald Trump each created a more genuine online connection with their audiences. *The New York Times* noted, "Mrs. Clinton has not always been totally hip, jiggy and on fleek with the cool kids."[85]

Clinton reminded people of what Trump said about her. Her use of such phrases and hashtags as #NastyWomen #LoveTrumpsHate reminded people of her opponent. Her campaign created a quiz where a user could simulate an insulting Trump tweet. She wanted to remind people of Trump's less-than-ideal personality traits, but, in the end, solidified Trump's story. Remember, #IGuessImWithHer appeared on Twitter because many Americans felt both candidate choices were less than ideal. Furthermore, #IGuessImWithHer proved people had not forgotten Hillary Clinton's past controversies. Studies have shown that "images of the future are shaped by the experience of the past."[86]

HILLARY AND MEDIA

Hillary Clinton was unavailable to the press, where Bernie Sanders and Donald Trump thrived in the media spotlight. Both Trump and Sanders did very little damage control after bad interviews; instead, Trump and Sanders kept repeating their message and telling their story through media. Hillary Clinton's rare media appearances did not help build her credibility. After her press conference on December 4, 2015, she did not hold a formal press conference for 250 days.[87] She had only eleven informal media interactions through July 2016.[88] The lack of media presence also created a weak connection to her supporters and to undecided voters.

Clinton's campaign defended the decision to stonewall the press, reiterating that Clinton made herself directly available to the American people: "They get to ask her questions every day. And she answers questions from journalists."[89] She did interact with potential voters, but one-on-one interviews with journalists are important because journalists ask questions that need addressing. Good journalism seeks out answers with questions that should reveal the politician's experience and leadership capabilities. In *Public Opinion*, Walter Lippman said the press is like "the beam of a searchlight that moves restlessly about, bringing one episode and then another out of darkness into vision."[90]

In 2008, the media had exposed Hillary Clinton's faults, and, as a result, Hillary Clinton's campaign shielded her from unscripted remarks in 2016. The result of Clinton's nearly nonexistent media presence produced third parties who were able to shape Clinton's campaign story, rather than Clinton taking an active storytelling role. As Kathleen Hall Jamieson explains,

When those communicating to the press provide inadequate definitions, play fast and loose with the facts, and fail to show the trade-offs inherent in governing, the task or reporters is made more complicated.[91]

Clinton held very few, if any, press conferences and limited her contact to journalists. She allowed the journalists to fill in the blanks for her rather than control and shape her own story. When politicians do not control their own story, "journalists need to help viewers and readers make sense of statements about fact while not losing sight of those facts, political actors are reluctant to acknowledge."[92]

Clinton's social media campaign was mundane at best, but her media presence could have kept her storyline from failing. Though Trump's campaign was unprofessional and at times looked amateurish, Trump's authenticity increased by his media savviness, especially his social media presence.[93] The *Columbia Journalism Review* interviewed journalists who covered the campaign. Susan Page, Washington Bureau Chief of *USA Today*, explained Donald Trump's victory was because he was accessible to the media:

One thing Donald Trump deserves credit for is that during the primaries, not so much now, he was available. He was more accessible than any leading candidate I've ever covered, and more willing to take questions when he had a bad story, not just a good story.[94]

Trump was accessible in not only the positive stories but also the negative stories. A study, which analyzed ten major news outlets, showed 43 percent of Hillary Clinton's press coverage during the general election focused on the "horserace" aspect of campaigning and was 19 percent focused on controversies.

In contrast, only 9 percent of Clinton's press coverage focused on her policy stances, and 2 percent focused on her experience.[95] The study found both candidates' press coverage was negative, but "overall, the coverage of [Clinton's] candidacy was 62 percent negative to 38 percent positive, while [Trump's] coverage was 56 percent negative to 44 percent positive."[96]

Both candidates became media targets because of their controversies, Clinton for her emails and Trump because of his bombastic rhetoric and failure to release his tax returns. As Thomas Patterson explains, "To journalists, the real issues of presidential politics are not the candidates' policy commitments but instead the controversies that ensnare them."[97] Clinton's past controversies, coupled with new controversies, overshadowed her traditional campaign. Her story did not overpower the negative press—the negative press took over due to her lack of presence. Moreover, she allowed the media to overtake her offline, real, authentic persona.

WHAT HAPPENED

Hillary Clinton released her book *What Happened* after the 2016 campaign. Hillary Clinton's book tour interviews showed her engaged in conversations where she was candid, funny, and passionate. Her book is her story, but her campaign was not. Clinton needed to show more of the authenticity that she showed during her book tour.

The 2016 presidential campaign showed a change in rhetoric, change in politics, and a change in how to create an authentic self. Clinton's political persona during the campaign failed to show her authentic self. Her political personality could not surpass a reality show celebrity, despite her experience.

At times during the campaign, Clinton tried to show her sense of humor. Her appearance on a satirical interview show, Zach Galifianakis's *Between Two Ferns,* in September 2016 garnered millions of views. Clinton had suggested appearing on *Between Two Ferns* because Barack Obama had also appeared on the show with great success.[98] The web series features Galifianakis asking uncomfortable mocking questions. *The Atlantic* reported,

> The biggest payoff for Clinton, a politician often caricatured as stiff and overly serious, was always going to be the simple fact that she agreed to participate in the show in the first place.[99]

Clinton rarely showed her humorous side during the election; she shrouded her authentic self amid the controversies and weakened her campaign story with a strict rhetorical strategy. Instead, Clinton looked reserved next to her opponent's unhinged personality and campaign. The Internet loved when Clinton unexpectedly shimmied her shoulders during a debate rebuttal against Donald Trump. The shimmy meme went viral.

When Clinton wrote *Living History*, Sidonie Smith said the book "ought to do the social work of convincing the voting public that a woman could assume national leadership."[100] A political autobiography should establish authenticity. Smith explains, "The narrating 'I' of *Living History* is the collective endeavor of Clinton herself, her three ghostwriters, and the editors(s) involved in its publication."[101] Ghostwriting is common but leads to generic, rather than authentic, prose. Smith explains, "The restlessness of generic modes also opens up the suspicion that it is impossible to locate the 'real' Hillary, and any ground of authenticity to this political personal, except the Exhibit A of ambition."[102]

Clinton's *What Happened* memoir on why she lost the 2016 election is different from her last two books, in which positioned herself as a valid, credible leader who listed her qualifications. *What Happened* is a book filled with what-ifs, such as "what if Hillary Clinton's campaign had introduced a new economic plan called 'Alaska for America.'"[103] She contemplates her decision:

"I wonder now whether we should have thrown caution to the wind."[104] *The Washington Post* said this type of information is dull for the reader:

> The reader, like Clinton, relies on media that prioritizes scandal and narrative over news. Trump, in the campaign and in power, never let go of the narrative; Clinton could never get her hands around it.[105]

Clinton tries to explain her defeat, but overall, she concluded her campaign message was not clear. She even wrote that President Obama said her campaign "needed more message discipline."[106]

Clinton said what many Republicans said in 2008 after losing to Barack Obama: they have to catch up digitally. "We need an 'always on' content distribution network that can match what the right-wing has built."[107] Clinton is correct when she says, "That most people get their news from screens, so we have to be there 24/7."[108]

Clinton's cyborg image taught future campaigns that modern communication technology could manipulate a campaign's story to their opponent's advantage. Clinton's conventional and distant approach to her message never created a relationship with citizens that produced a dialogical interaction as industrious as Trump's. Trump's repetitive narrative never lost focus, even during his campaign's snafus and controversies. Robin Lakoff's analysis of Clinton in her book *The Language War* was published in 2000 and is still true today:

> Hillary Rodham Clinton's role in the making of meaning is like everything else about her—complex and even contradictory. On the one hand, her action is negative: she subverts the attempts of traditional meaning makers to define her and control her by her ambiguity and ambivalence. On the other hand, she is a positive and active maker of meaning, a woman who—at least sometimes—chooses her own words, makes her own meaning, speaks for herself.[109]

Clinton's narrative never changed through the years. Academics, journalists, and politicians all assess her story in the same ways they did before 2016. As Trump broke the ritualistic political frame, Clinton kept the same conventional campaign story frame, not only of those who campaigned before her but also the story the media defined for her and the story she refused to redefine for herself.

NOTES

1. Amy Chozick, "Hillary Clinton Announces 2016 Presidential Bid," *New York Times*, April 12, 2015, https://www.nytimes.com/2015/04/13/us/politics/hillary-clint on-2016-presidential-campaign.html.

2. Karlyn Kohrs Campbell, "Feminist Rhetoric," in *Encyclopedia of Rhetoric*, ed. Thomas Sloane (Oxford: Oxford University Press, 2001), 303.

3. Bill Clinton and Hillary Clinton Interviewed by Steve Kroft, "Clinton on Flowers '92," *60 Minutes,* YouTube Video, 10:58, posted by Jim Heath, November 20, 2011, https://www.youtube.com/watch?v=lwXE52e9JFg.

4. Hillary Clinton, *Living History* (New York: Simon & Schuster, 2003), 119.

5. Sandra L. Combs, "FLOTUS," *Race, Gender & Class* 20, no. ½ (2013): 271.

6. "Double bind" is a term that Kathleen Hall Jamieson explored in her book *Beyond the Double Bind: Women and Leadership.* Hillary Clinton mentions both double bind and Kathleen Hall Jamieson in her book *Living History.* Video of Kathleen Hall Jamieson's interview with Charlie Rose in 1995 discussing the term "double bind" can be found here: https://charlierose.com/videos/9091.

7. Combs, "FLOTUS," 271.

8. Ibid., 267.

9. Gwen Ifill, "Trapped in a Spotlight, Hillary Clinton Uses It," *New York Times,* February 3, 1992.

10. Ibid.

11. Peter Baker, "First Lady Remains Vital Force in White House," *New York Times*, January 20, 1997.

12. Karlyn Kohrs Campbell, "The Discursive Performance of Femininity: Hating Hillary," *Rhetoric and Public Affairs* 1, no. 1 (1988): 11.

13. Ibid., 1.

14. Ibid., 4.

15. Aristotle, "Rhetoric," 1378a.

16. Peggy Noonan, "Declarations while McCain Watches," *Wall Street Journal*, April 19, 2008, W14.

17. Evan Thomas, "Hillary Milhous Clinton; The Similarities between Richard Nixon and Mrs. Clinton Go Well Beyond their Hostility Toward the Press," *Wall Street Journal*, June 9, 2015.

18. Wendy Wasserstein, "Hillary Clinton's Muddled Legacy," *New York Times*, August 25, 1998.

19. Ibid.

20. George Campbell, *The Philosophy of Rhetoric* (New York: Harper & Brothers, 1849), 120.

21. Hillary Clinton, "Clinton's Iraq Speech at GWU," *Real Clear Politics*, March 17, 2008, https://www.realclearpolitics.com/articles/2008/03/clintons_iraq_speech _at_gwu.html.

22. Glenn Kessler, "Recalling Hillary Clinton's Claim of 'Landing under Sniper Fire' in Bosnia," *Washington Post,* May 23, 2016, https://www.washingtonpost.com /news/fact-checker/wp/2016/05/23/recalling-hillary-clintons-claim-of-landing-under -sniper-fire-in-bosnia/.

23. Ibid.

24. Kathryn Kish Sklar, "A Women's History Report Card on Hillary Rodham Clinton's Presidential Primary Campaign, 2008," *Feminist Studies* 34, no. ½ (2008): 320–321.

25. Ibid.

26. Ibid.

27. Ibid, 321.

28. Mikhail Bakhtin explains a speaker, "Does not expect passive understanding that, so to speak, only duplicates his own idea in someone else's mind. Rather he expects response, agreement, sympathy, objection, execution, and so forth. . . . The desire to make one's speech understood is only an abstract aspect of the speaker's concrete and total speech plan. M. M. Bakhtin, *Speech Genres & Other Late Essays,* trans. Vern W. McGee, ed. Caryl Emerson and Michael Holquist (Austin: University of Texas Press, 1986), 69.

29. Rebecca S. Richards, "Cyborgs on the World Stage: Hillary Clinton and the Rhetorical Performances of Iron Ladies," *Feminists Formations* 23, no. 1 (Spring 2011): 2.

30. Margaret Thatcher, "Speech at Kensington Town Hall ("Britain Awake") (The Iron Lady)," *Margaret Thatcher Foundation,* January 19, 1976, https://www .margaretthatcher.org/document/102939.

31. Ibid., 627.

32. Jennifer J. Jones, "Talk Like a Man: The Linguistic Styles of Hillary Clinton, 1992–2013," *Perspectives on Politics* 14, no. 3 (2016): 636.

33. Ashley Ault, "A Symbol for Women's Progress: A Rhetorical Analysis of Hillary Rodham Clinton's Story as America's Story," *Michigan Academician,* XLII (2015): 121.

34. Ibid.

35. Keith V. Erickson and Stephanie Thomson, "Seduction Theory and the Recovery of Feminine Aesthetics: Implications for Rhetorical Criticism," *Communication Quarterly* 52, no. 3 (May 2009): 312.

36. Kenneth Burke explains, "You persuade a man only insofar as you can talk his language by speech, gesture, tonality, order, image, attitude, idea, identifying your ways with his," Burke, *Rhetoric of Motives,* 55.

37. Richards, "Cyborgs on the World Stage," 17.

38. Ibid., 18–19.

39. Ibid., 19.

40. Kimberley A. Strassel, "Hillary's Email Escapade," *Wall Street Journal,* March 6, 2015, Eastern Edition, A11.

41. Alexis Simendinger, "New Media as the Message," *National Journal* 40, no. 16 (April 19, 2008): 44.

42. Joseph E. Usincski and Lilly J. Goren, "What's in a Name? Coverage of Senator Hillary Clinton during the 2008 Democratic Primary," *Political Research Quarterly* 64, no. 4 (2011): 892.

43. Alexis Simendinger, "The XX Factor," *National Journal,* September 29, 2007, 48.

44. Frank Rich, "Hillary's St. Patrick's Day Massacre," *New York Times,* March 30, 2008, WK13.

45. Ibid.

46. R. Lawrence Butler, "Momentum in the 2008 Presidential Contests," *Palgrave Macmillan Journals* 41, no. 3 (2009): 340.

47. Christine Stansell, "All Fired Up: Women, Feminism, and Misogyny in the Democratic Primaries," *Dissent* 55, no. 4 (2008): 37.

48. Ibid., 36.

49. WMUR-TV, "Clinton Wells Up: 'This is Very Personal,'" *YouTube* video, posted by WMUR-TV, January 7, 2008, https://www.youtube.com/watch?v=pl-W3IXRTHU.

50. Robin Tolmach Lakoff, *The Language War* (Berkley: University of California Press, 2000), 163.

51. Barbara C. Burrell, "Hillary Rodham Clinton as First Lady: the People's Perspective," *Social Science Journal* 37, no 4 (2000): 530.

52. "The Clinton Mail Baggage; Are Hillary's Ethics Behind the Bernie Sanders Surge?" *Wall Street Journal* (Online), January 14, 2016.

53. Bernie Sanders, *Our Revolution* (New York: Thomas Dunne Books, 2016), 99–100.

54. Harold Meyerson, "The Democrats after Bernie," *Dissent* 63, no 3 (Summer 2016).

55. Gerhard Peters and John T. Woolley, "Democratic Candidates Debate in Las Vegas, Nevada," *The American Presidency Project,* October 13, 2015, https://www.presidency.ucsb.edu/node/311256.

56. Sanders, *Our Revolution,* 160.

57. Michael Grothaus, "Inside Bernie Sanders's Social Media Machine," *Fast Company,* April 11, 2016, https://www.fastcompany.com/3058681/inside-bernie-sanders-social-media-machine?itm_source=parsely-api.

58. Sanders, *Our Revolution,* 100.

59. Jenkins, *Convergence Culture,* 17.

60. Ibid., 219.

61. Ibid., 17.

62. Isie Lapowsky, "Here's How Facebook Actually Won Trump the Presidency," *Wired,* November 15, 2016, https://www.wired.com/2016/11/facebook-won-trump-election-not-just-fake-news/.

63. Ibid.

64. Donna Haraway, *The Haraway Reader* (New York: Routledge, 2004), 7.

65. Ibid., 26.

66. Ibid., 39.

67. Ibid., 34.

68. Kenya Downs, "#GirlIGuessImWithHer: Disappointed Voters Show Reluctant Support for Clinton," *PBS Newshour,* June 8, 2016, http://www.pbs.org/newshour/rundown/girliguessimwithher-disappointed-voters-show-reluctant-support-for-clinton/?utm_source=facebook&utm_medium=pbsofficial&utm_campaign=newshour.

69. Kenya Downs, "#GirlIguessImWithHer."

70. Ibid.

71. Amy Chozick and Patrick Healy, "Hillary Clinton Is Set Back by Decision to Keep Illness Secret," *New York Times*, September 12, 2016, https://www.nytimes.com/2016/09/13/us/hillary-clinton-pneumonia.html?mcubz=0.

72. Hillary Faints, "Hillary Faints-Proof of Hillary Clinton on Leg Braces," *YouTube*, Published on September 11, 2016, 57, https://www.youtube.com/watch?v=MgydvjoftJY.

73. "#HackingHillary," *Know Your Meme*, 2016, http://knowyourmeme.com/memes/hackinghillary. *Know Your Meme* is a website that tracks the origins of trending memes. The website shows several examples of Hillary Clinton coughing memes that went viral.

74. Annie Karni, "Clinton Sells Sick Days as Campaign Reset," *Politico*, September 15, 2016, http://www.politico.com/story/2016/09/hillary-clinton-sick-days-campaign-reset-228253.

75. WikiLeaks, "What is WikiLeaks?" About, *WikiLeaks*, November 3, 2015, https://wikileaks.org/What-is-WikiLeaks.html.

76. Chris Hables Gray, *Cyborg Citizen : Politics in the Posthuman Age* (New York: Routledge, 2001), 2.

77. Charlie Beckett and James Ball, *WikiLeaks: News in the Networked Era* (Cambridge: Polity, 2012).

78. James Comey, "Letter to Congress from F.B.I. Director on Clinton Email Case," *New York Times,* October 28, 2016, https://www.nytimes.com/interactive/2016/10/28/us/politics/fbi-letter.html.

79. Eliot Ness and Terence R. McAuliffe, "A Fine FBI-Clinton Mess; Comey Reopens the Email Probe 11 days before the Election," *Wall Street Journal*, October 28, 2016, https://www.wsj.com/articles/a-fine-fbi-clinton-mess-1477695528.

80. Haraway, *The Haraway Reader*, 106.

81. Jayeon Lee and Young-shin Lim, "Gendered Campaign Tweets: The Cases of Hillary Clinton and Donald Trump," *Public Relations Review* 42 (2016): 853.

82. Ibid.

83. Daniel Victor, "Clinton to Trump on Twitter: 'Delete Your Account,'" *New York Times*, June 9, 2016, https://www.nytimes.com/2016/06/10/us/politics/hillary-clinton-to-donald-trump-delete-your-account.html.

84. Ibid.

85. Ibid.

86. Amos Tversky and Daniel Kahneman, "Availability: A Heuristic for Judging Frequency and Probability," *Cognitive Psychology* 5 (1973): 230.

87. Luis Ferre Sadurni, "Clinton Historically Wary of the Press," *Reporters Committee for Freedom of the Press* (2016), http://www.rcfp.org.

88. Ibid.

89. Ibid.

90. Walter Lippman, *Public Opinion* (New York: Free Press Paperbacks, 1997), 229.

91. Kathleen Hall Jamieson, *The Press Effect: Politicians, Journalists, and the Stories that Shape the Political World* (Oxford: Oxford University Press, 2003), 194.

92. Ibid, 23.

93. Gunn Enli, "Twitter as Arena for the Authentic Outsider: Exploring the Social Media Campaigns of Trump and Clinton in the 216 US Presidential Election," *European Journal of Communication* 32, no. 1 (2017): 59.

94. Shelley Hepworth, Vanessa Gezari, Kyle Pope, Cory Schouten, Carlett Spike, David Uberti and Pete Vernon, "Covering Trump: An Oral History of an Unforgettable Campaign," *Columbia Journalism Review*, November 22, 2016, https://www.cjr.org/special_report/trump_media_press_journalists.php.

95. Ibid.

96. Ibid.

97. Ibid.

98. Ibid.

99. Clare Foran, "Hillary Clinton's Appearance on *Between Two Ferns* Wasn't Brave," *The Atlantic*, September 23, 2016, http://www.theatlantic.com.

100. Sidonie Smith, "'America's Exhibit A': Hillary Rodham Clinton's *Living History* and the Genres of Authenticity," *American Literary History*, June 6, 2012, https://academic.oup.com/alh/article/24/3/523/103133/America-s-Exhibit-A-Hillary-Rodham-Clinton-s?searchresult=1.

101. Ibid.

102. Ibid.

103. Hillary Clinton, *What Happened* (New York: Simon & Schuster, 2017), 293.

104. Ibid.

105. David Weigel, "Clinton's Account of How She was 'shivved in the 2016 Presidential Election," *The Washington Post*, September 12, 2017. https://www.washingtonpost.com/outlook/clintons-account-of-how-she-was-shivved-in-the-2016-presidential-election/2017/09/11/f6740438-957f-11e7-89fa-bb822a46da5b_story.html?utm_term=.498ba526092e.

106. Clinton, *What Happened*, 74.

107. Ibid., 422.

108. Ibid.

109. Lakoff, *The Language War*, 192.

Chapter 7

Donald Trump's Rhetrickery

In *The Art of the Deal*, Donald Trump says, "Sometimes it pays to be a little wild."[1] Trump published *The Art of the Deal* in 1987. Thirty years later, Trump seems to have the same mentality when he sealed the deal to become the United States' forty-fifth president. Trump's rhetorical choices have been dramatic and somewhat unpredictable. Trump's over-the-top personality, which turned him into a reality star, became his online and offline signature campaign-style. Future politicians must take note of the ways he used social media to connect to the electorate.

Donald Trump grew up with the talent for making deals. He inherited his Dad's business savvy and went on to create an empire of his own. According to *Art of the Deal*, Trump believed "success was defined—and created—in good measure by reputation and image."[2] Moreover, Trump found in building a strong brand early in his business career "an ever-morphing array of ways to send the message that Trump meant ambition, wealth, and distinctively personal expression of success."[3]

Trump's definition of success also meant building his own rhetorical style to fit his brand. Bombastic, and at many times, antagonistic describes Donald Trump's rhetorical style. He once told a crowd, "When a person screws you, you screw them back fifteen times harder."[4] Trump uses universal experiences to identify with citizens' experiences, which makes his rhetorical choices even more powerful. His tweets became national news within seconds of posting, and his rallies drew thousands of citizens. He has been a newsmaker most of his life—always appearing in the New York City media landscape and eventually moving into the role of celebrity via NBC's *The Apprentice*.

TRUMP'S RHETORICAL STRATEGY

Trump used not only mainstream media but social media with ease. He called news programs for impromptu interviews. He tweeted, and the mainstream media reported on that same tweet within minutes. Kenneth Burke writes, "The way in which language is used, its form and style, affects the audiences to which it is addressed."[5] Trump kept communicating with his audience through his Twitter account. L. Virginia Holland explains Kenneth Burke's theory, Dramatism:

> Man is an actor who purposively acts through certain means (symbolical or linguistic methods as well as physical), and he carries out his action against the backdrop of the historical scene—the time and place in which he lives.[6]

Trump's historical scene was the 2016 presidential campaign, and the media was his chosen way to communicate. Trump's rhetorical strategy motivated people to take action through sharing his social media posts. *The New York Times* reported,

> His online dominance is striking: Over the past two months, on Twitter alone, he has been mentioned in 6.3 million conversations, eight times as many as Republican rivals like Marco Rubio, Carly Fiorina, and Ben Carson—not to mention three times as many as Hillary Rodham Clinton and nearly four times as many as Bernie Sanders.[7]

Trump engaged his followers by retweeting them, and having his supporters take part in the conversation. His rhetorical style had audiences following him to see what he would say next. His rhetorical style motivated audiences to react both positively and negatively.

An orator must identify with the audience. Language can move us to tears, to laughter, and anger. Remember, "the language we select makes all of us act in particular ways rather than others, making language serve an important function of generating motives for action."[8] Trump's rhetorical strategy motivated those he called "the voiceless."

In the article "Explaining Donald Trump via Communication Style: Grandiosity, Informality, and Dynamism," the authors found, "Donald Trump dominated his more experienced competitors in the primaries."[9] The researchers explained even though political pundits had underestimated Donald Trump's chances to win the nomination, their study revealed: "that a populist communication style—grandiose, dynamic, and informal—may have 'trumped' a carefully-reasoned platform."[10] The study indicates that identifying with one's audience moves people to action.

The emotion that Donald Trump tapped into with his supporters was anger. Angry rhetoric is strategic. Aristotle says the orator must discover:

(1) what the state of mind of angry people is, (2) who the people are with whom they usually get angry, and (3) on what grounds they get angry with them.[11]

Trump created many scenes where his rhetoric incited his crowd's anger toward the media at his rallies; even journalists sometimes became scared for their safety while covering these events.

Trump kept describing the media as "dishonest" and "fake news."

@RealDonaldTrump: I am not running against Crooked Hillary Clinton, I am running against the very dishonest and totally biased media—but I will win! (August 6, 2016)

The media became Trump's rhetorical target to try to discredit journalists who wrote about his campaign.

He used similar rhetorical tactics against Hillary Clinton at a campaign rally in August 2016. Trump exclaimed:

Hillary wants to abolish—essentially abolish the Second Amendment. By the way, if she gets to pick, if she gets to pick her judges, nothing you can do, folks. Although the Second Amendment people, maybe there is, I don't know, but I tell you what, that will be a horrible day, if Hillary gets to put her judges in, right now we're tied.[12]

Many people interpreted Trump's words to insinuate Second Amendment supporters could use violence to stop Clinton. Trump's campaign later said the remark was a joke, but Trump's comment spurred a response from many critics, including Martin Luther King, Jr.'s daughter, who tweeted on August 9, 2016,

@BerniceKing: As the daughter of a leader who was assassinated, I find #Trump's comments distasteful, disturbing, dangerous. His words don't #LiveUp #MLK

Trump's rhetorical choices tapped into people's fears and anger. The Twitter conversation #wordsmatter was repeated throughout the campaign by people who understood, as Burke believed, that language moves people to action. Trump's words affected some people to tweet #wordsmatter to @realDonaldTrump

@*ChristaHazel:* Beyond irritated w/@realDonaldTrump for the discussion I've been forced to have with my teenage daughter. #WordsMatter 4 this #GOP-mom. (October 8, 2016)

@*candemcd:* Watch your actions, they become habits. Whatch your habits, they become your character. @realDonaldTrump #TrumpTapes #WordsMatter #NotOkay (October 7, 2018)

@*TheaWakanda:* @realDonaldTrump #wordsmatter airing direct clips of your own words is NOT unfair or misrepresentation #debatenight #FactsMatter

@*suekron:* (Replying to @annanavarro) When is enough ENOUGH? @realdonaldtrump repeatedly says incredibly ignorant things…now downright dangerous things. #Wordsmatter (August 9, 2016)

Colleen Shogan, the author of *The Moral Rhetoric of American Presidents*, said in an interview with *The Washington Post*, "It's a very difficult task to determine that someone acts in a particular way because of what has been argued by another person. It's more accurate to think about rhetoric as setting scripts or frameworks that justify action, rather than inciting action itself."[13]

The New York Times analyzed a week's worth of Trump's campaign transcripts and reported that Trump "relies on potent language to connect with and, often, stoke the fears and grievances of Americans."[14] After examining 95,000 words, *The New York Times* found that his language reflects language used by Joseph McCarthy, who infamously tapped into American fears about Communists.[15] Comparatively, Trump taps into American fears about terrorists. Kenneth Burke says, "You persuade a man only insofar as you can talk his language by speech, gesture, tonality, order, image, attitude, idea, *identifying* your ways with his."[16] Some of Trump's "supporters combine the distinct traits of a strong nationalist and ethnocentric identity with a deep suspicion of elites and cultural pretenses."[17] In the research article "Rise of the Trumpenvolk: Populism in the 2016 Election," critics accuse Trump "of being a fascist, an authoritarian, a demagogue, and a dangerous influence on American politics."[18] The authors found that Trump's rhetoric is simple and "quintessentially populist."[19] A trait of populist rhetoric is "proclaiming a crisis exists."[20] For example, during the campaign, Trump tweeted daily about how dangerous the world was and how only he could fix the problems Democrats wanted to ignore. Trump tweeted:

@*realdonaldtrump:* Shooting deaths of police officers up 78% this year. We must restore law and order and protect our great law enforcement officers. (July 27, 2016.)

@*realdonaldtrump:* Crooked Hillary Clinton wants to flood our country with Syrian immigrants that we know little or nothing about. The danger is massive. NO! (July 27, 2016)

@realdonaldtrump: Will CNN send its cameras to the border to show the massive unreported crisis now unfolding—or are they worried it will hurt Hillary? (August 1, 2016)

Trump used hyperbole, exaggerations, to amplify his message that America was in crisis mode. Trump's rhetorical strategy "is a style of political communication that utilizes particular communicative practices and routines that simultaneously connect and divide, and construct and reconstruct identities in the pursuits of power."[21] Michael Signer, in *Demagogue: The Fight to Save Democracy from Its Worst Enemies*, explains,

> Aristotle likened the demagogue to a gadfly, an insect that you cannot shake free, that has a bitter sting. In this metaphor, democracy is a beast bedeviled by the maddening pest, who goads and pesters and stings until the animal bolts—stampeding away, trampling everything underneath, perhaps rushing off a cliff.[22]

Trump's rhetoric is one where he goaded and pestered and stung his opponents. His demagogue rhetoric was persuasive because of the audience's preconceived beliefs.[23] Moreover, his audience, in return, offered support and votes.[24]

RHETRICKERY AND PROPAGANDA

Donald Trump's rhetorical style is far from refined. His many techniques in his social media presence suggest a propaganda style is his primary persuasion technique. Putting historical factors of propaganda aside for this chapter, we will concentrate on the implications modern propaganda has and the techniques Trump uses that make his tweets move people to action. People who read Trump's tweets either notice the tweets are propaganda-like or retweet the posts unknowingly, supporting the propagandist ideology. Rhetorician Wayne Booth might have defined Trump's tweets as "rhetrickery."

Wayne Booth defines "rhetrickery" as "the whole range of shoddy, dishonest communicative arts producing misunderstanding—along with other harmful results. The arts of making the worse seem the better cause."[25] Booth explains that

> Rhetoric makes realities, however temporary. And meanwhile it creates a multiplicity of judgments about what the realities really are. After every election or every war, there is never full agreement about what new reality has been created.[26]

Rhetoric makes and creates our realities, and "employing the term 'rhetrickery' for the worst forms can't disguise the fact that much of what we find repulsive is a form of rhetoric."[27]

Rhetrickery may evolve into propaganda but could also become the political persuasion tool called *spin*. Spin "reflects our mindfulness that politics is full of competing versions of events and ways of ordering reality."[28] A presidential candidate's spin can morph into a propagandist approach that reaches far beyond the spin campaign that gives many politicians a way to inform and persuade. Sometimes this technique is misleading. In Donna Woolfolk Cross's article, "Propaganda: How Not to Be Bamboozled," she explains how propaganda misleads and deceives people because they do not know "propaganda when they see it."[29]

Simply, "propaganda . . . means to disseminate or promote particular ideas."[30] Think of the propagandist as a gardener. The propagandist's goal is to plant a seed. The seed will then grow into either doubt or acceptance. Then the gardener (propagandist) waters and fertilizes the seeds to help the seeds grow. The propagandist uses techniques to frame (mis)information, so the (mis)information takes root in the audience's minds. The propagandist wants the audience to adopt their ideology as reality.

However, there are not many rhetoricians who discuss propaganda in a rhetorical context.[31] Kenneth Burke analyzed Hitler's propaganda and formed the Pentad or what he called "Dramatism." Kenneth Burke named the five elements of dramatism as Act, Scene, Agent, Agency, and Purpose.[32] To discover the motive behind the *why* Burke explains, "Any complete statement about motives will offer some kind of answers to these five questions: what was done (act), when or where it was done (scene), who did it (agent), how he did it (agency), and why (purpose)."[33] Trump's rhetorical approach "invites one to consider the matter of motives in a perspective that, being developed from the analysis of drama, treats language and thought primarily as modes of action."[34] The news reported that Trump routinely would shout to protestors, "Get Out!" On the day of the Iowa caucuses, he told an audience he would pay their legal fees if arrested for assaulting protestors.[35] One lawsuit accused Trump of inciting a riot at a Kentucky rally. Three protestors argued that "crowd members assaulted them upon Trump's command."[36]

Propaganda cannot be ignored as a rhetorical strategy because propaganda moves people to action. Jason Stanley explains two types of rhetorical strategies:

One kind of propaganda, demagogic speech, both exploits and spreads flawed ideologies. Hence demagogic speech threatens democratic deliberation. A different kind of propaganda, *civic rhetoric*, can repair flawed ideologies, potentially restoring the possibility of self-knowledge and democratic deliberation.[37]

To understand Trump's social media presence and influence, one must look at Trump's use of propaganda techniques, how Trump created a movement, and helped sow seeds of doubt in voters' minds about his opponent through propaganda techniques. Trump's rhetrickery helped him win the presidency.

Propaganda Techniques

In a 1945 article in the *American Journal of Sociology*, Alfred McClung Lee explained, "Propaganda grows out of and plays a part in social tensions and struggles."[38] Donald Trump showcased his supporters' tensions and struggles by framing his campaign rhetoric, especially his tweets, to tell people he understood their struggles. The Institute of Propaganda in the late 1930s identified seven propaganda techniques.[39] Donald Trump commonly used propaganda techniques during his 2016 presidential campaign.

1. Name-Calling: This technique "consists of labeling people or ideas with words of bad connotation."[40] Donald Trump liked to nickname his opponents: "Little Rubio," "Low-Energy Jeb," "Lying Cruz," and "Crooked Hillary." When repeated by Donald Trump and by news media, these names created a bad connotation in peoples' minds. Trump created these nicknames to remind people of his opponents' character flaws.

   @realDonaldTrump: Low energy Jeb Bush just endorsed a man he truly hates, Lyin' Ted Cruz. Honestly, I can't blame Jeb in that I drove him into oblivion. (March 23, 2016)

   @realDonaldTrump: I hope that Crooked Hillary picks Goofy Elizabeth Warren, sometimes referred to as Pocahontas, as her V.P. Then we can litigate her fraud! (July 17, 2016)

2. Glittering Generalities: The propagandist goal is to spark and stir emotions. Glittering generalities are no exception; it "is the practice of short-cutting discussion by associating an idea with a 'virtue word' in order to make us accept and approve the proposal without examining the evidence further."[41] For example, Trump tweeted about how a strong military stops wars.

   @realDonaldTrump: A strong military will stop wars. Peace through Strength! Let's Make America Great Again! (July 11, 2015)

3. Argumentum Ad Populum: This technique is used quite often in politics. The politician will discuss the popular sentiment by targeting a specific

population or making general comments. The lesson is to be careful when someone tells you exactly what you want to hear.

@realDonaldTrump: Our country does not feel "great already" to the millions of wonderful people living in poverty, violence and despair. (July 27, 2016)

@realDonaldTrump: I will bring our jobs back to the U.S., and keep our companies from leaving. Nobody else can do it. Our economy will "sing" again. (March 15, 2016)

4. Bandwagon: Have your parents ever asked, "If your friends jumped off a bridge, would you?" This propaganda technique is to convince people that others are accepting their idea.

For example, Donald Trump started calling his campaign a movement; he implied he had the best political strategy; he used repetition to overemphasize his support base. Trump even insinuated that Clinton's husband was one of his supporters: he said former president Bill Clinton disliked Obamacare as much as he did. Trump always took advantage of ways he could insinuate Democrats liked his ideas.

@realDonaldTrump: Wow, did you just hear Bill Clinton's statement on how bad ObamaCare is. Hillary not happy. As I have been saying, REPEAL AND REPLACE! (October 4, 2016)

@realDonaldTrump: Just leaving Florida. Big crowds of enthusiastic supporters lining the road that the FAKE NEWS media refuses to mention. Very dishonest! (February 12, 2017)

@realDonaldTrump: My supporters are the best! $18 million from hard-working people who KNOW what we can be again! Shatter the record. (September 27, 2016)

Twitter Propaganda

In a tweet on January 2, 2018, Professor Emeritus George Lakoff categorized Trump's tweets into several categories, as seen in Figure 7.1. Lakoff tweeted,

@*GeorgeLakoff:* Trump uses social media as a weapon to control the news cycle. It works like a charm. His tweets are tactical rather than substantive. They mostly fall into one of these four categories. (January 2, 2018)

Trump is always first to frame an idea and control the news cycle through his rhetrickery. As mentioned earlier in his text *Gorgias*, Plato explained that Socrates called rhetoric "cookery." In the excerpt below, Socrates worries rhetoric is just persuasion.

A Taxonomy of

TRUMP TWEETS

1 PREEMPTIVE FRAMING	**2** DIVERSION	**3** DEFLECTION	**4** TRIAL BALLOON
Be the first to frame an idea	*Divert attention from real issues*	*Attack messenger, change direction*	*Test public reaction*
EXAMPLE: The hacking of the DNC was the DNC's fault and Democrats lost by a wide margin. (when in fact it was one of the narrowest margins in US history).	**EXAMPLE:** Divert attention away from real issues around conflicts of interest and Russian hacking and toward Meryl Streep's speech at Golden Globe Awards.	**EXAMPLE:** Attack media in an attempt to erode public trust. Reframe story as "fake news" and establish Trump administration as source of truth.	**EXAMPLE:** Test public reaction to nuclear arms escalation.
JAN 7 @realDonaldTrump Only reason the hacking of the poorly defended DNC is discussed is that the loss by the Dems was so big that they are totally embarrassed!	JAN 9 @realDonaldTrump Meryl Streep, one of the most over-rated actresses in Hollywood, doesn't know me but attacked last night at the Golden Globes. She is a.....	JAN 11 @realDonaldTrump Intelligence agencies should never have allowed this fake news to "leak" into the public. One last shot at me. Are we living in Nazi Germany?	DEC 22 @realDonaldTrump The United States must greatly strengthen and expand its nuclear capability until such time as the world comes to its senses regarding nukes

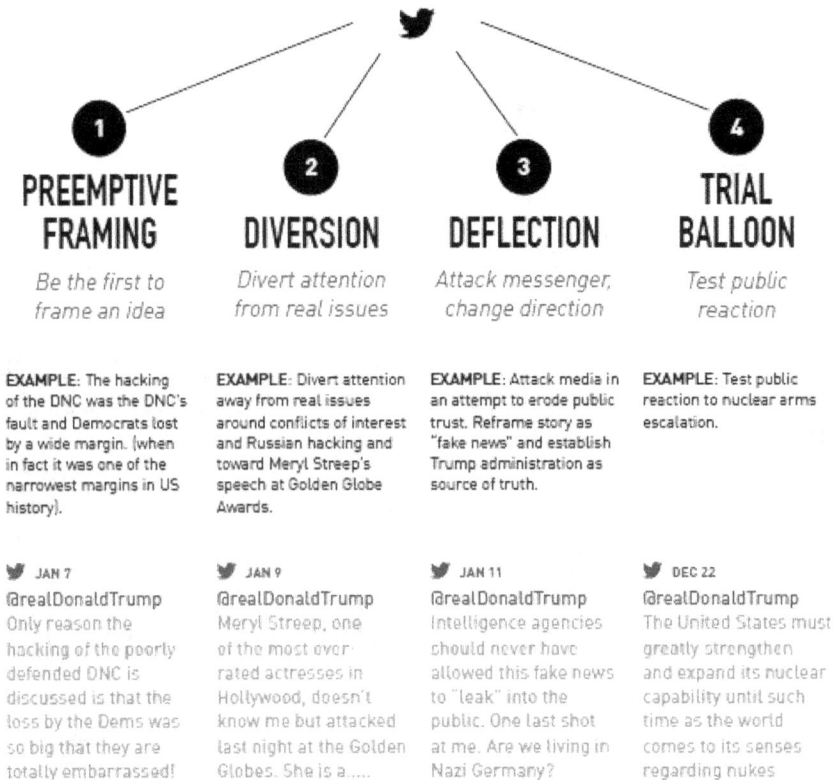

Figure 7.1   A Taxonomy of Trump Tweets. *Source*: Reprinted by permission from George Lakoff (Tweeted January 1, 2018).

Socrates: Then the case is the same in all the other arts from the orator and his rhetoric: There is no need to know the truth of the actual matters, but one merely needs to have discovered some device of persuasion which will make one appear to those who do not know to know better than those who know.[42]

Trump's "device of persuasion" is repetition when he believes there is no need for the actual truth. He leaves the audience with doubt by repeating the lie over and over. For example, Trump repeatedly created doubt that the election system was "rigged."

@realDonaldTrump: Crooked Hillary can't even close the deal with Bernie-and the Dems have it *rigged* in favor of Hillary. Four more years of this? No way! (May 20, 2016)

@realDonaldTrump: Bernie Sanders is being treated very badly by the Democrats-the system is *rigged* against him. Many of his disenfranchised fans are for me! (May 18, 2016)

@realDonaldTrump: I look so forward to debating Crooked Hillary Clinton! Democrat Primaries are *rigged*, e-mail investigation is rigged-so time to get it on! (May 17, 2016)

@realDonaldTrump: Do you think Crooked Hillary will finally close the deal? If she can't win Kentucky she should drop out of race. System *rigged*! (May 17, 2016)

@realDonaldTrump: Bernie Sanders is being treated very badly by the Dems. The system is *rigged* against him. He should run as an independent! Run Bernie, run. (May 16, 2016)

Trump kept using the word "rigged" As Lakoff suggests in Figure 7.1, Trump preemptively framed the story for the media as well as framed the story for the voters.

@realDonaldTrump: Crooked Hillary Clinton is "guilty as hell" but the system is totally *rigged* and corrupt! Where are the 33,000 missing emails? (July 4, 2016)

@realDonaldTrump: "THE SYSTEM IS *RIGGED*!" (July 3, 2016)

@realDonaldTrump: Crooked Hillary Clinton knew that her husband wanted to meet with the U.S.A.G. to work out a deal. The system is totally *rigged* and corrupt! (July 3, 2016)

The more Trump says the word "rigged," the more likely the word becomes part of Americans' vocabulary. The media even repeated the phrase "rigged election," while reporting on Trump's tweets. When Trump repeats "Crooked Hillary," "rigged election," and "dishonest media," these labels start to resonate in people's minds, who connect the negative aspects to what Trump describes without seeking out more information. The propagandist wants people to believe what they are saying to be true in order to instill doubt in people's minds and stir emotions to move people to action. George Lakoff, in his book *The Political Mind*, reminds us, "Say things not once, but over and over. Brains change when ideas are repeatedly activated."[43] Rhetrickery travels far in this social media age.

CELEBRITY POLITICIAN

Trump knew the importance of performing for an audience, as did Ronald Reagan. Reagan, a former actor, said in 1966—at the height of television's political influence—that "politics is just like show business."[44] Reagan knew performance mattered—and so did the Greek Sophists.

Greek rhetoric teachers, known as Sophists, knew performance and a grandiose style was vital to a successful speech. In Plato's *Gorgias*, Socrates argued to the Sophist Gorgias that rhetoric was nothing but cookery. In Athens's town square, politicians learned more effective ways to persuade, but they did not have Twitter to carry their message as far. Sophists did not persuade the masses—just the townspeople. Today's town square is your Facebook feed, your Twitter feed, or even your local news channel. Cookery is what we now call "spin." Moreover, images are everywhere and, to get noticed, one must create more than a speech, but an experience—a performance. Technology created a cultural phenomenon where politicians with achievements evolved into celebrities with charisma.

The Kardashian Effect

At the Newseum on July 11, 2016, a panel of journalists referred to the Trump phenomenon as the "Kardashian effect." CNN journalist John King explained:

> We process people through how we met them . . . but everybody met Donald Trump as a celebrity and a reality TV star, and so I call that the Kardashian effect. You know 80 percent of that is B.S. It's an act, and it's meant to drive your emotions. It's meant to make you do something and it's not real . . . they translate him differently because they met him differently.[45]

Trump's celebrity is how many voters knew him, and he never stopped performing. When Trump tweeted, his tweets became news. When Trump did not tweet, that became news. The media helped solidify Trump's celebrity status more than the political status the media reported on for other GOP candidates or Hillary Clinton. All of Trump's opponents had achieved job credibility as established politicians—not as celebrities.

Remember, Trump's celebrity status is not comparable to Tom Hanks's or Meryl Streep's, who have won Oscars for their achievements in acting. Both Hanks and Streep can proudly claim to be "movie stars." The Kardashian type of celebrities has television shows reflecting their real life. These types of celebrities are only celebrities because the media has told us they are.

In *Amusing Ourselves to Death: Public Discourse in the Age of Show Business*, Neil Postman says:

> Although it may go too far to say that the politician-as-celebrity has, by itself, made political parties irrelevant, there is certainly a conspicuous correlation between the rise of the former and the decline of the latter. Some readers may

remember when voters barely knew who the candidate was and, in any case, were not preoccupied with his character and personal life.[46]

New media brings new worries for politicians. Politicians may worry about what unflattering memes, YouTube videos, or tweets will go viral. Voters should be cautious as well because "as we become more dependent on electronic media for information and entertainment, our information environment is permeated not only with synthetic events but also with synthetic experience."[47] If a politician does not have a household name upon entering a campaign, that politician needs to work on his or her media presence. The best way to do so is through grassroots campaigns that create a viral message that transcends beyond mainstream media outlets. *The New York Times* Frank Bruni said that to appeal to voters' anger, "obnoxiousness is the new charisma."[48]

The celebrity-turned-politician is much different from a traditional politician. Media manufactures fame, but most career politicians run a campaign off achievement and experience. Daniel J. Boorstin, in his book *The Image: A Guide to Pseudo-Events in America,* explains, "Our power to fill our minds with more and more 'big names' has increased our demand for Big Names and our willingness to confuse the Big Name with the Big Man. Again, mistaking our powers for our necessities, we have filled our world with artificial fame."[49] Trump saying "you're fired" weekly on *The Apprentice* created an image of a no-nonsense, off-the-cuff businessman. *The Apprentice* helped solidify Trump's presidential campaign image. Boorstin adds,

> We can fabricate fame, we can at will (though usually at considerable expense) make a man or woman well-known; but we can never make him great. We can make a celebrity, but we can never make a hero.[50]

Not all presidential candidates can be a war hero like President Dwight D. Eisenhower. President Eisenhower's war hero status made him a celebrity. Eisenhower won by his name recognition, not by his less-than-eloquent speeches, but through his hero status. As Boorstin reiterates, "Celebrity-worship and hero-worship should not be confused."[51] Not many celebrities are heroes. The saying "unsung heroes" speaks volumes in the distinction between celebrity vs. hero. Not many heroes become celebrities or known for their accomplishments. In the end, "The danger of unrealistic expectations is that lack of fulfillment can lead to disappointment, frustration, and dissatisfaction."[52]

Throughout Donald Trump's campaign, chaotic moments deterred his performance. Trump added more dramatics for Twitter—watched by an audience of not only supporters but also observers checking in to watch what Trump would post next. The media kept Trump in the spotlight by reporting on his controversial tweets and taking his calls during news programs. Tweet by tweet, the media helped build upon Trump's already-solidified celebrity. Trump's unprecedented access and use of media outlets became a new way to campaign, saving Trump millions in campaign advertising dollars. In a February 2016 interview with Showtime's *The Circus: Inside the Greatest Political Show on Earth,* Trump said:

> One thing with me, they know me. They've known me for a long time. I sort of grew up with the American people. And . . . I have a voice. I have a strong voice. You add up Facebook, Twitter, Instagram, all of the things, I guess I have 13 million, 14 million people. Other people, there's no way of getting the word out unless you're willing to spend a million dollars for a commercial. With me, all I have to do is go bing, bing, bing, and I get the word out.[53]

Americans already knew him, and he believed that helped his successful campaign. Even Ronald Reagan, when he started to run for governor of California, said being an actor helped:

> Being an actor who was running for political office wasn't all drawbacks: many people develop an affection and feelings of friendship for someone they enjoy on the screen, and that could be an advantage for me.[54]

President Reagan acted in movies. Donald Trump appeared as himself on a reality show where "he is the master of sure quick-fire business decisions. In his own TV world, he is always the winner. Losing is for dummies."[55] Trump branded himself a winner, a businessman, a decision-maker—and his brand as a politician grew stronger during his campaign.

> *@realDonaldTrump:* I've dealt w/politicians throughout the world. My deals are multi-faceted transactions which involve many issues. I know the process & win! (May 8, 2015)

Trump believed his strategies could transcend over many campaign issues, much like the sophists believed that rhetoric "could be applied to any subject."[56] Gorgias, like Trump, "boasted that he did not need expert knowledge of a subject; he could persuade people to do things where experts had failed."[57]

Trump kept to his authentic self "because politicians are not the great actors who can play every role that is necessary, their persona needs to be close to their sense of self."[58] Trump valued his media presence and chastised Hillary Clinton for her lack of a media charisma:

> *@realDonaldTrump:* Crooked Hillary Clinton is being protected by the media. She is not a talented person or politician. The dishonest media refuses to expose! (August 14, 2016)

When politicians are not authentic, "their performance will be exposed as manufactured and artificial."[59]

Since Trump knew how to create a successful reality series, he knew that the story was an essential part of keeping people interested. Van Zoonen explains, "The campaign story, in fact, is built on a double quest: that of the candidate trying to reach his or her seat and of journalists trying to get hold of the candidate."[60] Trump positioned himself as the protagonist (the hero) and the journalists as the antagonists (the villains). Even his supporters played a role in the story as helpers, who eventually become "future marks."

TRUMP AND THE MEDIA

Donald Trump has a love/hate relationship with the media. Trump called into various news programs for impromptu interviews throughout his campaign and yet labeled the media as "dishonest" and "fake news." One of his first feuds started with Fox News anchor Megyn Kelly during the first Republican debate on August 6, 2015.[61] Soon after, Kelly interviewed Trump, which sparked much interest because of the hateful tweets Trump had directed toward Kelly after the debate. During a CNN interview about the "feud," Trump said,

> She gets out, and she starts asking me all sorts of ridiculous questions. You could see there was blood coming out of her eyes, blood coming out of her wherever. In my opinion, she was off base.[62]

Trump's comments elicited Twitter responses.

@*JoeTheFan1:* @JoeNBC @morningmika U have Trump lying and spinning his @megynkelly "Had Blood coming out of her . . . Wherever" comment. We know what he meant (August 9, 2015)

@*mare949:* I think @realDonaldTrump proved @megynkelly point with the "there was blood coming from . . wherever comment. Nasty comments to woman (August 8, 2015)

@*JaniceDean:* Wow. Comments about @megynkelly from @realDonaldTrump "blood coming from "whereever"?! He picked the wrong woman to mess with. (August 8, 2015)

Trump responded to the criticism:

@*realDonaldTrump:* Re Megyn Kelly quote: "you could see there was blood coming out of her eyes, blood coming out of her wherever" (NOSE). Just got on w/thought. (August 8, 2015.)

@realDonaldTrump: So many "politically correct" fools in our country. We have to all get back to work and stop wasting time and energy on nonsense! (August 8, 2015)

Trump may criticize the media, but Trump also needs the media to promote his message. *The Washington Post*'s Philip Bump reported that Trump:

> isn't running any ads, spending zero dollars on television (and getting outspent by the Green Party and Libertarian candidates). He isn't contacting voters on doors or on phones and has hardly any field offices. He isn't sending mail. He's tweeting, he's holding rallies, but not much else.[63]

Bump said Trump had a hard time transitioning from primary candidate to presidential candidate because his only messenger is Trump himself:

> Trump's problem is not that the "disgusting and corrupt media" is putting false meaning into things he says. The problem is that Trump's only messenger is himself, and that he says things that seem to objective observers inside and outside the media as questionable.[64]

Trump believed his messages were being misunderstood and misinterpreted by the media. Trump tweeted:

@realDonaldTrump: If the disgusting and corrupt media covered me honestly and didn't put false meaning into the words I say, I would be beating Hillary by 20% (August 14, 2016.)

@realDonaldTrump: The failing @nytimes talks about anonymous sources and meetings that never happened. Their reporting is fiction. The media protects Hillary! (August 14, 2016.)

@realDonaldTrump: I have always been the same person-remain true to self. The media wants me to change but it would be very dishonest to supporters to do so! (August 14, 2016)

@realDonaldTrump: "Stay on message" is the chant. I always do—trade, jobs, military, vets, 2nd A, repeal Ocare, borders, etc-but media misrepresents! (August 14, 2016)

His message was up for interpretation because his campaign did not advertise a clear message. Trump tweeted, held rallies, and sometimes did media interviews, either formal or impromptu. Trump believed his tweets and rallies were enough to get the message out, but his message became murky when he repeatedly had to clarify messages.

Tom Leonard says the media "have pounced on his every tweet and endlessly discussed each one."[65] Trump dominated media coverage—even during debates. If a debater mentions his opponent's name—the opponent may make a rebuttal. As Leonard points out, "As none of his rivals seems ever able to complete a sentence without mentioning the word 'Trump,' then inevitably, he is allowed to hog the camera."[66]

Trump, like Nixon, believed he was the victim of the media. Nixon's opinion became known as the "hostile media" effect. The hostile media effect is "the perception that the media are biased against one's candidate."[67] Lauren Feldman found "issue partisans do seem to have a bias against news bias—in instances where that news bias coheres with their pre-existing viewpoints."[68] She found, "even in the presence of blatant journalist opinionation, audiences filter their perceptions of news through the lens of their own partisanship."[69] The implications for these hostile media perceptions are that they "appear to foster widespread contempt for democratic institutions and contribute to emotionally charged, polarizing discourse."[70] The country was politically divided during the campaigns. The Pew Research Center in 2017 reported that 86 percent of people believed the country was more politically divided than in past years.[71] Only 12 percent of people said the country was no more politically divided than in past years.[72] In contrast, in 2009, before President Obama's inauguration, only 46 percent of people believed the country was more politically divided.[73]

Trump believes the media is to blame for any misunderstandings. In his book *Crippled America*, Trump wrote: "I've had meetings with reporters who faithfully recorded what I said, then changed the words and the meaning."[74] He continues to reflect on one experience:

> I had a so-called journalist from a well-known publication come up to my office and interview me and several of my executives. We gave him a pile of paperwork, we gave him financial reports and statements, anything he asked for—then he wrote one of the most inaccurate stories I've ever read. The public pays attention to a story for less than a week, especially when you get as many stories as I do. But the impression a bad story leaves lasts a lot longer.[75]

According to Trump, his issue with the media comes down to pride. Trump says, "I'm proud of what I've built, so when so-called journalists get it wrong. I have to respond."[76] However, Trump himself has spread conspiracy theories. On August 6, 2012, Trump tweeted, "An 'extremely credible source' has called my office and told me that @BarackObama's birth certificate is a fraud." As discussed above, throughout the election, he claimed the media was dishonest, and the election was rigged. Again, Trump tweets repetitive claims with no evidence, and the media had no idea how to handle his comments. *The Washington Post* reported that Trump supporters believed his conspiracy theory because:

talk of voter fraud is nearly always coupled with attacks on the media, which Trump and his supporters have accused of coordinating with Clinton's campaign, refusing to investigate scandals involving her and fabricating news about Trump's treatment of women over the years.[77]

The *Shorenstein Center on Media, Politics and Public Policy* found "over the full course of the election, it was Clinton, not Trump, who was more often the target of negative coverage . . . Overall, the coverage of her candidacy was 62 percent negative to 38 percent positive, while his coverage was 56 percent negative to 44 percent positive."[78] The horserace-style media coverage helped Trump: "as Trump rose from single digits in the polls and then won key primaries, he got favorable press. It was a story of growing momentum rising poll numbers, ever-larger crowds, and electoral success."[79]

Again, Trump's overall campaign narrative proved more forceful than Clinton's. Kathleen Hall Jamieson, in *Dirty Politics*, explains the campaign story process:

> The language through which the press reported on politics assumes that the American electorate selects a president through a process called a "campaign" seen as a "game" or "war" between a "front runner" and an "underdog" in which each "candidate's" goal is "winning."[80]

Jamieson explains the strategy schema is such that "candidates are seen as performers, reporters as theatrical critics, the audience as spectators."[81] Trump wanted to be the protagonist and to frame the media as the antagonists. Jamieson warns, "One danger in seeing candidates as actors is that they will be lured by our expectations into becoming the person they pretend to be."[82] Another danger is that the media shapes the expectations and encourages the performance.

Additionally, the media likes to capture the audience's attention by framing the presidential election as a horserace.[83] Shanto Iyengar believes:

> the real problem facing American journalism is not the intrusion of political motives into editorial decisions but rather the fact that journalism has become less motivated by the need to inform the public and more intent on offering programming that entertains.[84]

Journalists seized every opportunity to read Trump's tweets and replay his sound bites. Trump kept framing the media as the villain after unfavorable stories were published or broadcast about him. You can attribute Trump's campaign media success to how well he understands the media. Martin F. Nolan points out, "A president either masters a medium or the medium masters him.".[85] While the media helped Trump spread his message, they also became frustrated by his labels of "dishonest media" and "fake news." In October 2016, the Committee to Protect Journalists (CPJ) chairperson, Sandra Mims Rowe, condemned Trump's treatment of the press. She said,

> A Trump presidency would represent a threat to press freedom in the United States, but the consequences for the rights of journalists around the world could be far more serious . . . Through his words and actions, Trump has consistently demonstrated a contempt for the role of the press beyond offering publicity to him and advancing his interests.[86]

Trump may have changed the rules for journalists covering a presidential campaign. Amber E. Boydstun and Peter Van Aelst interviewed twenty-four journalists and political consultants and asked about the rules of campaign coverage. Boydstun and Van Aelst found that their interviewees "were most surprised that the rule of being a neutral adversary had no effect on the outcome of the 2016 election."[87] The journalists believed their coverage of Trump would dissuade the public. The journalists said Trump resonated "with large segments of America—a resonance that was more driven by emotions than facts, and that many journalists failed to fully appreciate or capture."[88] The journalists believed their audience missed their cues, and the rules of covering a campaign "changed" or "didn't matter."[89]

TRUMP TWEETS

Donald Trump's tweetstorms, a rapid series of tweets of indignation, became breaking news. In this way, Trump created one of the most hostile media environments. On August 1, 2016, Trump attacked CNN in a tweetstorm:

@realDonaldTrump: CNN will soon be the least trusted name in news if they continue to be the press shop for Hillary Clinton. (August 1, 2016)

@realDonaldTrump: When will we see stories from CNN on Clinton Foundation corruption and Hillary's pay-for-play at State Department? (August 1, 2016)

@realDonaldTrump: Will CNN send its cameras to the border to show the massive unreported crisis now unfolding—or are they worried it will hurt Hillary? (August 1, 2016)

@realDonaldTrump: The people who support Hillary sit behind CNN anchor chairs, or headline fundraisers—those disconnected from real life. (August 1, 2016)

@realDonaldTrump: People believe CNN these days almost as little as they believe Hillary . . . that's really saying something! (August 1, 2016)

CNN reported the tweetstorm came during an interview CNN did with Pat Smith, a Clinton critic and the mother of an American who died in 2012 in Benghazi, Libya.[90] Trump's tweets may have followed the news cycle. David Karpf explains, "Trump rarely was using Twitter in order to *bypass* the mainstream media. Instead, he was using social media in order to set the agenda for the mainstream media."[91] Karpf says Trump, through his use of social media, would increase the longevity of an article and decrease the longevity of a story.[92]

Barack Obama's campaign created the foundation for how a presidential candidate and the White House could use social media. Donald Trump built on that foundation to add ways a presidential candidate uses social media platforms. He broke the code for campaign strategists to online campaign "that foregoes costly, conventional methods of political communications and relies instead on the free, urgent, and visceral platforms of social media."[93] His campaign used Facebook as well, but the campaign's website was minimal compared to Hillary Clinton's.

Errors and all, Trump demonstrated what an authentic voice sounds like online. *Politico* reported, "Trump's errors pass for style. They add to the impression that he is unscripted, which is precisely what the Internet, and the American public, seems to be craving in this current media moment."[94] David A. Siegel found "social networks can also amplify media bias, leading to large swings in aggregate behavior made more severe when individuals can select into media outlets."[95] Trump's Twitter account is also a way people can receive information directly. His campaign strategy was to talk directly to the American citizen and amplify what he believed was media bias.

Trump is good at "directive uses of language."[96] Trump knows "with words . . . we influence and to an enormous extent control future events."[97] Trump's rhetoric is not dull and stirs emotions. As S. I. Hayakawa and Alan R. Hayakawa explain,

> If directive language is to direct effectively, it cannot be dull or uninteresting. If it is to influence our conduct, it must make use of the affective element available in language: dramatic variations in tone of voice, rhyme and rhythm, purring and snarling, words with strong affective annotations, endless repetition.[98]

Trump's rhetoric, online and offline, is rarely dull or uninteresting, but almost always repetitive. David Robinson's text analysis revealed that Trump might not be responsible for writing all of his tweets. Robinson concluded that an Android phone is used to send angrier tweets, and an iPhone is used to send informational tweets.[99] Robinson observed that posts from the Android phone do not use hashtags, and "emotionally charged words, like 'badly,' 'crazy,' 'weak,' and 'dumb' were overwhelmingly more common on Android."[100] Robinson also found instances when an iPhone was used to tweet in Trump's "voice" and style, which makes Robinson wonder who is behind the messages sent from the iPhone.

Trump's Twitter philosophy is all press is good press, and he can set the media's agenda with one tweet. During the Republican National Convention, amid accusations that Melania Trump's speechwriters had plagiarized Michelle Obama's speech, Trump tweeted:

@realDonaldTrump: Good news is Melania's speech got more publicity than any in the history of politics especially if you believe that all press is good press! (July 20, 2016)

Trump always talks about television ratings, and so his Twitter analytics must be of importance as well.

Trump's tweets show he concentrated on *polls*, *crowds*, and using the word *totally*. In a review of 10,106 tweets sent from March 2015 until Election Day, November 8, 2016, Trump's tweets' top theme was the keyword *polls*.

@realDonaldTrump: Wow, my *poll* numbers have just been announced and have gone through the roof! (December 10, 2015)
@realDonaldTrump: I am attracting the biggest crowds, by far, and the best *poll* numbers also by far. Much of the media is totally dishonest. So sad! (September 20, 2015)

The word *total* is the second-most used word in Trump's tweets. He uses the word to amplify his point.

@realDonaldTrump: Explain how the women on the View, which is a *total* disaster since the great Barbara Walters left, ever got their jobs. @abc is wasting time. (March 24, 2016)
@realDonaldTrump: Wow, Jeb Bush, whose campaign is a *total* disaster, had to bring in mommy to take a slap at me. Not nice! (February 6, 2016)
@realDonaldTrump: I'm turning down millions of dollars of campaign contributions—feel *totally* stupid doing so, but hope it is appreciated by the voters. (September 1, 2015)

  Donald Trump loves an audience and his third most common word from his tweets was *crowd*.

@realDonaldTrump: So sad that @CNN and many others refused to show the massive *crowd* at the arena yesterday in Oklahoma. Dishonest reporting! (January 21, 2016)

@realDonaldTrump: Will be at venue in Wonderful South Carolina, very soon. Big traffic back-up. Tremendous *crowd*! Will be wild! (January 8, 2016)

@realDonaldTrump: Word is that Crooked Hillary has very small and unenthusiastic *crowds* in Pennsylvania. Perhaps it is because her husband signed NAFTA? (July 30, 2016)

The three most common themes from Trump's tweets emphasized how popular he was and emphasized his derogatory comments toward others.

Trump's tweets during the campaign built his support by creating a frame of success. His tweets suggest he knew that the more he created outrageous and exciting posts about his campaign, the more support he could garner through retweets. These retweets helped him spread his message further than any television news broadcast. Trump's genuine approach, making grammatical/spelling mistakes on Twitter, and creating a plain-folk, no-nonsense style gravitated voters toward the dramatic rather than the pragmatic.

Kenneth Burke explains there is a distinction between scientific language and dramatistic language.[101] The difference is "language as definition, and language as act."[102] Trump's rhetorical style leans toward the dramatistic—as act. Burke says, "Even if any given terminology is a *reflection* of reality, by its very nature as a terminology it must be a *selection* of reality; and to this extent, it must function as a *deflection* of reality."[103] When Trump tweets about "rigged" elections, his reflection of reality becomes a deflection of reality.

@realDonaldTrump: The election is absolutely being rigged by the dishonest and distorted media pushing Crooked Hillary—but also at many polling places— SAD (October 16, 2016)

@realDonaldTrump: This election is being rigged by the media pushing false and unsubstantiated charges, and outright lies, in order to elect Crooked Hillary! (October 15, 2016)

Trump kept tweeting that if he lost the election, it was not his fault—it was the fault of a rigged system. He took on the role of a dramatist. As Burke explains,

If *action* is to be our key term, then *drama*; is the culmination form of action . . . But if *drama*, then *conflict*. And if *conflict,* then *victimage*. Dramatism is always on the edge of this vexing problem, that comes to a culmination in tragedy, the song of the scapegoat.[104]

Trump's campaign story dominated the news headlines. The other candidates were not dramatists. Other candidates, including Clinton, were defining themselves, whereas Trump used his platform to deflect reality to change the news cycle. The more his tweets deflected reality, the more the media reported on his Twitter posts. George Lakoff and Mark Johnson explain, "In allowing us to focus on one aspect of a concept, a metaphorical concept can keep us from focusing on other aspects of the concept that are inconsistent with that metaphor."[105] His tweets kept the media and voters focused on other aspects of the campaign, inconsistent with what people knew as truth. The campaign strategy—instilling doubt, fear, and drama—worked by using the repetition of words and phrases to embed ideas in the national conversation.

CONCLUSION

Trump won the election. Almost four years later, Trump's rhetorical strategy has not wavered. His campaign strategy came under scrutiny: a special White House counsel, led by former FBI director Robert Mueller, investigated and found possible connections from Russian influences to the Trump campaign.[106] Additionally, In April 2018, Facebook's CEO, Mark Zuckerberg, testified before Congress about the political consulting firm Cambridge Analytica, which had worked with Trump's campaign. Cambridge Analytica used Facebook data and created targeted advertisements that honed in on voters' emotions.

I. Hayakawa and Alan R. Hayakawa, in *Language in Thought and Action,* said, "If one is disillusioned by the acts of a politician, sometimes the politician is to blame, but sometimes the voter is to blame for having entertained the illusion to start with—for having confused different levels of abstraction."[107] An increasing number of voters affirm their beliefs through online news instead of an assortment of information they may need to make a more informed decision. Trump's campaign strategists played on people's illusions.

The Republican National Convention created a fear-based platform, and their "law and order" theme became the basis for saying America was out of control. During the 1968 presidential campaign, Richard Nixon had also adopted the "law and order" slogan. Louis Menand explains, "It was a brilliant political slogan, a whistle heard by many dogs. It transposed political issues like civil rights and Vietnam into what appeared to be a straightforward legal position: crime is wrong and criminals should be punished."[108] Trump's tweets and his speeches at rallies created doubt in people's minds about safety. No one was safe from being attacked. The drama Trump manufactured became his story.

Trump's demeanor surprised no one because he never changed; he never tried to be presidential. Trump acted like he did any other time he was interviewed or had acted on his reality show, *The Apprentice.* Instead, he played the outsider wanting to disrupt the inside. When Ronald Reagan first ran for governor of California, he was an outsider, but when he ran for president, he was an insider. Although Reagan was known as an actor, he also became an accomplished politician before running for president. As for Trump, he was known as a no-nonsense businessman with a reality show; Trump's run for president was his first attempt to run for any political office. Trump framed his story—the outsider who alone, could fix America.

Trump's tweets are what sets the news agenda for the day. His rhetorical style is the same: react and attack. Trump also likes to be different. At a rally in March 2018, Trump mentioned that Peggy Noonan, a former advisor to Ronald Reagan and now political analyst, had said he was not very presidential. Trump reacted by imitating how a president should act. *New York Times* reporter Charles Homans observed, "We were watching a sitting American president imitating an American president."[109] Homans said Trump's rally still had the conventional speech elements, but his speech was entertaining for other reasons:

It was fun to listen to because Trump—and this is still perhaps the most incredible thing about his candidacy, in retrospect—was somehow the first politician in however many decades of modern American political oratory to capitalize on the fact that nobody likes listening to modern American political oratory . . . watching Trump onstage in Phoenix, the instincts he was following seemed to be much more those of an entertainer than those of a demagogue.[110]

Politicians will have to create more compelling stories and more mass appeal. Liesbet van Zoonen warns, "Political parties and candidates now have to *produce* their constituencies on the basis of their appeal rather than relying on already existing social commonalities."[111]

Moreover, as a public, more people need to understand propaganda "to expose its rhetrickery and educate human beings in how to resist and challenge it."[112] Wayne Booth explains the paradigms of rhetoric—the good and the bad—in *The Rhetoric of Rhetoric*. Booth says, "Some even praise an outburst as *eloquent* without meaning to suggest excessiveness or true dodging of rationality."[113] Booth also points out that the rhetrickery list of harmful rhetoric is long:

propaganda, bombast, jargon, gibberish, rant, guff, twaddle, grandiloquence, purple prose, sleaze, crud, bullshit, ranting, gutsy gambit, palaver, fluff, prattle, scrabble, harangue, tirade, verbiage, balderdash, rodomontade, flapdoodle, nonsense: "full of sound and fury, signifying nothing."[114]

If a person read Trump's Twitter feed, one could find an example of rhetrickery from Booth's list. Trump's rhetorical style during the presidential campaign was unique and unconventional compared to presidential campaign rhetoric of the past. Trump's words and campaign-style created an array of emotional responses and reminded us that words matter online and offline.

NOTES

1. Donald Trump and Tony Schwartz, *The Art of the Deal* (New York: Ballantine Books: 1987), 5.

2. Michael Kranish and Marc Fisher, *Trump Revealed* (New York: Scribner, 2016), 121.

3. Ibid., 121.

4. Ibid., 260.

5. Kenneth Burke, *On Symbols and Society* (Chicago: The University of Chicago Press, 1989), 18.

6. L. Virginia Holland, "Kenneth Burke's Dramatistic Approach in Speech Criticism," *The Quarterly Journal of Speech* 41, no. 4 (1955): 353.

7. Michael Barbaro, "Pithy, Mean and Powerful: How Donald Trump Mastered Twitter for 2016," *New York Times*, October 5, 2015, https://www.nytimes.com/2015/10/06/us/politics/donald-trump-twitter-use-campaign-2016.html?referringSource=articleShare.

8. Sonja K. Foss, Karen A. Foss, and Robert Trapp, *Contemporary Perspectives on Rhetoric* (Prospect Heights, IL: Waveland Press, 1991), 181.

9. Sara Ahmadian, Sara Azarshahi, and Delroy L. Paulhus, "Explaining Donald Trump via Communication Style: Grandiosity, Informality, and Dynamism," *Personality and Individual Differences* 107, no. C (March 1, 2017): 49–53.

10. Ibid., 52.

11. Aristotle, "Rhetoric," 1378a.

12. Tami Luhby and Jim Sciutto, "Secret Service spoke to Trump Campaign about 2nd Amendment Comment," *CNN*, August 11. 2016, http://www.cnn.com/2016/08/10/politics/trump-second-amendment/index.html.

13. Janell Ross, "Just how unique is the political rhetoric of the Donald Trump era?" *Washington Post*, December 7, 2015, https://www.washingtonpost.com/news/the-fix/wp/2015/12/07/is-our-out-of-control-political-rhetoric-really-all-that-extraordinary/?utm_term=.ad47a60b2887.

14. Patrick Healy and Maggie Haberman, "95,000 Words, Many of Them Ominous, From Donald Trump's Tongue," *New York Times,* December 5, 2015, https://www.nytimes.com/2015/12/06/us/politics/95000-words-many-of-them-ominous-from-donald-trumps-tongue.html?_r=0&login=email&auth=login-email.

15. Ibid.

16. Kenneth Burke, *Rhetoric of Motives* (Los Angeles: University of California Press, 1962),55.

17. J. Eric Oliver and Wendy M. Rhan, "Rise of the Trumpenvolk: Populism in the 2016 Election," *The Annals of the American Academy*, 667 (2016): 202.

18. Ibid.

19. Ibid.

20. Ibid., 191.

21. Elena Block and Ralph Negrine, "The Populist Communication Style: Toward a Critical Framework," *International Journal of Communication* 11 (2017): 191.

22. Michael Signer, *Demagogue: The Fight to Save Democracy from Its Worst Enemies* (New York: Palgrave MacMillan, 2009), 34.

23. "Since Aristotle, the demagogue has been described as a *leader of the people* who wins the masses," Sigmund Neumann, "The Rule of the Demagogue," *American Sociological Review* 3, no. 4 (1938): 487.

24. Ibid.

25. Wayne Booth, *The Rhetoric of Rhetoric: The Quest for Effective Communication* (Oxford: Blackwell Publishing, 2004), 11.

26. Ibid., 16.

27. Ibid., 9.

28. David Greenberg, *Republic of Spin* (New York: Norton, 2016), 9.

29. Donna Woolfolk Cross, "Propaganda: How Not To Be Bamboozled," in *Reading Pop Culture*, ed. Jeff Ousborne (Boston, MA: Bedford/St. Martin's, 2013), 72.

30. Garth S. Jowett and Victoria O'Donnell, *Propaganda and Persuasion* (Thousand Oaks, CA: Sage Publications, 1999), 2.

31. Ibid., 41.

32. Burke, *A Grammar of Motives*, xv.

33. Ibid.

34. Ibid., xxii.

35. Meghan Keneally, "A Look Back at Trump Comments Perceived by Some as Encouraging Violence," *ABC News*, October 19, 2018, https://abcnews.go.com/Politics/back-trump-comments-perceived-encouraging-violence/story?id=48415766.

36. Avi Selk, "The Violent Rally Trump Can't Move Past," *Washington Post*, April 3, 2017, https://www.washingtonpost.com/news/the-fix/wp/2017/04/03/the-violent-rally-trump-cant-move-past/?utm_term=.1f22e040ef3c.

37. Jason Stanley, *How Propaganda Works* (Princeton, NJ: Princeton University Press, 2015), 5.

38. Alfred McClung Lee, "The Analysis of Propaganda: A Clinical Summary," *American Journal of Sociology* 51, no. 2 (1945): 126–135.

39. See Garth S. Jowett and Victoria O'Donnell, *Propaganda and Persuasion*, (Thousand Oaks, CA: Sage Publications, 1999), 232.

40. Cross, "Propaganda: How Not To Be Bamboozled," 72.

41. Lee, "The Analysis of Propaganda," 126–135.

42. Plato, "Gorgias," in *The Rhetorical Tradition Readings from Classical Times to the Present*, 2nd ed., ed. Patricia Bizzell and Bruce Herzberg (Boston, MA: Bedford /St. Martin's, 2001), 95.

43. Lakoff, *The Political Mind*, 116.

44. Elizabeth Drew, *Portrait of an Election: The 1980 Presidential Campaign* (New York: Simon and Schuster, 1981), 263.

45. Freedom Forum, "'Inside Politics' with CNN's John King at the Newseum," *YouTube* video, 1:27:18, posted by Newseum, July 12, 2016, https://www.youtube.com/watch?v=rfBNWqenB44.

46. Postman, *Amusing Ourselves to Death*, 133.

47. G. Ray Funkhouser and Eugene F. Shaw, "How Synthetic Experience Shapes Social Reality," in *Media Power in Politics*, ed. Doris A. Graber (Washington, DC: CQ Press, 2000), 59.

48. Frank Bruni, "Obnoxiousness Is the New Charisma," *New York Times*, January 9, 2016, https://www.nytimes.com/2016/01/10/opinion/sunday/obnoxiousn ess-is-the-new-charisma.html?rref=collection%2Fcolumn%2Ffrank-bruni&action= click&contentCollection=opinion&region=stream&module=stream_unit&version=la test&contentPlacement=229&pgtype=collection.

49. Daniel J. Boorstin, *The Image: A Guide to Pseudo-Events in America* (New York: Vintage Books, 1987), Kindle Edition, 755.

50. Ibid., 778.

51. Ibid.

52. Funkhouser and Shaw, "How Synthetic Experience Shapes Social Reality," 62.

53. Donald Trump, "Donald Trump on His Huge Social Media Following," *YouTube*, 1:27, posted by *The Circus on Showtime*, February 16, 2016, https://www.youtube.com/watch?v=b3LQEU8h07I.

54. Reagan, *An American Life*, 151.

55. Jane Suiter, "Post-Truth Politics," *Political Insight* 7, no. 3 (December 2016): 27.

56. Steve Johnson, "Skills, Socrates and the Sophists: Learning from History," *Journal of Educational Studies* 46, no. 2 (1998): 207.

57. Ibid.

58. Liesbet van Zoonen, *Entertaining the Citizen* (Lanham, MD: Rowman & Littlefield, 2005), 74.

59. Ibid.

60. Ibid., 110.

61. Philip Rucker, "Trump says Fox's Megyn Kelly had 'Blood Coming Out of Her Wherever,'" *Washington Post*, August 8, 2015, https://www.washingtonpost.com/news/post-politics/wp/2015/08/07/trump-says-foxs-megyn-kelly-had-blood-coming-out-of-her-wherever/?utm_term=.1bef3846e828.

62. Ibid.

63. Philip Bump, "Donald Trump Blames the Media for his Own Failure to Run a General Election Campaign," *Washington Post*, August 14, 2016, https://www.washingtonpost.com/news/the-fix/wp/2016/08/14/donald-trump-blames-the-media-for-his-own-failure-to-run-a-general-election-campaign/.

64. Ibid.

65. Ibid., 17.

66. Ibid., 19.

67. Larry Powell and Joseph Cowart, *Political Campaign Communication: Inside and Out*, (Boston, MA: Pearson, 2013), 85.

68. Lauren Feldman, "Partisan Differences in Opinionated News Perception: A Test of the Hostile Media Effect," *Political Behavior* 33 (2011): 430.

69. Ibid., 428.

70. Lauren Feldman, "The Hostile Media Effect," *Oxford Handbooks Online*, August 2017, http://www.oxfordhandbooks.com/view/10.1093/oxfordhb/9780199 793471.001.0001/oxfordhb-9780199793471-e-011.

71. Pew Research Center, "On Eve of Inauguration, Americans Expect Nation's Deep Political Divisions to Persist," *Pew Research Center*, January 19, 2017, http:// www.people-press.org/2017/01/19/on-eve-of-inauguration-americans-expect-nations -deep-political-divisions-to-persist/.

72. Ibid.

73. Ibid.

74. Donald Trump, *Crippled America* (New York: Threshold Editions, 2015), 145.

75. Ibid., 145–146.

76. Ibid., 148.

77. Jenna Johnson, "Donald Trump says the Election is 'Rigged.' Here's What His Supporters Think That Means," *Washington Post*, October 18, 2016, https:// www.washingtonpost.com/news/post-politics/wp/2016/10/18/donald-trump-says-the -election-is-rigged-heres-what-his-supporters-think-that-means/?utm_term=.fbe55e 717bde.

78. Thomas E. Patterson, "News Coverage of the 2016 General Election: How the Press Failed the Voters," *Shorenstein Center on Media, Politics and Public Policy*, December 7, 2016, https://shorensteincenter.org/news-coverage-2016-genera l-election/?platform=hootsuite#Trumps_Coverage.

79. Ibid.

80. Jamieson, *Dirty Politics*, 165.

81. Ibid., 166.

82. Ibid., 171.

83. Iyengar, *Media Politics*, 87.

84. Ibid., 87.

85. Martin F. Nolan, "Orwell Meets Nixon: When and Why "The Press" became "The Media,"" *Press/Politics* 10, no. 2 (2005): 73.

86. CPJ, "CPJ Chairman Says Trump is Threat to Press Freedom," *Committee to Protect Journalists*, October 13, 2016, https://cpj.org/2016/10/cpj-chairman-says-tru mp-is-threat-to-press-freedom/.

87. Amber E. Boydstun and Peter Van Aelst, "New Rules for an Old Game? How the 2016 U.S. Election Caught the Press off Guard," *Mass Communication and Society: Media Theory and the 2016 U.S. Election* 21 (2018): 689.

88. Ibid., 689.

89. Ibid., 682.

90. Brian Stelter, "Donald Trump Attacks CNN in Tweetstorm," *CNN*, August 1, 2016, https://money.cnn.com/2016/08/01/media/donald-trump-attacking-cnn/inde x.html.

91. David Karpf, "Digital Politics after Trump," *Annals of the International Communication Association,* 41, no. 2 (2017): 3.

92. Ibid.

93. Barbaro, "Pithy, Mean and Powerful."

94. Virginia Heffernan, "How the Twitter Candidate Trumped the TelePrompTer," *Politico,* May/June 2016, https://www.politico.com/magazine/story/2016/04/2016 -heffernan-twitter-media-donald-trump-barack-obama-teleprompter-president -213825.

95. David A. Siegel, "Social Networks and the Mass Media," *American Political Science Review* 107, no. 4 (2013): 803.

96. S. I. Hayakawa and Alan R. Hayakawa, *Language in Thought and Action* (San Diego, CA: A Harvest Original, 1990), 65.

97. Ibid.

98. Ibid., 65–66.

99. David Robinson, "Text Analysis of Trump's Tweets Confirms He Writes Only the (Angrier) Android Half," *Variance Explained,* August 9, 2016, http://var ianceexplained.org/r/trump-tweets/.

100. Ibid.

101. Kenneth Burke, *Language as Symbolic Action* (Berkeley: University of California Press, 1966), 45.

102. Ibid.

103. Ibid., 46.

104. Ibid., 54

105. George Lakoff and Mark Johnson, *Metaphors We Live By* (Chicago: The University of Chicago Press, 1980), 10.

106. See Robert S. Mueller, III, "Report on the Investigation into Russian inter- ference in the 2016 Presidential Election," *U.S. Department of Justice*, March 2019, https://www.justice.gov/storage/report.pdf.

107. Hayakawa, *Language in Thought and Action*, 73.

108. Louis Menand, "Been There," *The New Yorker*, January 8, 2018, 74.

109. Charles Homans, "The Post-Campaign Campaign of Donald Trump," *New York Times,* April 9, 2018, https://www.nytimes.com/2018/04/09/magazine/donald -trump-rallies-campaigning-president.html.

110. Ibid.

111. Zoonen, *Entertaining the Citizen*, 59.

112. Gae Lyn Henderson and M. J. Braun, *Propaganda and Rhetoric in Democracy: History, Theory, Analysis* (Carbondale: Southern Illinois University Press, 2016), 14.

113. Booth, *The Rhetoric of Rhetoric*, 11.

114. Ibid., 11–12.

Chapter 8

Conclusion

This book's central thesis is as media evolved, so has presidential campaign rhetoric. U.S. presidential candidates adapted their rhetorical performances for new media. Some presidential candidates failed at using media to persuade, like Al Smith and Hillary Clinton. In contrast, other presidential candidates revolutionized the presidential media campaign, as did Franklin D. Roosevelt and Barack Obama.

When George Washington stood for election in 1788, he worried American citizens would perceive him as wanting to be king. He tried to instill faith in his audience by not campaigning but allowing the electorate to choose their president with little to no influence on his part. Washington ran on his reputation as a general. As American politics matured, so did the technologies that enabled us to reach a mass audience—first, newspapers, radio, and then television created the foundation for the social media frenzy where political rhetoric thrives. Digital media allows presidential campaigns to use big data to target a specific American voter political profile. Presidential campaigns created a more interactive relationship with the electorate through new media. As we navigate each media advancement, Bakhtin's words ring true today, "Everything that is said, expressed, is located outside the 'soul' of the speaker and does not belong only to him."[1]

It takes time for new media to transform and saturate our everyday lives. Four walls do not confine our political opinions, but through global media channels that the intended audience holds in their hands. U.S. presidential candidates use mobile apps to connect with the electorate. The presidential candidate creates their own media outlets separate from the traditional media. Information from a plethora of sources seems to swirl around our heads at once. At times the truth gets muddled. News travels fast. Digital natives have very little news brand loyalty. The information from social media newsfeeds becomes fragmented. The Internet allows ordinary citizens to participate in the conversation. A mobile device transforms an average citizen into a citizen journalist, and often a political pundit. This creates a lot of media noise between the electorate and the politician, but we can also determine a presidential candidate's media success through follows, retweets, likes, and shares.

Onetime presidential candidate Barack Obama tested social media's power to campaign using Facebook, blogs, YouTube, and Twitter. Before Barack Obama's 2008 campaign, presidential candidates did not use the Internet as a viable tool during their campaigns. Barack Obama created an online community. Barack Obama's campaign blog started an extension to his offline campaign. Barack Obama's campaign strategy was to be where his audience might be. Facebook, Twitter, and YouTube were new territory for a candidate. Still, to reach multiple audiences, Barack Obama's digital campaign is an example for future candidates. Future candidates should learn to use all the media channels to spread a consistent campaign message to various audiences. This strategy resulted in a successful grassroots campaign where Obama's supporters organized events and generated personal fundraising pages. Obama's new media allowed the traditional narrative framed "I" campaign to become a "we" campaign by using all available media. Social media's direct access to voters in both the 2008 and 2012 elections enriched the dialogue and the interest in political campaigns that television, radio, and newspapers could not achieve.

Every presidential campaign tells a story. The story arc is the same for the most part. Until 2016, the traditional presidential campaign story remained consistent. In 2016, Donald Trump took the conventional story arc and changed the trajectory of current campaigns. As Barack Obama set a precedent for an online campaign, Donald Trump set the example for a presidential candidate who talked directly to his supporters. Donald Trump never filters his messages. The 2016 campaign taught journalists that a candidate could and will set the news agenda for the day. Trump's campaign story involved drama, intrigue, and curiosity. The audience is always curious about what Trump might say next. The untraditional, new campaign narrative that Trump created throughout the 2016 campaign succeeded in comparison to Hillary Clinton's lackluster campaign narrative that did not connect to voters in the same way.

Former first lady, senator, and secretary of state Hillary Clinton became a cyborg, a fictional character within the media. Hillary Clinton's campaign failed to build a robust, credible image. Hillary Clinton became her own meme. Clinton's strong political background came with a scandalous past. Her rhetorical techniques were to hide her female vulnerability and create a more masculine persona. Through Clinton's campaign, we learned that modern technology, through a foreign influence, could manipulate a story to the advantage of their opponent. Clinton's indirect approach to media failed.

She failed to use all possible means to spread her campaign message as consistently as Trump did.

As Clinton avoided the media, Donald Trump consistently tweeted and called into broadcast news shows. Trump's past success as a reality star proved to help him navigate the media landscape. His Twitter use proved effective because journalists and voters for or against his campaign responded to his messages. Journalists treated his tweets as news, and his supporters retweeted and shared his messages. Trump's campaign is an example for future presidential candidates that the rhetorical tool repetition is critical. His campaign narrative never changed across media. His tweets became news just by his use of colloquial language and the simplicity of his argument. Donald Trump proved bluntness and propaganda techniques could become a rhetorical weapon. Trump's primary rhetorical tool was planting seeds of doubt in the minds of voters. His consistent, repetitive tweets about *rigged elections* and *fake news* created uncertainty in the minds of voters. Trump used media against the media to blur the truth.

TRUTH CRISIS

Trump's 2016 campaign showed social media's weakness. Fake news is easy to create and spread. Fake news is defined as "news articles that are intentionally and verifiably false and could mislead readers."[2] Information becomes distorted when media gatekeepers are no longer present. Fact-checking is the crux of journalism's credibility. Journalists now must defend their profession in a time when ordinary citizens can write and post information that may or may not be real about a presidential candidate. It is even more challenging when the presidential candidate influences and promotes the fake news narrative.

The Internet allows users to get in the habit of gathering only news that confirms your own beliefs. This phenomenon, confirmation bias, "connotes the seeking or interpreting of evidence in ways that are partial to existing beliefs, expectations, or a hypothesis in hand."[3]

These biases are how fake news penetrates our psyche. People have fallen into the habit of only visiting websites that confirm their beliefs instead of challenging their assumptions. Brooks Jackson and Kathleen Hall Jamieson, in *Un-Spun Finding Facts in a World of [Disinformation]*, suggest, "To avoid being deceived (or deceiving ourselves), we have to make sure the pictures in our heads come as close to reflecting the world outside as they reasonably can."[4] To combat someone else's perspective, the authors suggest to counterargue "the other side's point of view as well as their own—they are more likely to accept new evidence rather than reject it."[5]

The 2016 presidential campaign did make people rely more on traditional media than social media. *Knight/Gallup Foundation Survey* reported that Americans now have more confidence in traditional media such as television news and newspapers.[6] Moreover, even though the information is at most people's fingertips, 58 percent of Americans believed it is harder to be well informed.[7]

The study "Social Media and Fake News in the 2016 Election" found anti-Trump fake stories had been shared on Facebook 7.6 million times—versus the 30.3 million shares anti-Clinton fake articles.[8] The study explains the two motivations for disseminating fake news. The first is monetary: "news articles that go viral on social media can draw significant advertising revenue when users click to the original site."[9] The second motivation is ideological because "some fake news providers seek to advance candidates they favor."[10] The researchers also found partisan attachment predicts who believes what story.[11] For example, a Democrat would likely believe a pro-Clinton story than a pro-Trump story, and a Republican would probably believe a pro-Trump story than a pro-Clinton story.[12]

The American Press Institute's *Media Insight Project* research shows the main problem between the public and the press is miscommunication.[13] The *Media Insight Project* explains, "The public is confused by some basic concepts of news."[14] The project also points out that "4 in 10 did not know what the term 'attribution' means and close to 3 in 10 do not know the difference between an 'editorial' and a 'news story.'"[15] The study also showed that the public wants more news and less commentary; both the public and the journalists agree they want "verified facts, supplemented by some background and analysis."[16]

Unfortunately, smoke and mirrors and exaggerating the truth are a constant nuisance even before the Internet existed. Word-of-mouth (or gossip) spreads rumors—today, word-of-mouth chatter is equivalent to a share on social media. The new watercooler is your Twitter newsfeed or your Facebook feed. A fake news story can travel to hundreds of followers at a time, who then send the misleading information to hundreds of more followers in turn. Moreover, foreign influences infiltrate our news feeds daily, feeding fake news to amplify messages and promote more divisiveness to create an unstable democracy.

JOURNALISM COMBATING FAKE NEWS

The purpose of journalism in our democracy is to question our leaders, which supports the check-and-balance system upholding our democracy. One could define "the ideal journalist is one who seeks to know what the facts are, and then impartially informs the public, allowing the chips to fall where they may."[17] During the 2016 campaign, *The New York Times* and *The Washington Post* continued to tell the story and allow the "chips to fall where they may." These two newspapers "spelled out and criticized Trump's insinuations in their news columns, without attributing the criticism to an 'other hand.'"[18] Journalists may blame false equivalence for explaining how they reported the 2016 presidential campaign. False equivalence presents "two reasonable alternatives, when they are not."[19] Usually, journalists will try to find a balance, but what if you know the candidate is lying? Many mainstream media interviewers during the 2016 election season stopped trying, and "rather than letting Trump spinners repeat or try to sanitize his incorrect statements [. . .] interviewers had begun to question or make fun of these efforts."[20] These journalists presented the truth to Trump's lies to the public as the story—allowing the "chips to fall where they may." Journalists' jobs are more demanding, primarily when they cover unhinged tweets and campaign speeches that are more than occasionally untruthful.

DIGITAL CITIZENSHIP

Trump shattered traditional messaging and traditional political narratives. Colloquial, combative messages sent via Twitter replaces the formal syntax of past presidential candidate messages. Presidential candidates' rhetorical choices and patterns through social media are worth noting and researching, especially when no other presidential candidate has used media quite the same way Trump has. Trump is one of the first incumbents whose presidency became a four-year reelection campaign.

Both scholars and professionals in the journalism field need to inform the public about sources, news-gathering, and discerning differences between editorial content and a news story. It is not surprising that the public cannot discern a journalist from an opinion commentator. Media literacy education is critical for the public to distinguish between fake news and real news. American citizens are trying to navigate a new digital political rhetoric normal, whether it is defining journalism or understanding if a presidential candidate's tweets are factual. Neil Postman and Steve Powers warned us about consuming television news, "We do not have time to reflect on any piece of news, and we are rarely helped. . . . We become information junkies, addicted to news, demanding (even requiring) more and more of it but without any notion of what to do with it."[21] We evolved into a society addicted to screens we hold in our hands.

Digital governing is a responsibility. Being a digital citizen is a responsibility. Future presidential campaigns and White House administrations will know how social media can create productive and inspiring digital citizens and how social media can destroy any productive dialogue between citizens. Hopefully, future presidential candidates and White House administrations will choose to create a digital community that harnesses the potential for productive dialogue.

As digital citizens, we must protect our First Amendment rights, especially as people challenge truth-telling. As legendary journalist Walter Cronkite reminds us, "The First Amendment, with its guarantees of free speech and a free press, has been at the heart of the American success story. It must be guarded zealously if we are to gird for the challenges of the new century ahead."[22]

NOTES

1. Bakhtin, *Speech Genres & Other Late Essays*, 121–122.
2. Hunt Allcott and Matthew Gentzkow, "Social Media and Fake News in the 2016 Election," *Journal of Economic Perspectives* 31, no. 2 (Spring 2017): 213.
3. Raymond S. Nickerson, "Confirmation Bias: A Ubiquitous Phenomenon in Many Guises," *Review of General Psychology* 2, no. 2 (1998): 175–220.
4. Jackson and Jamieson, *Un-Spun: Finding Facts*, 81.
5. Ibid.
6. Gallup/Knight Foundation, "American Views: Trust, Media and Democracy a Gallup/Knight Foundation Survey," *Knight Foundation*, 2018, https://kf-site-prod uction.s3.amazonaws.com/publications/pdfs/000/000/242/original/KnightFounda tion_AmericansViews_Client_Report_010917_Final_Updated.pdf.
7. Ibid.
8. Allcott and Gentzkow, "Social Media and Fake News," 212.
9. Ibid., 217.
10. Ibid.
11. Ibid.
12. Ibid., 230.
13. Media Insight Project, "Americans and the News Media: What They Do—and Don't—Understand About Each Other," *American Press Institute*, June 11, 2018, https://www.americanpressinstitute.org/publications/reports/survey-research/amer icans-and-the-news-media/.
14. Ibid.
15. Ibid.
16. Ibid.
17. John C. Merrill and S. Jack O'Dell, *Philosophy and Journalism* (New York: Longman, 1983), 49.
18. Marjorie Randon Hershey, "The Media: Covering Donald Trump," in *The Elections of 2016,* ed. Michael Nelson (Los Angeles, CA: Sage, 2018), 121.
19. Ibid.
20. Ibid., 123.
21. Neil Postman and Steve Powers, *How to Watch TV News* (London: Penguin Books, 1992), 153.
22. Cronkite, *A Reporter's Life*, 380.

Bibliography

"1960 Kennedy vs. Nixon." *The Living Room Candidate: Presidential Campaign Commercials 1952–2016,* Accessed August 24, 2018. http://www.livingroomcand idate.org/commercials/1960/nixons-experience.

Abramowitz, Alan I. and Walter J. Stone. "The Bush Effect: Polarization, Turnout, and Activism in the 2004 Presidential Election." *Presidential Studies Quarterly* 36, no. 2 (June 1, 2006): 141–154.

Ahmadian, Sara, Sara Azarshahi, and Delroy L Paulhus. "Explaining Donald Trump via Communication Style: Grandiosity, Informality, and Dynamism." *Personality and Individual Differences* 107, no. C (March 1, 2017): 49–53.

Alexander, Jeffrey C. "Heroes, Presidents, and Politics." *Contexts* 9, no. 4 (September 2010): 16–21.

Alexovich, Ariel. "Clinton's National Security Ad." *The New York Times*, February 29, 2008. https://thecaucus.blogs.nytimes.com/2008/02/29/clintons-national-secur ity-ad/.

Allan, Stuart. "Reweaving the Internet: Online news of September 11." In *Journalism After September 11*, edited by Barbie Zelizer and Stuart Allan, 119–140. New York: Routledge, 2002.

Allcott, Hunt and Matthew Gentzkow. "Social Media and Fake News in the 2016 Election." *Journal of Economic Perspectives* 31, no. 2 (Spring 2017): 213.

Altschull, J. Herbert. *From Milton to McLuhan: The Ideas behind American Journalism*. New York: Longman, 1990.

Applebaum, Yoni. "I Alone Can Fix It." *The Atlantic*, July 21, 2016. http://www.thea tlantic.com/politics/archive/2016/07/trump-rnc-speech-alone-fix-it/492557/.

Aristotle. "Metaphysics." In *The Basic Works of Aristotle,* edited by Richard McKeon. New York: The Modern Library, 2001, 689.

———. "Nicomachean Ethics." In *The Basic Works of Aristotle*, edited by Richard McKeon. New York: The Modern Library, 2001, 1068.

———. "Rhetoric." In *The Basic Works of Aristotle*, edited by Richard McKeon. New York: The Modern Library, 2001, 1129, 1329, 1380, 1408, 1422.

Assange, Julian. "Conspiracy as Governance." *iq.org*, December 3, 2006. http://web
.archive.org/web/20070129125831/http://iq.org/conspiracies.pdf.

Auerbach, Jonathan. "McKinley at Home: How Early American Cinema Made
News." *American Quarterly* 51, no. 4 (1999): 797–832. https://muse.jhu.edu/article
/2414.

Ault, Ashley. "A Symbol for Women's Progress: A Rhetorical Analysis of Hillary
Rodham Clinton's Story as America's Story." *Michigan Academician* 42, no. 1
(January 2015): 119–130. doi:10.7245/0026-2005-42.1.119.

Baker, Peter. "First Lady Remains Vital Force in White House." *New York Times*,
January 20, 1997.

Bakhtin, M. M. *The Dialogic Imagination: Four Essays*. Edited by Michael Holquist.
Translated by Caryl Emerson and Michael Holquist. Austin, TX: University of
Texas Press, 1981, 293, 337, 353.

———. *Problems of Dostoevsky's Poetics*. Edited by and translated by Caryl
Emerson. Minneapolis: University of Minnesota Press, 1984. 87–88.

———. *Speech Genres & Other Late Essays*. Edited by Caryl Emerson and Michael
Holquist. Translated by Vern W. McGee. Austin, TX: The University of Texas
Press, 1986, 69, 121–122.

Ballard, Daniel. "Presidential Election 1948." In *Encyclopedia of American Political
Parties and Elections*, edited by Larry J. Sabato and Ernst Howard, 353. New
York: Checkmark Books, 2007.

"Barack Obama's Presidential Announcement." *YouTube* video, 22:03. Uploaded
on December 10, 2007 by BarackObama.com. https://m.youtube.com/watch?v=
gdJ7Ad15WCA.

Barbaro, Michael. "Pithy, Mean and Powerful: How Donald Trump Mastered Twitter
for 2016." *New York Times*, October 5, 2015. https://www.nytimes.com/2015/10
/06/us/politics/donald-trump-twitter-use-campaign-2016.html.

Barlow, Aaron. *The Rise of the Blogosphere*. Westport, CT: Praeger, 2007.

Baym, Geoffrey. "The Daily Show: Discursive Integration and the Reinvention of
Political Journalism." *Political Communication* 22, no. 3 (July 1, 2005): 259–276.
http://www.tandfonline.com/doi/abs/10.1080/10584600591006492.

Beckett, Charlie and James Ball. *Wikileaks: News in the Networked Era*. Cambridge,
MA: Malden, 2012.

Beckwith, Ryan Teague. "Transcript: Read the Full Text of the Primetime Democratic
Debate." *Time,* October 26, 2015. http://time.com/4072553/democratic-debate-tra
nscript-primetime-cnn/?iid=sr-link1.

Benedikt, Amelie Frost. "On Doing the Right Thing at The Right Time: Toward an
Ethics of Kairos." In *Rhetoric and Kairos: Essays in History, Theory, and Praxis*,
edited by Phillip Sipiora and James S. Baumlin, 232. Albany, NY: State University
of New York Press, 2002.

Bitzer, Lloyd F. "The Rhetorical Situation." *Philosophy & Rhetoric* 1, no. 1 (1968):
1–14. Accessed July 20, 2020. www.jstor.org/stable/40236733.

Bleeker, Andrew and Nathaniel Lubin. "Growing Power: Digital Marketing in
Politics." In *Margin of Victory: How Technologists Help Politicians Win Elections*,
edited by Nathaniel G. Pearlman, 53. Santa Barbara, CA: Praeger, 2012.

Block, E. and R. Negrine. "The Populist Communication Style: Toward a Critical Framework." *International Journal of Communication* 11, no. 1 (2017): 178–197.

Boorstin, Daniel J. *The Image: A Guide to Pseudo-Events in America.* New York: Vintage Books, 1987. Kindle Edition.

Booth, Wayne. *The Rhetoric of Rhetoric: The Quest for Effective Communication.* Oxford: Blackwell Publishing, 2004.

Boydstun, Amber E. and Peter Van Aelst. "New Rules for an Old Game? How the 2016 U.S. Election Caught the Press Off Guard." *Mass Communication and Society: Media Theory and the 2016 U.S. Election* 21, no. 6 (November 2, 2018): 671–696. http://www.tandfonline.com/doi/abs/10.1080/15205436.2018.1492727.

Brady, Kevin M. "Presidential Election 1840." In *Encyclopedia of American Political Parties and Elections,* edited by Larry J. Sabato and Howard R. Ernst, 312–313. New York: Checkmark Books, 2007.

Brennen, Bonnie S. *Qualitative Research Methods for Media Studies.* New York: Routledge, 2013.

Brown, Elisha. "How a Freelance Journalist Broke the Melania Trump Plagiarism Story in 3 Tweets." *Vox,* July 21, 2016. https://www.vox.com/2016/7/21/12247504/jarrett-hill-melania-trump-plagiarism.

Bruni, Frank. "Obnoxiousness Is the New Charisma." *New York Times,* January 9, 2016. https://www.nytimes.com/2016/01/10/opinion/sunday/obnoxiousness-is-the-new-charisma.html?rref=collection%2Fcolumn%2Ffrank-bruni&action=click&contentCollection=opinion&region=stream&module=stream_unit&version=latest&contentPlacement=229&pgtype=collection.

Bruns, Axel and Jean Burgess. "Researching News Discussion on Twitter: New Methodologies." *Journalism Studies: The Future of Journalism 2011: Developments and Debates* 13, no. 5/6 (October 1, 2012): 801–814. http://www.tandfonline.com/doi/abs/10.1080/1461670X.2012.664428.

Brummett, Barry. *Techniques of Close Reading.* Los Angeles, CA: Sage, 2019.

Bugeja, Michael. "Making Whole: The Ethics of Correction." *Journal of Mass Media Ethics* 22, no. 1 (April 30, 2007): 49–65. http://www.tandfonline.com/doi/abs/10.1080/08900520701315285.

Buhite, Russell and David W. Levy. "Introduction." In *FDR's Fireside Chats*, edited by Russell Buhite and David W. Levy, xiii. Norman, OK: University of Oklahoma Press, 1992.

———. "A Pre-Election Appeal to Farmers and Laborers." In *FDR's Fireside Chats*, edited by Russell Buhite and David W. Levy, 74. Norman, OK: University of Oklahoma Press, 1992.

Bump, Philip. "Donald Trump Blames the Media for His Own Failure to Run a General Election Campaign." *Washington Post*, August 14, 2016. https://www.washingtonpost.com/news/the-fix/wp/2016/08/14/donald-trump-blames-the-media-for-his-own-failure-to-run-a-general-election-campaign/.

Burke, Kenneth. *A Grammar of Motives.* Berkley, CA: University of California Press, 1969.

———. *Language as Symbolic Action.* Berkley, CA: University of California Press, 1966.

———. *On Symbols and Society*. Chicago, IL: The University of Chicago Press, 1989.

———. *Rhetoric of Motives*. Berkley, CA: University of California Press, 1969.

Burrell, Barbara C. "Hillary Rodham Clinton as First Lady: The People's Perspective." *The Social Science Journal* (Fort Collins) 37, no. 4 (December 1, 2000): 529–546. http://www.tandfonline.com/doi/abs/10.1016/S0362-3319(00)00094-X.

Butler, R. Lawrence. "Momentum in the 2008 Presidential Contests." *Palgrave Macmillan Journals* 41, no. 3 (2009): 340.

Butts, Robert. "Presidential Election 1896." In *Encyclopedia of American Political Parties and Elections*, edited by Larry J. Sabato and Ernst Howard, 332. New York: Checkmark Books, 2007.

Campbell, George. *The Philosophy of Rhetoric*. New York: Harper & Brothers, 1849.

Campbell, Karlyn Kohrs. "The Discursive Performance of Femininity: Hating Hillary." *Rhetoric & Public Affairs* 1, no. 1 (1998): 1–20. https://muse.jhu.edu/article/373390.

———. "Feminist Rhetoric." In *Encyclopedia of Rhetoric*, edited by Thomas Sloane, 303. Oxford: Oxford University Press, 2001.

Carey, James W. *Communication as Culture: Essays on Media and Society*. New York: Routledge, 1989.

Carleton, William G. "The Revolution in the Presidential Nominating Convention." *Political Science Quarterly* 72, no. 2 (June 1, 1957): 224–240.

Carpini, Michael X., Delhi Scott Keeter, and Sharon Webb. "The Impact of Presidential Debates." In *Politics and Press: The News Media and Their Influence*, edited by Pippa Norris, 145. Boulder, CO: Lynne Reiner Publishers, 1997.

Charles, Willis Thompson. "Radio Takes the Bunk Out of Campaigns." *New York Times*, October 26, 1930.

Chen, Gina Masullo. "Tweet This: A Uses and Gratifications Perspective on How Active Twitter Use Gratifies a Need to Connect with Others." *Computers in Human Behavior* 27 (2011): 760.

Cheney, George. "The Rhetoric of Identification and the Study of Organizational Communication." *Quarterly Journal of Speech* 69, no. 2 (May 1, 1983): 143–158. http://www.tandfonline.com/doi/abs/10.1080/00335638309383643.

Cho, Jaeho and Syng Pom Choy. "From Podium to Living Room: Elite Debates as an Emotional Catalyst for Citizen Communicative Engagements." *Communication Research* 38 no. 6 (2011): 794.

Chozick, Amy. "Hillary Clinton Announces 2016 Presidential Bid." *New York Times*, April 12, 2015. https://www.nytimes.com/2015/04/13/us/politics/hillary-clinton -2016-presidential-campaign.html.

Chozick, Amy and Patrick Healy. "Hillary Clinton Is Set Back by Decision to Keep Illness Secret." *New York Times*, September 12, 2016. https://www.nytimes.com/2 016/09/13/us/hillary-clinton-pneumonia.html?mcubz=0.

Cillizza, Chris. "What George W. Bush's chief speechwriter thinks of the Melania Trump Mess." *Washington Post*, July 19, 2016. https://www.washingtonpost.com /news/the-fix/wp/2016/07/19/what-george-w-bushs-chief-speechwriter-thinks-of -the-melania-trump-mess/?utm_term=.0ab54b06a69e.

Clinton, Bill and Hillary Clinton interviewed by Steve Kroft. "Clinton on Flowers '92." *60 Minutes,* YouTube Video, 10:58, posted by Jim Heath, November 20, 2011. https://www.youtube.com/watch?v=lwXE52e9JFg.

Clinton, Hillary. "Clinton's Iraq Speech at GWU." *Real Clear Politics*, March 17, 2008. https://www.realclearpolitics.com/articles/2008/03/clintons_iraq_speech_at_gwu.html.

Clinton, Hillary. *Living History.* New York: Simon & Schuster, 2003.

Clinton, Hillary. *What Happened.* New York: Simon & Schuster, 2017.

"CMU Researchers Analyze Twitter Sentiments." *Communications of the ACM* 53, no. 7, (2010): 18.

Coenen, Craig R. "The Election of 1960." In *American Presidential Campaigns and Elections,* edited by William G. Shade, Campbell C. Ballard, and Craig R. Coenen, 856. Armonk, NY: Sharpe Reference, 2003.

Conger, Kate. "Twitter Posts another Profit as User Numbers Drop." *The New York Times*, October 25, 2018. https://www.nytimes.com/2018/10/25/technology/twitter-quarterly-earnings.html.

Combs, Sandra. "FLOTUS: Media Darling or Monster?" *Race, Gender & Class* 20, no. 1/2 (January 1, 2013): 266–280. http://search.proquest.com/docview/1464752343/.

Cooper, Troy B. "The Impromptu Rhetorical Situation." *Communication Teacher* 33, no. 4 (October 2, 2019): 262–265. http://www.tandfonline.com/doi/abs/10.1080/17404622.2019.1575429.

Corbett, Edward P. J. *Classical Rhetoric for the Modern Student.* Oxford: Oxford, 1990.

Coulson, T. "Is Television Ripe for Picking?" *Forum and Century* XC, no. 1. (1933): 35.

Cowen, Tyler. "Three Tweets for the Web." *The Wilson Quarterly (1976-)* 33, no. 4 (October 1, 2009): 54–58.

CPJ. "CPJ Chairman says Trump is Threat to Press Freedom." *Committee to Protect Journalists*, October 13, 2016. https://cpj.org/2016/10/cpj-chairman-says-trump-is-threat-to-press-freedom/.

Cronkite, Walter. *A Reporter's Life.* New York: Alfred A. Knopf, 1996.

Cross, Donna Woolfolk. "Propaganda: How Not to Be Bamboozled." In *Reading Pop Culture,* edited by Jeff Ousborne, 72. Boston, MA: Bedford/St. Martin's, 2013.

Daly, Christopher B. *Covering America: A Narrative History of a Nation's Journalism.* Amherst, MA: University of Massachusetts Press, 2012.

Daye, Alison. "Shimmying and Sniffling: Social Reaction to the Presidential Debate." *CNN*, September 27, 2016. http://www.cnn.com/2016/09/27/politics/presidential-debates-social-media-reaction/.

Dean, Howard. "How the Internet Taught Me that You Have the Power: Interview with Howard Dean." By Thomas Streeter and Zephyr Teachout. In *Mousepads, Shoe Leather, and Hope,* edited by Zephyr Teachout and Thomas Streeter, 15. Boulder, CO: Paradigm Publishers, 2008.

"Democratic Candidates Debate in Las Vegas, Nevada." *The American Presidency Project,* October 13, 2015. http://www.presidency.ucsb.edu/ws/index.php?pid=11 0903.

Dewey, John. *The Public & It's Problems.* Athens: Swallow Press, 1927.

Doctor, Vanessa. "Hashtag History: When and What Started It?" *Hashtags.org,* May 30, 2013. Accessed May 13, 2016. https://www.hashtags.org/featured/hashtag-his tory-when-and-what-started-it/.

Donaldson, Gary. *The First Modern Campaign: Kennedy, Nixon, and the Election of 1960.* Lanham, MD: Rowman & Littlefield, 2007.

Downs, Kenya. "#GirlIGuessImWithHer: Disappointed Voters Show Reluctant Support for Clinton." *PBS Newshour,* June 8, 2016. http://www.pbs.org/newshour/ rundown/girliguessimwithher-disappointed-voters-show-reluctant-support-for-clint on/?utm_source=facebook&utm_medium=pbsofficial&utm_campaign=newshour.

Drew, Elizabeth. *Portrait of an Election: The 1980 Presidential Campaign.* New York: Simon and Schuster, 1981.

Duffus, R. L. "Our Radio Battle for the Presidency." *New York Times,* October 28, 1928, 139.

Dutta-Bergman, Mohan J. "Complementarity in Consumption of News Types Across Traditional and New Media." *Journal of Broadcasting & Electronic Media* 48, no. 1 (March 1, 2004): 41–60. http://www.tandfonline.com/doi/abs/10.1207/s155068 78jobem4801_3.

Eisenhower, Dwight D. "241-Television Broadcast: 'The People as the President' 1956." *The American Presidency Project,* edited by John T. Woolley and Gerhard Peters, October 5, 2009. http://www.presidency.ucsb.edu/ws/index.php?pid=10640 &st=Eisenhower&st1=television.

"Election 2012: Romney on Pay Equity for Women: 'Binders Full of Women'." Posted October 16, 2012 by *The New York Times* on *YouTube.* https://www.you tube.com/watch?v=wfXgpem78kQ.

Ellis, Joseph J. *His Excellency: George Washington.* New York: Alfred A. Knopf, 2004.

Enda, Jodi. "Campaign Coverage in the Time of Twitter." *American Journalism Review* 33, no. 2 (October 1, 2011): 14–22.

Enli, Gunn. "Twitter as Arena for the Authentic Outsider: Exploring the Social Media Campaigns of Trump and Clinton in the 2016 US Presidential Election." *European Journal of Communication* 32, no. 1 (February 2017): 50–61.

Erickson, Keith V. and Stephanie Thomson. "Seduction Theory and the Recovery of Feminine Aesthetics: Implications for Rhetorical Criticism." *Communication Quarterly* 52, no. 3 (May 2009): 312.

Fahnstock, Jeanne. *Rhetorical Figures in Science.* Oxford: Oxford University Press, 1999.

———. *Rhetorical Style: The Uses of Language in Persuasion.* Oxford: Oxford University Press, 2011.

Fahrenthold, David A. "Trump Recorded Having Extremely Leased Conversation about Women In 2005." *Washington Post,* October 8, 2016. https://www.washingt onpost.com/politics/trump-recorded-having-extremely-lewd-conversation-about

-women-in-2005/2016/10/07/3b9ce776-8cb4-11e6-bf8a-3d26847eeed4_story.h
tml?utm_term=.e643d0e6561c.

Fama, Jilian. "Twitter has Become a Favorite of Republicans in Congress." *ABC News*, June 21, 2012. http://abcnews.go.com/Politics/republicans-tweet-democrats -congress/story?id=16619963#.T-PfF44yCI4.

Farrell, Kathleen and Marilyn J. Young. "The Rhetorical Situation." In *Rhetorical Criticism: Perspectives in Action*, edited by Jim A. Kuypers, 35. Lanham, MD: Lexington Books, 2009.

Farrell, Thomas B. "Political Conventions as Legitimation Ritual." *Communication Monographs: Campaign '76 Communication Studies of the Presidential Campaign* 45, no. 4 (November 1, 1978): 293–305. http://www.tandfonline.com/doi/abs/10 .1080/03637757809375975.

Fedeli, Sophia and Katerina Eva Matsa. "Use of Mobile Devices for News Continues to Grow, Outpacing Desktops and Laptops." *Pew Research Center*, July 17, 2018. http://www.pewresearch.org/fact-tank/2018/07/17/use-of-mobile-devices-for-n ews-continues-to-grow-outpacing-desktops-and-laptops/.

Feezell, Jessica T. "Agenda Setting through Social Media: The Importance of Incidental News Exposure and Social Filtering in the Digital Era." *Political Research Quarterly* 71, no. 2 (June 2018): 482–494. doi:10.1177/1065912917744895.

Feldman, Jeffrey and George Lakoff. *Framing the Debate: Famous Presidential Speeches and How Progressives Can Use Them to Change the Conversation (And Win Elections)*. Brooklyn, NY: IG Publishing, 2007.

Feldman, Lauren. "The Hostile Media Effect." *Oxford Handbooks Online*, August 2017. http://www.oxfordhandbooks.com/view/10.1093/oxfordhb/9780199793471 .001.0001/oxfordhb-9780199793471-e-011.

Feldman, Lauren. "Partisan Differences in Opinionated News Perceptions: A Test of the Hostile Media Effect." *Political Behavior* 33, no. 3 (September 2011): 407–432.

Fisher, Walter. "Narration as a Human Communication Paradigm." In *Contemporary Rhetorical Theory*, edited by John Louis Lucaites, Celeste Michelle Condit and Sally Caudill, 274. New York: The Guilford Press, 1999.

Foran, Clare. "Hillary Clinton's Appearance on *Between Two Ferns* Wasn't Brave." *The Atlantic*, September 23, 2016. http://www.theatlantic.com.

Foss, Sonja K. *Rhetorical Criticism: Exploration & Practice*. Long Grove, IL: Waveland Press, 2004.

Foss, Sonja K., Karen A. Foss, and Robert Trapp. *Contemporary Perspectives on Rhetoric*. Prospect Heights, IL: Waveland Press, 1991.

Foucault, Michel. "What is an Author?" In *Language, Contemporary, Practices: Selected Essays and Interviews by Michel Foucault*, edited by Donald F. Bouchard, 124. Ithaca, NY: Cornell University Press, 1977.

Fowler, Mayhill. "Obama: No Surprise That Hard-Pressed Pennsylvanians Turn Bitter." *HuffPost*, April 11, 2008. https://www.huffingtonpost.com/mayhill-fowler /obama-no-surprise-that-ha_b_96188.html.

Fox, Susannah, Lee Rainie, and Deborah Fallows. "The Internet and the Iraq war." *Pew Research Center Internet, Science & Tech*, April 1, 2003. http://www.pewI nternet.org/2003/04/01/the-Internet-and-the-iraq-war/#.

Frum, David. "Ten Reasons Why Melania Trump's Speech Will Have a Lasting Impact." *The Atlantic*, July 19, 2016. http://www.theatlantic.com/politics/archive /2016/07/melania-trumps-speech-matters/492038/.

Fry, Jason. "The Age of Internet Politics." *Wall Street Journal*, November 6, 1996.

Funkhouser, G. Ray and Eugene F. Shaw. "How Synthetic Experience Shapes Social Reality." In *Media Power in Politics*, edited by Doris A. Graber, 59. Washington, DC: CQ Press, 2000.

Gainous, Jason and Kevin. M. Wagner. *Tweeting to the Power: The Social Media Revolution in American Politics*. Oxford: Oxford University Press, 2014. Kindle e-book, chap 1.

Gallup/Knight Foundation. "American Views: Trust, Media and Democracy a Gallup/Knight Foundation Survey." *Knight Foundation*, 2018. https://kf-site-prod uction.s3.amazonaws.com/publications/pdfs/000/000/242/original/KnightFounda tion_AmericansViews_Client_Report_010917_Final_Updated.pdf.

Garret, Mary and Xiaosui Xiao. "The Rhetorical Situation Revisited." *Rhetoric Society Quarterly* 23, no. 2, (1993): 39. www.jstor.org/stable/3885923.

Gillespie, Tarleton. "Algorithms, Click Workers, and the Befuddled Fury around Facebook Trends." *Neiman Lab*, May 19, 2016. http://www.niemanlab.org/2016/ 05/algorithms-clickworkers-and-the-befuddled-fury-around-facebook-trends/.

Gillmor, Dan. *We the Media: Grassroots Journalism by the People, for the People*. Beijing: O'Reilly, 2004.

Goffman, Erving. *Frame Analysis: An Essay on the Organization of Experience*. Boston, MA: Northeastern University Press, 1974.

Goldzwig, Steven R. *Truman's Whistle-Stop Campaign*. College Station, TX: Texas A&M University Press, 2008.

Gomes, Lee. "Does the Web Deserve the Power it Gained to Influence Politics?" *Wall Street Journal*, March 26, 2008.

Gottfried, Jeffrey, Michael Barthélemy, Elisa Shearer, and Amy Mitchell. "The 2016 Presidential Campaign—A News Event That's Hard to Miss." *Pew Research Center: Journalism & Media*, February 4, 2016. http://www.journalis m.org/2016/02/04/the-2016-presidential-campaign-a-news-event-thats-hard-to-miss/.

Gould, Jack. "What is Television Doing to Us?" *New York Times*, June 12, 1949.

Graham, David. "Clinton Keeps Her Cool." *The Atlantic*, September 26, 2016. https ://www.theatlantic.com/liveblogs/2016/09/first-presidential-debate-clinton-trump -2016/501647/.

Gray, Chris Hables. *Cyborg Citizen: Politics in the Posthuman Age*. New York: Routledge, 2001.

Greenberg, Andy. "Want to Know Julian Assange's Endgame? He Told You a Decade Ago." *Wired*, October 14, 2016. https://www.wired.com/2016/10/want-know-julian-assanges-endgame-told-decade-ago/.

Greenberg, David. *Republic of Spin*. New York: Norton, 2016.

Grizzell, Craig. "Public Opinion and Foreign Policy: The Effects of Celebrity Endorsements." *The Social Science Journal* 28 (2011): 315.

Gronbeck, Bruce E. "The Presidential Campaign Dramas of 1984." *Presidential Studies Quarterly*, 15, no. 2 (1985): 391.

Grothaus, Michael. "Inside Bernie Sander's Social Media Machine." *Fast Company*, April 11, 2016. https://www.fastcompany.com/3058681/inside-bernie-sanders-social-media-machine?itm_source=parsely-api.

Hacker, Kenneth L. "Introduction: The Continued Importance of the Candidate Image Construct." In *Presidential Candidate Images*, edited by Kenneth L. Hacker, 11. New York: Rowan & Littlefield Publishers, 2004.

Hagan, Joe. "Truth or Consequences." *Texas Monthly*, May 2012. http://www.texasmonthly.com/story/truth-or-consequences.

Haggerty, James A. "Nixon's Speech 'Shot in Arm' to the G.O.P., Survey Finds." *New York Times*, September 29, 1952, 1.

Hamburger, Tom and Karen Tumulty. "Hacked Emails are Posted Online as Democrat's Convention Nears." *Washington Post,* July 22, 2016. https://www.washingtonpost.com/politics/2016/07/22/117f0574-504f-11e6-a422-83ab49ed5e6a_story.html.

Haraway, Donna. *The Haraway Reader.* New York: Routledge, 2004.

Harpine, William D. *From the Front Porch to the Front Page: McKinley and Bryan in the 1896 Presidential Campaign.* College Station, TX: Texas A & M University Press, 2005.

Hayakawa, S. I. and Alan R. Hayakawa. *Language in Thought and Action.* San Diego, CA: A Harvest Original, 1990.

Hayes, Danny. "Has Television Personalized Voting Behavior?" *Political Behavior* 31, no. 2 (June 2009): 231–260.

———. "Media and Elections, Internet." In *Encyclopedia of American Political Parties and Elections*, edited by Larry J. Sabato and Ernst Howard, 224. New York: Checkmark Books, 2007.

Healy, Patrick and Maggie Haberman. "95,000 Words, Many of Them Ominous, From Donald Trump's Tongue." *New York Times,* December 5, 2015. https://www.nytimes.com/2015/12/06/us/politics/95000-words-many-of-them-ominous-from-donald-trumps-tongue.html?_r=0&login=email&auth=login-email.

Heath, Robert L. "Identification." In *Encyclopedia of Rhetoric*, edited by Thomas Sloan, 377. Oxford: Oxford University Press, 2001.

Heath, Robert L. and Jennings Bryant. *Human Communication Theory and Research.* Mahwah, NJ: Lawrence Erlbaum Associates, Publishers, 2000.

Heffernan, Virginia. "How the Twitter Candidate Trumped the TelePrompTer." *Politico,* May/June 2016. https://www.politico.com/magazine/story/2016/04/2016-heffernan-twitter-media-donald-trump-barack-obama-telemprompter-president-213825.

Heinrichs, Jay. *Thank You for Arguing: What Aristotle, Lincoln, and Homer Simpson Can Teach Us About the Art of Persuasion.* New York: Three Rivers Press, 2007.

Henderson, Gae Lyn and M. J. Braun. *Propaganda and Rhetoric in Democracy: History, Theory, Analysis.* Carbondale, IL: Southern Illinois University Press, 2016.

Hendricks, John Allen and Robert E. Denton Jr. *Communicator-in–Chief: How Barack Obama Used New Media Technology to Win the White House.* New York: Lexington Books, 2010.

Hepworth, Shelley, Vanessa Gezari, Kyle Pope, et al. "Covering Trump: An Oral History of an Unforgettable Campaign." *Columbia Journalism Review*, November 22, 2016. https://www.cjr.org/special_report/trump_media_press_journalists.php.

Hershey, Marjorie Randon. "The Media: Covering Donald Trump." In *The Elections of 2016,* edited by Michael Nelson, 121. Los Angeles: Sage, 2018.

Heyboer, Kelly. "Web Feat." *American Journalism Review* 20, no. 9 (November 1, 1998): 26–28. http://search.proquest.com/docview/216863605/.

Himelboim, Itai, Derek Hansen, and Anne Bowser. "Playing in the Same Twitter Network." *Information, Communication & Society* 16, no. 9 (2013): 1393.

Hitlin, Paul. "Internet, Social Media Use and Device Ownership in U.S. have Plateaued after Years of Growth." *Pew Research Center*, September 28, 2018. http://www.pewresearch.org/fact-tank/2018/09/28/Internet-social-media-use-and-device-ownership-in-u-s-have-plateaued-after-years-of-growth/.

Holland, L. Virginia. "Kenneth Burke's Dramatistic Approach in Speech Criticism." *Quarterly Journal of Speech* 41, no. 4 (December 1, 1955): 352–358. http://www.tandfonline.com/doi/abs/10.1080/00335635509382094.

Holquist, Michael. *Dialogism.* New York: Routledge: 1990.

Homans, Charles. "The Post-Campaign Campaign of Donald Trump." *New York Times,* April 9, 2018. https://www.nytimes.com/2018/04/09/magazine/donald-trump-rallies-campaigning-president.html.

Hunter, Leslie L. "The Role of Music in the 1840 Campaign of William Henry Harrison." *The Bulletin of Historical Research in Music Education* 10, no. 2 (July 1989): 110.

Ifill, Gwen. "Trapped in a Spotlight, Hillary Clinton Uses It." *New York Times,* February 3, 1992.

"'Inside Politics' with CNN's John King at the Newseum." *YouTube* video, 1:27:18, posted by Newseum, July 12, 2016. https://www.youtube.com/watch?v=rfBNWqenB44.

Issenberg, Sasha. "How Obama's Team Used Big Data to Rally Voters." *MIT Technology Review*, December 19, 2012. https://www.technologyreview.com/s/509026/how-obamas-team-used-big-data-to-rally-voters/.

Iyengar, Shanto. *Media Politics: A Citizen's Guide.* New York: W.W. Norton & Company, 2011.

Jackson, Brooks and Kathleen Hall Jamieson. *Un-Spun: Finding Facts in a World of [Disinformation].* New York: Random House, 2007.

James, Frank. "Obama and Romney Respond to Sandy With Election (And Katrina) In Mind." *NPR*, October 29, 2012. https://www.npr.org/sections/itsallpolitics/2012/10/29/163862168/obama-and-romney-respond-to-sandy-with-election-and-katrina-in-mind.

James, William. *Pragmatism: A New Name for Some Old Ways of Thinking.* 1907: *Project Gutenberg*, 2004, Lecture 1. http://www.gutenberg.org/files/5116/5116-h/5116-h.htm#link2H_4_0003.

Jamieson, Kathleen Hall. *Dirty Politics: Deception, Distraction, and Democracy.* Oxford: Oxford University Press, 1992.

———. "Discourse and the Democratic Ideal." *Proceedings of the American Philosophical Society* 137, no. 3 (September 1, 1993): 332–338.

———. *Eloquence in an Electronic Age: The Transformation of Political Speechmaking.* New York: Oxford University Press, 1988.

———. "Generic Constraints and the Rhetorical Situation." *Philosophy & Rhetoric* 6, no. 3 (1973): 162–170. Accessed July 20, 2020. www.jstor.org/stable /40236849.

———. *Packaging the Presidency.* Oxford: Oxford Press, 1996.

———. *The Press Effect: Politicians, Journalists, and the Stories that Shape the Political World.* Oxford: Oxford University Press, 2003.

Jamieson, Kathleen Hall and David S. Birdsell. *Presidential Debates the Challenge of Creating an Informed Electorate.* New York: Oxford University Press, 1988.

Janofsky, Michael. "Internet Helps Make Candidate a Contender." *New York Times,* July 5, 2003.

Jefferson, Thomas. "Second Inaugural Address—March 4, 1805." In *the Life and Selected Writings of Thomas Jefferson,* edited by Adrienne Koch and William Peden, 316. New York: Random House, 1993.

Jefferson, Thomas. *Thomas Jefferson.* New York: Library of America, 1984.

Jenkins, Henry. *Convergence Culture: Where Old and New Media Collide.* New York: New York University Press, 2006.

Johnson, Janet. "Blogs and Dialogism in the 2008 United States Presidential Campaign." *ProQuest Dissertations Publishing,* 2010. http://search.proquest.com /docview/597861508/.

Johnson, Jenna. "Donald Trump says the Election is 'Rigged.' Here's What his Supporters Think That Means." *Washington Post,* October 18, 2016. https:// www.washingtonpost.com/news/post-politics/wp/2016/10/18/donald-trump-says -the-election-is-rigged-heres-what-his-supporters-think-that-means/?utm_term=.f be55e717bde.

Johnson, Steve. "Skills, Socrates and the Sophists: Learning from History." *British Journal of Educational Studies* 46, no. 2 (June 1, 1998): 201–213. http://www.tand fonline.com/doi/abs/10.1111/1467-8527.00079.

Jones, Jennifer J. "Talk 'Like a Man': The Linguistic Styles of Hillary Clinton, 1992–2013." *Perspectives on Politics* 14, no. 3 (2016): 625–642. doi:10.1017/ S1537592716001092.

Jordan, John W. "Disciplining the Virtual Home Front: Mainstream News and the Web During the War in Iraq." *Communication and Critical/Cultural Studies* 4, no. 3 (September 1, 2007): 276–302. http://www.tandfonline.com/doi/abs/10.1080/14 791420701459707.

Jowett, Garth S. and Victoria O'Donnell. *Propaganda and Persuasion.* Thousand Oaks, CA: Sage Publications, 1999.

Karni, Annie. "Clinton Sells Sick Days as Campaign Reset." *Politico,* September 15, 2016. http://www.politico.com/story/2016/09/hillary-clinton-sick-days-campaign -reset-228253.

Karpf, David. "Digital Politics after Trump." *Annals of the International Communication Association* 41, no. 2 (2017): 198–207.

Kendall, Kathleen E. "Presidential Debates through Media Eyes." *American Behavioral Scientist* 40, no. 8 (August 1997): 1193–1207.

Keneally, Meghan. "A Look Back at Trump Comments Perceived by Some as Encouraging Violence." *ABC News*, October 19, 2018. https://abcnews.go.com/Politics/back-trump-comments-perceived-encouraging-violence/story?id=48415766.

Kenski, Kate, Bruce W. Hardy, and Kathleen Hall Jamieson. *The Obama Victory: How Media, Money, and Message Shaped the 2008 Election.* Oxford: Oxford University Press, 2010.

Kessler, Glenn. "Recalling Hillary Clinton's claim of 'landing under sniper fire' in Bosnia." *Washington Post,* May 23, 2016. https://www.washingtonpost.com/news/fact-checker/wp/2016/05/23/recalling-hillary-clintons-claim-of-landing-under-sniper-fire-in-bosnia/.

Killingsworth, M. Jimmie. "Rhetorical Appeals: A Revision." *Rhetoric Review* 24, no. 3 (2005): 249–264. https://doi.org/10.1207/s15327981rr2403_1.

Koczanowicz, Leszek. "Beyond Dialogue and Antagonism: A Bakhtinian Perspective on the Controversy in Political Theory." *Theory and Society* 40, no. 5 (2011): 558.

Kosterlitz, Julie. "The Internet Shows Its Muscles." *National Journal* 35, no. 40 (October 4, 2003): 3060–3061. http://search.proquest.com/docview/200328708/.

Kovach, Bill and Tom Rosenstiel. *Blur: How to Know What's True in the Age of Information Overload.* New York: Bloomsbury, 2010.

Kranish, Michael and Marc Fisher. *Trump Revealed.* New York: Scribner, 2016.

Kreiss, Daniel. *Prototype Politics: Technology-Intensive Campaigning and the Data of Democracy.* Oxford: Oxford University Press, 2016.

———. "Seizing the Moment: The Presidential Campaigns' Use of Twitter during the 2012 Electoral Cycle." *New Media & Society* 18, no. 8 (September 2016): 1473–1490.

Lakoff, George. *The Political Mind: A Cognitive Scientist's Guide to Your Brain and Its Politics.* New York: Penguin Books, 2008.

Lakoff, George and Mark Johnson. *Metaphors We Live By.* Chicago, IL: The University of Chicago Press, 1980.

Lakoff, Robin Tolmach. *The Language War.* Berkley, CA: University of California Press, 2000.

Lanham, Richard. *A Handlist of Rhetorical Terms.* Berkley, CA: University of California Press, 1991.

Lapowsky, Isie. "Here's How Facebook Actually Won Trump the Presidency." *Wired*, November 15, 2016. https://www.wired.com/2016/11/facebook-won-trump-election-not-just-fake-news/.

Leach, Joan. "Rhetorical Analysis." In *Qualitative Researching with Text, Image and Sound*, edited by Martin W. Bauer and George Gaskell, 224. London: Sage Publications, 2002.

Lee, A. "The Analysis of Propaganda: a Clinical Summary." *American Journal of Sociology* 51 (September 1, 1945): 126–135. http://search.proquest.com/docview/58591827/.

Lee, Jayeon and Young-Shin Lim. "Gendered Campaign Tweets: The Cases of Hillary Clinton and Donald Trump." *Public Relations Review* 42, no. 5 (December 2016): 849–855.

Leighton, Kyle and David Taintor. "Hashtags are the New Lawn Signs: Why Twitter Won't Predict Political Success in the 2012 Cycle." *Neiman Journalism Lab*, March 23, 2012. http://www.niemanlab.org /2012/03/hashtags-are-the-new-lawn-signs-why-twitter-wont-predict-political-success-in-the-2012-cycle/.

Leubsdorf, Carl P. "Reporting the Tube Campaign." *Columbia Journalism Review* 14, no. 6 (March 1, 1976): 8–10.

Levinson, Paul. *New New Media*. Boston: Pearson, 2013.

Lichtblau, Eric and Eric Schmitt. "Hack of Democrats' Accounts was Wider Than Believed, Officials Say." *New York Times*, August 10, 2016. http://www.nytimes.c om/2016/08/11/us/politics/democratic-party-russia-hack-cyberattack.html.

Liebovich, Louis. *Bylines in Despair: Herbert Hoover, the Great Depression, and the U.S. News Media*. Westport, CT: Praeger, 1994.

Lippmann, Walter. *Public Opinion*. New York: Free Press Paperbacks, 1922.

Los Angeles Times Staff. "Donald Trump's Complete Convention Speech, Annotated." *Los Angeles Times,* July 21, 2016. http://www.latimes.com/politics /la-na-pol-donald-trump-convention-speech-transcript-20160721-snap-htmlstory .html.

Luhby, Tami and Jim Sciutto. "Secret Service Spoke to Trump Campaign about 2nd Amendment Comment." *CNN*, August 11, 2016. http://www.cnn.com/2016/08/10/ politics/trump-second-amendment/index.html.

Lule, Jack. *Daily News, Eternal Stories: The Mythological Role of Journalism*. New York: Guilford Press, 2001.

Media Insight Project. "Americans and the News Media: What they Do—and Don't—Understand about Each Other." *American Press Institute*, June 11, 2018. https://www.americanpressinstitute.org/publications/reports/survey-research/americans-and-the-news-media/.

Melber, Ari. "Web War." *The Nation* 287, no. 7 (September 15, 2008): 25–27. http://search.proquest.com/docview/231408834/.

Menand, Louis. "Been There." *The New Yorker*, January 8, 2018, 74.

Meraz, Sharon. "Analyzing Political Conversation on the Howard Dean Candidate Blog." In *Blogging, Citizenship, and the Future of Media*, edited by Mark Tremayne, 77. New York: Routledge, 2007.

Merrill, John C. and S. Jack O'Dell. *Philosophy and Journalism*. New York: Longman, 1983.

McCarthy, Rory. "Salam's story." *The Guardian,* May 30, 2003. http://www.theg uardian.com/world/2003/may/30/iraq.digitalmedia.

McKeown, Carol Anne, and Kenneth D. Plowman. "Reaching Publics on the Web during the 1996 Presidential Campaign." *Journal of Public Relations Research* 11, no. 4 (October 1, 1999): 321–347. http://www.tandfonline.com/doi/abs/10.1207/s1 532754xjprr1104_03.

McKinley, William and Joseph P. Smith. *McKinley, the People's Choice the Congratulations of the Country, the Calls of Delegations at Canton, the Addresses by Them: His Eloquent and Effective Responses*. Canton, OH: Repository Press, 1896.

McKinnon, Mark. "It's Storytelling, Stupid: What Made Donald Trump Smarter than Hillary Clinton." *The Daily Beast*, (November 24, 2016). http://www.thed ailybeast.com/articles/2016/11/24/what-made-donald-trump-smarter-than-hillary -clinton.html.

McLuhan, Marshall. *Understanding Media: The Extensions of Man*. Cambridge, MA: MIT Press, 2001.

Media Matters Staff. "MSNBC Panel on Melania Trump's Plagiarized Speech: "This Turns this Night into a Catastrophe."" *Media Matters for America* video of MSNBC's *The Place for Politics*, July 19, 2016. http://mediamatters.org/video/2016/07/19/ msnbc-panel-melania-trump-s-plagiarized-speech-turns-night-catastrophe/211677.

Meyerson, Harold. "The Democrats after Bernie." *Dissent* (New York) 63, no. 3 (2016): 26–34. https://muse.jhu.edu/article/622111.

Minow, Newton N. and Lee Mitchell. "Putting on the Candidates: The Use of Television in Presidential Elections." *The Annals of the American Academy of Political and Social Science* 486 (July 1986): 150.

Nagourney, Adam. "With Conventions behind Us, Our Takeaways." *New York Times*, July 29, 2016. http://www.nytimes.com/2016/07/30/us/politics/convention -highlights.html.

Ness, Eliot and Terence R. McAuliffe. "A Fine FBI-Clinton Mess; Comey Reopens the Email Probe 11 Days before the Election." *Wall Street Journal*, October 28, 2016. https://www.wsj.com/articles/a-fine-fbi-clinton-mess-1477695528.

Neumann, Sigmund. "The Rule of the Demagogue." *American Sociological Review* 3, no. 4 (August 1, 1938): 487–498.

New York Times. "Candidates to Use Radio in Presidential Campaign." June 29, 1924, XX15.

New York Times. "Letter to Congress from F.B.I. Director on Clinton Email Case." October 28, 2016. https://www.nytimes.com/interactive/2016/10/28/us/politics/fbi -letter.html

New York Times. "Radio is Changing Campaign Tactics-Broadcasting Has Taken Politics into the Family Circle, Contends Major White—Five More Talks by Smith: Two by Hoover Radio Is Switching Votes. Final Speeches on Nov. 5." October 28, 1928, 154.

New York Times. "Transcript: Hillary Clinton's Speech at the Democratic Convention." July 28, 2016. http://www.nytimes.com/2016/07/29/us/politics/hillary-clinton-dnc -transcript.html?_r=0.

New York Times. "Transcript of the Republican Presidential Debate in Detroit." March 4, 2016. https://www.nytimes.com/2016/02/14/us/politics/transcript-of-the- republican-presidential-debate.html.

Nickerson, Raymond S. "Confirmation Bias: A Ubiquitous Phenomenon in Many Guises." *Review of General Psychology*, 2, no. 2 (1998): 175–220.

Nielsen, Rasmus Kleis. *Ground Wars: Personalized Communication in Political Campaigns*. Princeton, NJ: Princeton University Press, 2012.

Nixon, Richard. "Address of Senator Nixon to the American People: The "Checkers Speech" Santa Barbara, CA September 23, 1952." In *the American Presidency Project*. Online by John T. Woolley and Gerhard Peters, September 16, 2009. http://www.presidency.ucsb.edu/ws/index.php?pid=24485.

Nolan, Martin F. "Orwell Meets Nixon: When and Why 'The Press' Became 'The Media.'" *Harvard International Journal of Press/Politics* 10, no. 2 (April 2005): 69–84. doi:10.1177/1081180X05277630.

Noonan, Peggy. "Declarations while McCain Watches." *Wall Street Journal*, April 19, 2008, W14.

———. "So Much to Savor." *Wall Street Journal*, November 4, 2004. http://www.wsj.com/articles/SB122460651917154585.

Nunez, Michael. "Former Facebook Workers: We Routinely Suppressed Conservative News." *Gizmodo*, May 9, 2016. http://www.gizmodo.com.

Oliver, J. Eric, Wendy M Rahn, and Larry M Bartels. "Rise of the Trumpenvolk: Populism in the 2016 Election." *The ANNALS of the American Academy of Political and Social Science* 667, no. 1 (September 2016): 189–206.

Pan, Joann. "Will You be Twitter's 500 Millionth User?" *Mashable*, February 22, 2012. http://mashable .com/2012/02/22/twitters-500-million-user/.

Paolino, Philip and Daron R. Shaw. "Can the Internet Help Outsider Candidates Win the Presidential Nomination?" *Political Science and Politics* 36, no. 2 (April 2003): 193–197.

Parker, Ashley. "In Nonstop Whirlwind of Campaigns, Twitter is a Critical Tool." *The New York Times,* January 28, 2012. https://www.nytimes.com/2012/01/29/us/politics/twitter-is-a-critical-tool-in-republican-campaigns.html.

Patterson, Thomas E. "News Coverage of the 2016 General Election: How the Press Failed the Voters." *Shorenstein Center on Media, Politics and Public Policy*, December 7, 2016. https://shorensteincenter.org/news-coverage-2016-general-election/?platform=hootsuite#Trumps_Coverage.

Patterson, Thomas E. *The Vanishing Voter: Public Involvement in an Age of Uncertainty.* New York: Vintage, 2003.

Paulson, Michael. "The Drama of Ted Cruz: A Little Bit of Shakespeare in That Speech?" *New York Times,* July 21, 2016. http://www.nytimes.com/2016/07/22/theater/ted-cruz-speech-rnc-shakespeare.html.

Pax, Salam. "I blame the profane perfect Arab blogger." *The Guardian*, September 9, 2003. http://www.theguardian.com/world/2003/sep/09/iraq.biography.

Peachum, Henry. *The Garden of Eloquence (1593): A Facsimile Reproduction.* Gainesville, FL: Scholars' Facsimiles & Reprints, 1954.

Petre, Elizabeth A. "Encouraging Identification with the Larger Campaign Narrative: Grassroots Organizing Texts in Barack Obama's 2008 Presidential Campaign." *Communication Quarterly* 66, no. 3 (May 27, 2018): 283–307. http://search.proquest.com/docview/2044058080/.

Pew Research Center. "On Eve of Inauguration, Americans Expect Nation's Deep Political Divisions to Persist." *Pew Research Center*, January 19, 2017. http://www.people-press.org/2017/01/19/on-eve-of-inauguration-americans-expect-nations-deep-political-divisions-to-persist/.

Pew Research Center: Journalism and Media Staff. "Election 2016: Campaigns as a direct Source of News." *Pew Research Center*, July 18, 2016. https://www.journalism.org/2016/07/18/election-2016-campaigns-as-a-direct-source-of-news/.

Plato. *Gorgias*. In *The Rhetorical Tradition Readings from Classical Times to the Present*, 2nd ed., edited by Patricia Bizzell and Bruce Herzberg, 95. Boston, MA: Bedford /St. Martin's, 2001.

Plouffe, David. *The Audacity to Win*. New York: Penguin Books, 2010.

Politico Staff. "Full transcript: First 2016 presidential debate." *Politico,* September 27, 2016. http://www.politico.com/story/2016/09/full-transcript-first-2016-presidential-debate-228761.

Politico Staff. "Full transcript: Second 2016 presidential debate." *Politico,* October 10, 2016. http://www.politico.com/story/2016/10/2016-presidential-debate-transcript-229519.

Politico Staff. "Full transcript: Third 2016 Presidential Debate." *Politico*, October 20, 2016. http://www.politico.com/story/2016/10/full-transcript-third-2016-presidential-debate-230063.

Politico Staff. "Full Text Donald Trump 2016 RNC Draft Speech Transcript." *Politico*, July 21, 2016. https://www.journalism.org/2016/07/18/election-2016-campaigns-as-a-direct-source-of-news/.

Politico Staff. "Full Text Hillary Clinton's DNC speech." *Politico*, July 28, 2016. https://www.politico.com/story/2016/07/full-text-hillary-clintons-dnc-speech-226410.

Postman, Neil. *Amusing Ourselves to Death: Public Discourse in the Age of Show Business*. New York: Penguin Books, 1985.

Postman, Neil and Steve Powers. *How to Watch TV News*. London: Penguin Books, 1992.

Powell, Larry and Joseph Cowart. *Political Campaign Communication: Inside and Out*. Boston: Pearson, 2013.

Preston, Jennifer. "Campaigns Rapid Response Efforts Get a Little More Rapid." *New York Times*, August 1, 2012. https://thecaucus.blogs.nytimes.com/2012/08/01/campaigns-rapid-response-efforts-get-a-little-more-rapid/.

Rama, Padmananda. "Want Thousands of Twitter Followers? Put A Meme On it." *NPR*, October 17, 2012. https://www.npr.org/sections/itsallpolitics/2012/10/16/163054345/want-thousands-of-twitter-followers-put-a-meme-on-it.

Rather, Dan. *Rather Outspoken: My Life in the News*. New York: Grand Central Publishing, 2012. Nook e-book, chap. 2.

Reagan, Ronald. *An American Life*. New York: Simon and Schuster, 1990.

Reagan, Ronald. "Televised Campaign Address A Visual Economy: Jobs, Growth, and Progress for Americans." In *The American Presidency Project*, edited by John T. Woolley and Gerhard Peters, November 18, 2009. http://www.presidency.ucsb.edu/ws/?pid=85201.

Rein, Irving. "Campaigns." In *Encyclopedia of American Political Parties and Elections*, edited by Larry J. Sabato and Ernst Howard, 77. New York: Checkmark Books, 2007.

Rheingold, Howard. *Net Smart*. Cambridge: MIT Press, 2012.

Rich, Frank. "Hillary's St. Patrick's Day Massacre." *New York Times*, March 30, 2008, WK13.

Richards, Rebecca S. "Cyborgs on the World Stage: Hillary Clinton and the Rhetorical Performances of Iron Ladies." *Feminist Formations* 23, no. 1 (April 1, 2011): 1–24.

Riker, William H. "Campaign Rhetoric." *Bulletin of the American Academy of Arts and Sciences* 46, no. 5 (February 1, 1993): 41.

Robertson, Andrew W. *The Language of Democracy: Political Rhetoric in the United States and Britain, 1790–1900.* Ithaca, NY: Cornell University Press, 1995.

Robinson, David. "Text Analysis of Trump's Tweets Confirms He Writes Only the (Angrier) Android Half." *Variance Explained,* August 9, 2016. http://varianceexplained.org/r/trump-tweets/.

Robinson, Will. "The Digital Revolution: Campaigns and New Media Communications." In *Margin of Victory: How Technologists Help Politicians Win Elections,* edited by Nathaniel G. Pearlman, 5. Santa Barbara, CA: Praeger, 2012.

Roosevelt, Franklin D. "123-Fireside Chat." In *The American Presidency Project,* online by Gerhard Peters and John T. Woolley, September 6, 1936. http://www.presidency.ucsb.edu/ws/index.php?pid=15122.

Ross, Janell. "Just How Unique is the Political Rhetoric of the Donald Trump Era?" *Washington Post,* December 7, 2015. https://www.washingtonpost.com/news/the-fix/wp/2015/12/07/is-our-out-of-control-political-rhetoric-really-all-that-extraordinary/?utm_term=.ad47a60b2887.

Rucker, Philip. "Trump says Fox's Megyn Kelly had 'Blood Coming Out of Her Wherever.'" *Washington Post,* August 8, 2015. https://www.washingtonpost.com/news/post-politics/wp/2015/08/07/trump-says-foxs-megyn-kelly-had-blood-coming-out-of-her-wherever/?utm_term=.1bef3846e828.

Sadurni, Luis Ferro. "Clinton historically wary of the press." *Reporters Committee for Freedom of the Press* (2016). http://www.rcfp.org.

Sanders, Bernie. *Our Revolution.* New York: Thomas Dunne Books, 2016.

Savage, Neil. "Twitter as Medium and Message." *Communications of the ACM* 54, no. 3, (2011): 18.

Schatz, Amy. "BO, UR so Gr8: How a Young Tech Entrepreneur Translated Barack Obama into the Idiom of Facebook." *Wall Street Journal,* May 26, 2007.

Schroeder, Alan. "Watching between the Lines: Presidential Debates as Television." *Press/Politics* 1, no. 4 (1996): 59.

Selk, Avi. "The Violent Rally Trump Can't Move Past." *Washington Post,* April 3, 2017. https://www.washingtonpost.com/news/the-fix/wp/2017/04/03/the-violent-rally-trump-cant-move-past/?utm_term=.1f22e040ef3c.

Siegel, David A. "Social Networks and the Mass Media." *The American Political Science Review* 107, no. 4 (November 1, 2013): 786–805.

Signer, Michael. *Demagogue: The Fight to Save Democracy from Its Worst Enemies.* New York: Palgrave MacMillan, 2009.

Simendinger, Alexis. "New Media as the Message." *National Journal* 40, no. 16 (April 19, 2008): 44.

———. "The XX Factor." *National Journal,* September 29, 2007, 48.

Sklar, Kathryn Kish. "A Women's History Report Card on Hillary Rodham Clinton's Presidential Primary Campaign, 200." *Feminist Studies* 34, no. ½ (2008): 320–321.

Smith, Craig. "*Ethos* Dwells Pervasively: A Hermeneutic Reading of Aristotle on Credibility." In *The Ethos of Rhetoric*, edited by Michael J. Hyde, 13. Columbia, SC: University of South Carolina, 2004.

Smith, Sidonie. ""America's Exhibit A": Hillary Rodham Clinton's *Living History* and the Genres of Authenticity." *American Literary History*, June 6, 2012. https://academic.oup.com/alh/article/24/3/523/103133/America-s-Exhibit-A-Hillary-Rodham-Clinton-s?searchresult=1.

Stack, Liam. "Donald Trump Featured Paula Jones and 2 Other Women Who Accused Bill Clinton of Sexual Assault." *New York Times,* October 9, 2016. https://www.nytimes.com/2016/10/10/us/politics/bill-clinton-accusers.html?_r=0.

Standage, Tom. *Writing on the Wall: Social Media—the First 2,000 Years.* New York: Bloomsbury, 2013.

Stanley, Jason. *How Propaganda Works.* Princeton: Princeton University Press, 2015.

Stansell, C. "All Fired Up Women, Feminism, and Misogyny in the Democratic Primaries." *Dissent* 55, no. 4 (2008): 34–39.

Starr, Paul. *The Creation of the Media: Political Origins of Modern Communications.* New York: Basic Books, 2004.

Stelter, Brian. "Candidates Responding Almost as Fast as they can Attack." *New York Times*, March 4, 2008.

———. "Donald Trump Attacks CNN in Tweetstorm." *CNN*, August 1, 2016. https://money.cnn.com/2016/08/01/media/donald-trump-attacking-cnn/index.html.

———. "The Facebooker Who Friended Obama." *New York Times*, July 7, 2008. https://www.nytimes.com/2008/07/07/technology/07hughes.html.

Stephens, Mitchell. *A History of News.* Fort Worth: Harcourt Brace, 1997.

Stephens-Davidowitz, Seth. *Everybody Lies: Big Data, New Data, And What the Internet Can Tell Us About Who We Really Are.* New York: HarperCollins, 2017.

Strassel, Kimberley A. "Hillary's Email Escapade." *Wall Street Journal*, March 6, 2015, Eastern Edition, A11.

Stromer-Galley, Jennifer. *Presidential Campaigning in the Internet Age.* Oxford: Oxford University Press, 2014.

Suiter, Jane. "Post-Truth Politics." *Political Insight* 7, no. 3 (December 2016): 25–27.

Talbot, David. "How Obama Really did It." *Technology Review*, August 19, 2008. https://www.technologyreview.com/s/410644/how-obama-really-did-it/.

Tannen, Deborah. *The Argument Culture.* New York: Random House, 1998.

Team Fix. "The Fox News GOP Debate Transcript, Annotated." *Washington Post*, March 3, 2016. https://www.washingtonpost.com/news/the-fix/wp/2016/03/03/the-fox-news-gop-debate-transcript-annotated/?utm_term=.e20044394246.

Teten, Ryan. "Presidential Election 1804." In *Encyclopedia of American Political Parties and Elections*, edited by Larry J. Sabato and Ernst Howard, 301. New York: Checkmark Books, 2007.

Thatcher, Margaret. "Speech at Kensington Town Hall ("Britain Awake") (The Iron Lady)." *Margaret Thatcher Foundation,* January 19, 1976. https://www.margaret thatcher.org/document/102939.

Thomas, Evan. "Hillary Milhous Clinton; the Similarities between Richard Nixon and Mrs. Clinton Go Well Beyond their Hostility Toward the Press." *Wall Street Journal,* June 9, 2015.

Thompson, Charles Willis. "Radio Takes the Bunk out of Campaigns." *New York Times,* October 26, 1930, SM6.

Thornton, Lee. "New Media and the Man." *American Journalism Review* (December 2009). http://ajrarchive.org/Article.asp?id=4654.

Todsen, John P. "Presidential Election 1796." In *Encyclopedia of American Political Parties and Elections,* edited by Larry J. Sabato and Ernst Howard, 298–299. New York: Checkmark Books, 2007.

Toulmin, Stephen. *The Uses of Argument.* Cambridge: Cambridge University Press, 2003.

Trent, Judith S., Robert V. Friedenberg, and Robert E. Denton, Jr. *Political Campaign Communication: Principles & Practice.* New York: Rowman & Littlefield, 2011.

Troy, Gil. "The Campaign Triumph." *Wilson Quarterly* 36 no. 3 (Summer 2012): 20.

———. *See How They Ran: The Changing Role of the Presidential Candidate.* New York: Free Press, 1991.

Truman, Harry S. "Harry S. Truman: Radio Remarks in Independence on Election Eve, Santa Barbara, CA, November 1, 1948." *The American Presidency Project,* online by Gerhard Peters and John T. Woolley, September 16, 2009. http://www .presidency.ucsb.edu/ws/?pid=13082.

Trump, Donald. "Donald Trump on His Huge Social Media Following." *YouTube,* 1:27, posted by *The Circus on Showtime,* February 16, 2016. https://www.youtube. com/watch?v=b3LQEU8h07I.

Trump, Donald and Tony Schwartz. *The Art of the Deal.* New York: Ballantine Books: 1987.

———. *Crippled America.* New York: Threshold Editions, 2015.

Tsfati, Yaris. "Debating the Debate: The Impact of Exposure to Debate News Coverage and Its Interaction with Exposure to the Actual Debate." *Press/Politics* 8, no. 3 (2003): 70–86.

Tumasjan, Andranik and Timm O. Sprenger, Philipp G. Sandner and Isabell M. Welpe. "Election Forecasts with Twitter: How 140 Characters Reflect the Political Landscape." *Social Science Computer Review* 29, no. 4, (2010): 414.

Tumulty, Karen. "Twitter becomes a key real-time tool for campaigns." *The Washington Post,* April 26, 2012. https://www.washingtonpost.com/politics/twitt er-becomes-a-key-real-time-tool-for-campaigns/2012/04/26/gIQARf1TjT_story.h tml

Tversky, Amos and Daniel Kahneman. "Availability: A Heuristic for Judging Frequency and Probability." *Cognitive Psychology* 5, no. 2 (1973): 207–232.

Uberti, David. "Twitter and Factchecking Don't Mix During Debates." *Columbia Journal Review,* July 21, 2014. http://archives.cjr.org/behind_the_news/twitter_an d_fact-checking_dont.php

Uscinski, Joseph E. and Lilly J. Goren. "What's in a Name? Coverage of Senator Hillary Clinton during the 2008 Democratic Primary." *Political Research Quarterly* 64, no. 4 (2011): 884–896. Accessed July 21, 2020. www.jstor.org/stable /23056354.

Valley, David B. "Significant Characteristics of Democratic Presidential Nomination Acceptance Speeches." *Central States Speech Journal* 25, no. 1 (March 1, 1974): 56–62. http://www.tandfonline.com/doi/abs/10.1080/10510977409367769.

VanderMeer, Philip R. "Presidential Election 1952." In *Encyclopedia of American Political Parties and Elections*, edited by Larry J. Sabato and Ernst Howard, 824. New York: Checkmark Books, 2007.

Vasilew, Eugene. "The Real vs. The Mythical Campaign." *Today's Speech* 8, no. 4 (1960): 25.

Vatz, Richard E. "The Myth of the Rhetorical Situation." *Philosophy & Rhetoric* 6, no. 3 (1973): 154–161. Accessed July 20, 2020. www.jstor.org/stable/40236848.

Victor, Daniel. "Clinton to Trump on Twitter: 'Delete Your Account'." *New York Times*, June 9, 2016. https://www.nytimes.com/2016/06/10/us/politics/hillary-clint on-to-donald-trump-delete-your-account.html.

Wall Street Journal (Online). "The Clinton Mail Baggage; are Hillary's Ethics Behind the Bernie Sanders Surge?" January 14, 2016.

Walther, Joseph B. "Virtual Audiences." In *Encyclopedia of Rhetoric*, edited by Thomas Sloan, 72. Oxford: Oxford University Press, 2001.

Warner, Benjamin R., Diana B. Carlin, Kelly Winfrey, James Schnoebelen, and Marko Trosanovski. "Will the 'Real' Candidates for President and Vice President Please Stand Up? 2008 Pre- and Post-Debate Viewer Perceptions of Candidate Image." *American Behavioral Scientist* 55, no. 3 (March 2011): 232–52. doi:10.1177/0002764210392160.

Washington Post. "Melania Trump's 2016 Speech vs. Michelle Obamas' 2008 Speech." *Washington Post* video, July 19, 2016. https://www.washingtonpost.com /video/c/embed/ce608edc-4d71-11e6-bf27-405106836f96.

Washington Post. "Seeing Hoover By Radio." September 8, 1928.

Washington Post Staff. "Annotated transcript: The Aug. 6 GOP debate." *Washington Post,* August 6, 2015. https://www.washingtonpost.com/news/post-politics/wp/20 15/08/06/annotated-transcript-the-aug-6-gop-debate/?utm_term=.74ef6d077a90.

Wasserstein, Wendy. "Hillary Clinton's Muddled Legacy." *New York Times*, August 25, 1998.

Weigand, Edda. "Power in Dialogic Interaction." *Language and Dialogue* 1, no. 2 (2011): 234.

Weigel, David. "Clinton's Account of How She was 'Shivved in the 2016 Presidential Election." *The Washington Post*, September 12, 2017. https://www.washingtonpos t.com/outlook/clintons-account-of-how-she-was-shivved-in-the-2016-presidential -election/2017/09/11/f6740438-957f-11e7-89fa-bb822a46da5b_story.html?utm _term=.498ba526092e.

Wheeler, Tom. *Mr. Lincoln's T-Mails: The Untold Story of How Abraham Lincoln Used the Telegraph to Win the Civil War.* New York: Collins, 2006.

White, J. Andrew. "Hoover vs. Smith as Radio Orators." *New York Times*, September 16, 1928, 164.

White, Ronald C. *A. Lincoln: A Biography*, 1st ed. New York: Random House, 2009.

Wikileaks. "What is WikiLeaks?" About *Wikileaks*, November 3, 2015. https://wikileaks.org/What-is-WikiLeaks.html.

Wijfjes, Huub. "Spellbinding and Crooning: Sound Amplification, Radio, and Political Rhetoric in International Comparative Perspective, 1900–1945." *Technology and Culture* 55, no. 1 (January 1, 2014): 165. http://search.proquest.com/docview/1559006048/.

Wilentz, Sean. *The Rise of American Democracy: Jefferson to Lincoln*. New York: Norton, 2005.

Williams, Andrew Paul, Kaye D. Trammell, Monica Postelnicu, Kristen D. Landreville, and Justin D. Martin. "Blogging and Hyperlinking: Use of the Web to Enhance Viability During the 2004 US Campaign." *Journalism Studies: Content and Effects of Media in the 2004 US Presidential Campaign* 6, no. 2 (May 1, 2005): 177–186. http://www.tandfonline.com/doi/abs/10.1080/14616700500057262.

Wilson, Douglas L. "Lincoln's Rhetoric." *Journal of the Abraham Lincoln Association* 34, no. 1 (January 1, 2013): 5.

Winfield, Betty Houchin. *FDR and the news media*. Urbana, IL: University of Illinois Press, 1990.

WMUR-TV. "Clinton Wells Up: 'This is Very Personal.'" *YouTube* video, posted by WMUR-TV, January 7, 2008. https://www.youtube.com/watch?v=pl-W3IXRTHU.

Zitner, Aaron. "5 Takeaways from Final Donald Trump, Hillary Clinton Debate; Presidential Nominees Trade Barbs Over Character, Effectiveness; a Question Over Election Results." *Wall Street Journal,* October 20, 2016.

Zoonen, Liesbet van. *Entertaining the Citizen.* Lanham, MD: Rowman & Littlefield, 2005.

Index

About the Author

Dr. Janet Johnson is a lecturer at the University of Texas at Dallas. She brings over twenty years of experience in media and strategic communications. Her research passion is media in the political process, especially how social media is changing political rhetoric. Through her research, she seeks to provide professional communicators with a deeper understanding of how effective and powerful new media is to our political and media culture. Dr. Johnson graduated with a PhD in rhetoric from Texas Woman's University and a master of arts in journalism from the University of North Texas. Her BA is in broadcast communication from the University of Texas at Arlington.

www.ingramcontent.com/pod-product-compliance
Lightning Source LLC
Chambersburg PA
CBHW050646280326
41932CB00015B/2797